Girls, Performance, and Activism

D1231176

Girls, Performance, and Activism offers artists, activists, educators, and scholars a comprehensive analysis, celebration, and critique of the ways in which teenage girls create and perform activist theater.

Girls, particularly Black and Latinx teenagers, are using the tools of performance to share their stories, devise new ones, and use the stage to advocate for social change. Interweaving interviews, poetic text, drama, and theory, this book provides readers with a comprehensive understanding of how and why this field erupted and the ways in which girls are using performance to transform themselves and enact change in their communities. As a white woman who has collaboratively created theater with hundreds of girls of color over the past 20 years, Dana Edell offers strategies for engaging with girls across difference through an intersectional lens in order to acknowledge the ways in which race, gender, age, class, ability, and sexuality influence girls' experiences and relationships with adult collaborators as they work to create meaningful, impactful, and often personal activist performances.

This is the go-to handbook for teachers, theater directors, and performance makers who want to create politically engaged work with teenage girls.

Dana Edell is an assistant professor of Applied Theatre at Emerson College in Boston, Massachusetts.

"The book is a pleasure to read, exuding the energy and panache of teenage girls. It does not skimp on theory but is clear in its exposition. Writing at the intersection of performance, activism, and girls' studies, Edell balances an overview with firsthand experience. She expresses a love for the subject while being critical. She lets the reader in on her own questions and struggles, and the girls' successes and challenges. Assessing the work's impact on the girls themselves, their friends and family, and the 'world' beyond gets the reader thinking about what performance can and cannot do."

—Jan Cohen-Cruz, writer and teacher, socially engaged performance

"In *Girls, Performance, and Activism*, girls are a force to be reckoned with. All the world's a stage for their urgent messages, whether they're performing at a United Nations meeting, in a neighborhood park, at a protest rally, a school cafeteria, or in a TikTok video. Freely voiced and fully embodied, activism is their first language. Dana Edell offers us all a masterclass in girl-driven theater as a praxis of liberation and a vehicle for social change. She confronts the complexities of partnering with girls across difference and incites us all to bear critical witness to girls' imagination, rage, creativity, and joy."

—Lyn Mikel Brown, Professor of Education, Colby College; author of *Powered by Girl: A Field Guide for Supporting Youth Activists*

Girls, Performance, and Activism

Demanding to be Heard

Dana Edell

Routledge
Taylor & Francis Group

LONDON AND NEW YORK

First published 2022
by Routledge
2 Park Square, Milton Park, Abingdon, Oxon OX14 4RN

and by Routledge
605 Third Avenue, New York, NY 10158

Routledge is an imprint of the Taylor & Francis Group, an informa business

British Library Cataloguing-in-Publication Data
A catalogue record for this book is available from the British Library

Library of Congress Control Number: 2021939421

ISBN: 978-0-367-42709-2 (hbk)
ISBN: 978-0-367-42711-5 (pbk)
ISBN: 978-0-367-85456-0 (ebk)

Typeset in Bembo
by Newgen Publishing UK

For Mom, Dad, Wilder, and Forrest:
my past, present, and future

Contents

Acknowledgments

I have been dreaming of writing this book for nearly 20 years, and there are significant, wondrous people who have helped shape my understanding of theater, activism, and girl-driven work. My first theater teacher was Trina Tjersland: you set the bar high for showing me how an adult can collaborate with teenagers with respect and love. Ev Corum, David Montee, Robin Ellis, and Reed Zitting at Interlochen treated us crazy, theater-obsessed kids with care and taught me professional standards and an indefatigable work ethic. I am so grateful that I got through high school without cellphones or internet and that left quite literally to our own devices, we just kept devising and making art in the woods. Other theater scholars, directors, and professors that ignited my love for this blazing art form were, at Brown, Tori Haring-Smith: you helped me understand feminist performance and Oskar Eustis: you shared your insights and experiences of activist theater. I had the life-changing privilege to study directing with Anne Bogart and Robert Woodruff at Columbia: your complimentary styles and deep passion for theatrical innovation pushed me to listen to and cultivate my own creative voice. I am ever grateful that I was able to study with Augusto Boal and other founding jokers at the Center for Theatre of the Oppressed in Rio and will never forget the exquisite joy he brought to the work. At NYU, I learned about feminist ethnography with Deborah Kapchan and applied theatre with Phillip Taylor and Nan Smithner.

As soon as I got to NYU's campus, I showed up at the door of one of my academic heroes, Carol Gilligan and you not only let me in, but invited me to study with you and guided my understandings of patriarchy, relationships, and girls' voices. Niobe Way, studying with you, teaching with you, writing with you, and being part of your research team changed the way I understand research. You showed me how listening is an act of resistance, an act of love, and can change the world. Lyn Mikel Brown is another hero who never let me down. Your brilliance, generosity, and friendship have been transformative. You have been a stalwart voice for demanding we listen to girls and partnering with you was literally a dream come true. My co-conspirators in SPARK who taught me what antiracist, feminist activism really looks like in practice. Deb Tolman, thank you for co-founding this movement with Lyn and inviting me to join you. Shelby Knox and Jamia Wilson: you taught me what feminist activism looks like in practice and Melissa Campbell, you were my true partner in our messy, witchy, magic girls' work. Other feminist activists ignited my curiosity and passion and educated me when I needed it most. Thank you: Courtney, Emily, Jaclyn, Jenn, Monica, Samhita. You probably didn't realize that when you came as guest experts for our SPARK trainings, you were educating me too. And much gratitude to Candice, Crystal, Dana, Bailey, and Shareeza, and all the SPARKteam girls over the years who blew me away with your passion, feminist rabble-rousing energy, and indefatigable commitment to fighting for what you believe.

My fellow grad students, coffee shop dwelling buddies, and writing partners helped me work through theory and practice and have some fun through the process. I am so grateful for you: Dani, Desiree, Anna, Jennifer, and Kevin. The deep friendships that blossomed from surviving PhD programs together cannot be understated. Joseph Nelson, my teaching partner, and comrade through the world of research and writing, your support and enthusiasm always lifted my spirits. Nirit Gordon, we met studying the Listening Guide and you have proven to be the greatest listener and a dear friend in the trenches with me through the dual stresses and joys of motherhood and academia. Lizzy Davis, how I wish we were writing side by side at the Flying Saucer, thank you for your mother/ scholar/ professor wisdom and love. Ruth Nicole Brown, we met on an NWSA panel and I have been in awe of your groundbreaking work and so grateful for your friendship through the years. Aimee Cox, a co-director and confidante, your wisdom, humor, generosity, and golden energy lights up every space, and I also thank you for inviting me to contribute to your *Gender: Space* book with my chapter, "Theatre and Girls Resistance," and for granting me permission to reprint an excerpt from that piece here. I additionally acknowledge with gratitude Cengage Learning Inc.[1]

Thank you to my brilliant colleagues in CUNY's Applied Theatre program: Chris Vine, Helen White, Michael Wilson, Amy Green, Herukhuti Williams, and Ah-Keisha McCants for modeling how to teach this work and inspiring the next generation of practitioners. And all my undergraduate and graduate students through the years, you have asked the deep and provocative questions about theater, activism, antiracism, and feminism that have pushed me to bolder and braver responses. Your energy and passion give me hope for our field!

My oldest friends have been my lifeline, particularly as I've navigated the isolation and physical distancing of the Covid pandemic. You have listened to my rantings and offered guidance, advice, distraction, love, and laughter. I love you: David, Dan, Heather, Helen, Jill (and for reading a draft!), Justine, Kate, Katie, Megan, Martie, and Piper. And my mama friends Crystal, Dana, Kelly, and Melanie who helped me keep my sanity while trying to write during lockdown with two littles and no childcare.

Thank you to viBe co-founder chandra thomas, you taught me much about making theater with girls and viBe's program directors through the years: Katie, Ellen, Sarah, Renee, and Noelle shaped me as a director and through witnessing your transformative work with girls, I learned and grew.

I am forever in gratitude to the approximately 1,000 teenage girls whose stories and voices and creative energy have impacted everything I do. To all who sat with me over hot chocolate or over Zoom or spoke into tape recorders ten+ years ago to share your thoughts and feelings about our work together, thank you! Alex, Amber, Amee, Anais, Aniaha, Arlyn, Arianne, Ashanti, Brittney, Courtney, Daisy, Desiree, Elaina, Ericka, Erika, Genna, Imani, Izzy, Key, Kuenique, Leo, Mawia, Monique, Orchidea, Rukiya, Sinead, Stephanie, Tahiris, Tiffany, Theresa, Tinaya, Unique, Veronica, Xera, Zaidy, and Zola.

Thank you to Wakumi Douglas from S.O.U.L. Sisters Leadership Collective for both talking with me about and *doing* healing, activist creative work that should be the model we all aspire to. Thank you Ash Marinaccio for being open and vulnerable and sharing your experiences of creating theater with girls. Thank you, Catherine Connors for talking with me about girls and their innate hunger to perform and create. Thank you, Quenna Lené Barrett for sharing your wisdom and thoughts about Black queer femme theater and Zoom activist performance.

And thank you, Toya Lillard and Monique Letamendi! You stepped up and stepped into leadership at viBe and rebuilt, transformed, improved, and reimagined this mighty, little organization teaching me about the necessary power of Black woman leadership. I learn from you every day what it truly means to foster community, listen to Black girls and shift the culture to support them.

Thank you Ben Piggott and Zoe Forbes at Routledge for your faith and support in this project, your helpful feedback, and generous compassion in working with this single mom of two boys under four trying to write during a pandemic! To Abby Pasternack, the brilliant book cover designer, you are an AMAZING artist, and getting to collaborate with a teenage girl on this cover was so special and meaningful. Thank you for your work!

And to Jan Cohen-Cruz, you were my professor, mentor, advisor, co-professor, and now dear friend. You have generously read every chapter of this book in every draft, given amazingly useful feedback, and been my greatest support through this process. Thank you! Thank you, NYU research assistants, Jade O'Halloran Siena Yusi, and Katherine Rawlinson. Thank you Onnie Rogers and Chrissy Foo. Chrissy, you jumped in at the end of this process and read this manuscript offering exactly the commentary I needed. Thank you to Shanti Rose and Jessica Cortez, my brilliant former students who accepted my humble request to read drafts of this manuscript and gave excellent, generous, necessary feedback. You made this a better book!

And, finally, to my family without whom I would not have been able to follow my dreams. Mom and Dad, you supported me endlessly even when I know you wished I had just gone to law school or gotten a "real job." I never doubted your love and faith in me. I very literally would not have been able to write this book if you hadn't invited us back home and provided shelter, food, love, and childcare as I wrote and wrote and wrote. Thank you for taking my little monkeys to the park and the backyard while "Mommy's working." To my sisters Erica and Jane who listened to me and put up with my middle child drama through the decades, I love you. And to Wilder and Forrest, my sweet, magical little performers who give me reasons to laugh every day and have shattered any previous understanding I might have had about gender and girls.

Note

1 Reproduced by permission. www.cengage.com

Introduction

Picture three teenage girls standing on milk crates on a street corner in a gentrifying neighborhood, a bodega next to a laundromat next to an overpriced café. They are performing a play they have written for a growing crowd of audience members and passersby. Enraged by the gender-based violence they and their friends have endured, motivated to challenge the sexualization of girls they see the media perpetuating, and inspired by girls around the world demanding action, they speak.

GRACE: Listen.
LAILA: Listen.
MICHELLE: Listen.
GRACE, LAILA, & MICHELLE: LISTEN!
GRACE: It's our turn.
MICHELLE: We are tired of the silence you force upon us.
LAILA: We are tired of waiting for our turn to talk.
GRACE: Because – guess what? – I DON'T CARE!
MICHELLE: I don't care that you feel entitled to my smile when I'm in a public space you have been taught is yours.
GRACE: I don't care if you think I'm a slut.
LAILA: or a prude.
GRACE, LAILA, & MICHELLE: So here we are.
LAILA: In this unsafe space that every day we fight to survive in.
MICHELLE: But I am not alone anymore. Today I fight with a sisterhood.
GRACE: We find strength in our experiences.
LAILA: We lean on each other when the weight of these traumas grows too heavy.
MICHELLE: And we are demanding more from this world which feels entitled to our bodies and dismisses our words.
GRACE, LAILA, & MICHELLE: You cannot silence us any longer![1]

As their words leap through the air, I look around to try to assess their impact. A woman with a stroller rushes past, her gaze focused on her crying baby. A cluster of teenagers snaps their fingers and cheers at the performers.

A couple of hipster college students linger and listen as they sip their frothy coffee drinks. Men turn towards them. Men look away. A boy gives a thumbs up. Women raise their fists. These girls are taking up space. Regardless of those who ignore them or glare at them, they are determined to reach anyone who *will* listen. They are shouting their truths, demanding to be heard. This play is one example of many where girls are using the tools of performance to share their stories, devise new ones, and in the process advocate for social change.

Who are the girls[2] who create activist performances? Why do they gravitate to theater, this ancient and urgent art form? What impact does performing have on them? On their audiences and communities? On policy? Does it work? These are the questions I have been obsessing over for the better part of the past two decades. This book is my attempt to answer them.

Self-identified "radical feminist-of-color" ethnographers and anthropologists Cherríe Moraga, Gloria Anzaldúa, and Ruth Behar write about the tension from the academy when integrating personal experiences as a lens through which the reader can see and process the deeper theories within our research (Moraga & Anzaldúa, 1981; Behar, 1996). These Black and Latinx women bravely challenged the historically white and male canon of ethnography and anthropology and used the poetry, beauty, passion, and rage of their own lives as the language of their scholarship. They blazed a trail singed with the fire of their words that decades of future scholars, including myself, are grateful to follow.

In addition to case studies of activist theater projects I have co-created, historical and theoretical analysis, and in-depth qualitative interviews, I use an autoethnographic framework as part of my methodology to "integrate emotional, spiritual, and moral parts of [myself] with the intellectual and analytical in order to hold on to the personal connection to [my] experience" (Ellis & Bochner, 2017, p. vii). My own path winds through girlhood studies, theater and performance, and activism, and I situate this book in all three. I grab onto different branches of these fields, rip off buds and land finally in the messy, fiery heat at the intersection of all three: girl-driven activist performance. This is not where I started, but it is definitely where I begin. I cannot untangle my own work and experiences from the theories and histories of these intersecting fields. So, I won't. Girls' voices will saturate this text as it is their words and actions, dreams and struggles that help us understand how they can and are changing the world, along with themselves. The girl's voice that I start with, is my own.

Before I share any other details about me, there are some things you need to know. As readers of my book, you are already looking at the stories I will share through my lens. You are reading only what I have chosen to share with you and as this book has been 20-odd years in the making, there is much that I have left out. Yet, as we begin this journey together, I want to help you understand the lens you are looking through. My eyes, a hazel-ish brown come from my father whose mother's eyes were robin eggshell blue. My peachy beige fingers with chipped fuchsia nail polish click across my overpriced MacBook Pro keyboard. I am whiteness. I am cisgender girlhood. I am born from a social worker-lawyer-marched-in-the-1960s-stay-at-home mother and a working-class-raised, took-on-multiple-jobs-to-get-himself-through-college-and-medical-school father. I am solid middle class, never been hungry except during my trying-to-lose-weight, overachieving-and-stressed out, disordered-eating years in college. I am privileged. This lens is important as you read through my experiences and decide when and if to trust me. I will tell you the truth. But of course, even liars say that. My truths will be bookends to the stories I share about the girls I have known. As Black and Brown girls growing up in New York City, their backgrounds, upbringings, culture, and ancestors are vastly different from mine. Their voices will sit on these pages, and speak for themselves. As I take my first steps on this journey, I invite you to walk with me. I'll point out what I want you to notice, but you'll likely see your own landscape as well. So, let us begin.

My journey

The feminist in me cringes a little as I admit this, but like many girls of my generation, I grew up creating fantastical worlds inhabited by my cherished Barbie dolls. In my imagination (and obviously the imaginations of Mattel toy designers), Barbie was the boss, the hero, the protagonist. I would play for hours and hours spinning stories about her relationships with Skipper, with Christie, with Ken, with her teachers, friends, boyfriend, and parents. When I experienced something unfair in my life, I would restage the event with my dolls warping the truth into the outcome that I wanted. As the playwright, director and performer, I was in total control. But once I had cut off all their hair, redesigned and marker-ed on all their clothes, scribbled tattoos on all their shiny peach or brown limbs, I grew bored with their frozen plastic smiles. And by that time, I had found the real-life space where I could play similar games of make-believe, but live and with other kids. I had found the theater.

From middle school until today, not a year has gone by when I haven't been in some way involved with a theater production. I have been a director, an actor, a set, lighting, costume, sound, and props designer, a stage manager, and a producer. I had an urgent passion to make theater, so fierce that as a 14-year-old, without telling my parents, I applied, auditioned for, and was accepted to a private boarding school for the arts in Michigan. My mother found out when she received the first tuition bill. After much pleading, persuading, and making the teary case for why I *had* to study theater and be surrounded by artists, my open-hearted, unwaveringly supportive parents let me go, and I was off. By my senior year, with dozens of productions already under my belt, I was growing more and more fed up with the ways that gender inequality permeated the art form. Though there always seemed to be more girls than boys interested in participating in theater, the plays usually had more juicy roles for the boys. And the roles that were available to the girls stung with stereotypes. While the boys had their Odysseuses, Hamlets, and Willy Lomans, we girls seemed stuck as the women waiting behind, taking care of the home while the men went off on adventures. I remember as a teenager playing Helena in Shakespeare's *A Midsummer Night's Dream* in an acting class scene. My male teacher critiqued my performance choices by saying, "A woman wouldn't behave like that!" His words enraged me as I felt insulted that a man was trying to assert that he knew more than I did about being a girl. This was a turning point for me: I realized I could continue to speak lines written by men and be told how to behave by them, or I could create my own work. Though I knew that not every man was trying to silence girls, in that moment, as a tempestuous adolescent, I decided that I would walk away from acting and become a director. I wanted to use the stage to tell stories about girls, created by girls.

In college, I was intensely active in the theater community and directed, produced, or designed more than 50 productions. After my sheltered childhood and adolescence in the middle-class, segregated, white part of Wilmington, Delaware and the elite arts boarding school in Interlochen, Michigan, I arrived at Brown University in what seemed to me a booming urban center: Providence, Rhode Island. I started to notice injustice all around me from the people experiencing homelessness asking me for money on my way to class everyday to the stories of women I was reading about in my feminist theory classes. My middle-class, white privilege shone through as I stumbled, but I started to connect the obvious dots between racism and oppression and felt an urgent pull towards activism. I did not yet know how, but I desperately felt that I wanted to try to *do something*.

In my earnest, naïve wanderings from one activist group to the next trying to find where I might fit and make a difference, I joined the International Socialist Organization during my freshman year. I was looking for a community of like-minded social justice crusaders, but was disappointed by ISO's lack of creativity, aggressive recruitment techniques, and propensity for standing on street corners shouting angrily at passersby to sign their petitions which always seemed to be flying off their clipboards and blowing away in the wind. I finally found my ideal merging of theater and activism as a volunteer in the Space in Prison for the Arts and Creative Expression (SPACE) Program with incarcerated women at the Rhode Island Adult Correctional Institution. SPACE was created by playwright Paula Vogel in 1986 for Brown students to facilitate performing arts and creative writing workshops with women in prison. I saw first-hand how valuable it was for the women I worked with to have the space and basic guidance to express themselves through writing and performance, as many scholars since have documented (Balfour, 2004; Fraden, 2001; Thompson, 1998; Winn, 2011). Though as I drove from Providence to Cranston every week, I was logging more than miles. I was starting to see and understand what my presence as a white woman meant in spaces filled with Black and Brown women. It took me years to begin to shed my internalized "White Savior Complex" where I felt smugly proud that I was using my privilege and resources to "help" and yes, "save" poor Black women. I had so many unchecked assumptions about the women I worked with and at the time, was too insecure and ashamed to name them. When asked, I would ramble on and on about how creative the women were and how I was just there to make some great theater with people who had good stories to tell. I probably also said shallow statements such as, "They have no other creative outlet, except us." There was so much I did not yet understand about power, privilege, racism, poverty, and the prison industrial complex and I regret now that at that time, I did not do the necessary work to educate myself.

I was collaborating with women from their teens to their 70s and was most drawn to the 18-, 19-, and 20-year-olds whose energy ricocheted off the concrete walls, and whose ages at least matched mine and provided a means of connection despite so many other differences between my life and theirs. These girls' writing pulsed with hope, dreams, and faith in their future "on the outside." I partnered with Katie Eastburn, another white college student, dear friend, and SPACE volunteer and together we designed, organized, and launched a sister program with teenage girls at the Rhode Island Training School, a juvenile "justice" facility. Though I had yet to develop a more comprehensive understanding of how racism impacted the work we were doing, I persisted. We began to develop a curriculum that braided performing arts work with adolescent girls' social and emotional development. Smitten by the exuberance, creativity, and urgent need I saw in these girls to express their feelings, share their voices and demonstrate their agency, Katie and I continued this work after we graduated. With funding from a public service fellowship, we relocated to San Francisco and co-founded Inside/Out Performing Arts, a playmaking program with girls affected by the juvenile justice system in the San Francisco Bay Area. We continued building and re-focusing our mission and our activities as we led workshops and directed original theater projects with girls at juvenile halls, group homes, and community centers. Inspired by the work of Rhodessa Jones and her Medea Project for Incarcerated Women (Fraden, 2001), we used Greek mythology and cultural narratives as inspiration for the girls' personal writing about social justice issues in their lives.

At this point in my journey as a young director, I was thirsty for training and education in theater collaboration and directing. I believed that community-based performance work needed new vocabularies and language to critique it (Cohen-Cruz, 2005), but as a passionate theater creator, I was haunted by criticism that this work was a lesser art than professional theater created by trained artists and craved the space and training for my own artistic development and education. I was also conflicted about how I could be most useful to the girls I was working with. At one point, I had three different piles of grad school applications as I was considering whether to apply to law school, for a master's in social work or an MFA in theater directing. After some deep soul searching and conversations with my closest friends and family, I realized that at my core, I see the world through the lens of art and that I believe I could contribute the most as an artist, collaborating with and creating theater with girls.

I was introduced to the work of theater director Anne Bogart and was particularly interested in her unique theories of creative collaboration and her development of the Viewpoints technique for ensemble-building in rehearsal and collaborative staging for performance (Bogart, 2001; Bogart & Landau, 2005). I moved to New York City to pursue my degree in theater directing at Columbia University under Bogart's mentorship. There, I honed my skills as a director by creating and directing more than 40 projects in three years, including assigned projects by Euripides, Shakespeare, Chekhov, Strindberg, Witkiewicz, and Arthur Miller, all dead white men. In addition to feeling that my creative practice was worlds away from the "on-pause" work with teenage girls, I was frustrated by the lack of community engagement at Columbia. The "walled fortress" of the ivy-covered, white-bodied campus jutted up against the historically African American Harlem neighborhood. These feelings reached fever pitch after the terrorist attacks on the World Trade Center on September 11, during which I had been holed up in the library researching early twentieth-century Polish theater as my city smoldered 130 blocks south. In retrospect, I can hear that familiar "White Savior Complex" bell ringing inside me as I sought out opportunities to re-engage with young people of color. I acknowledge that I still had not yet done the personal and deeply necessary work to understand how white supremacy culture had devastated so many of the schools and neighborhoods of the Black and Latinx high school students I began to collaborate with, and that my presence, though well-intentioned, could do as much harm as good. These years were my training time and I still have some aches of regret over how I wish I had done things differently, while I am also deeply proud of the creative work I was a part of. This book is part of my attempt to reconcile and acknowledge how unprepared so many white people are to do ethical, useful and creative work with teenagers of color, in theater and beyond.

It is 2002. I start working as a teaching artist in the Bronx, Manhattan, and Brooklyn, and clock hundreds of hours in high school hallways saturated with teenage shrieking, giggling, sweating bodies sliding past each other, climbing and falling in vertical elevator dances as they check each other out, up and down and up and down. The eyes of the girls are outlined in smudged blacks and purples, hidden naked behind glasses frames or gazing up from under eyelash extensions. Denim stretches like saran across hips, calves, and shoulders. Bodies contort in shapes to illuminate curves, swells, lips, and hair or to mask bulges, ripples, or blemishes. I listen to pulsing whispers, hushed voices, squirting cackles, and a buzzing drone of voices dangling in the air above their corn-rowed, extension plaited, twisted, straightened, curling, bleached, rainbowed, and natural hairdos. Amidst the swirls of stray glitter sparkling in the air, and hip-hop beats leaking muffled from earbuds, pairs and clumps of teenage girls huddle in conversations, sharing stories of heartbreak, abuse, injustice, love, desire, and betrayal. Stories upon stories upon stories flow out of them like breath.

Their beats, rhythms, and lyrics are like a song I can't shake from my head. My ears are tuned to the nuances and poetry of their word choices as they struggle to be understood, listened to, and believed. They join me to create theater so that these stories can float up above these intimate clusters like hot air balloons above the hallways, schools, and street corners, witnessed by thousands pointing up at the sky. And as a theater director, I am particularly attentive to how they mine the drama from their lives and spin it into drama for the stage. I am trained to look at the spaces between their bodies, to analyze the rhythms and pitches of their voices, to reconstruct the missing narratives from the snippets of stories they share, to question who needs to sit in the audience seats to hear them and then to guide them to consider how to craft and mold their stories in order to assure the greatest impact.

Dismayed by the lack of creative opportunities for these girls in the Harlem neighborhoods cocooning Columbia, chandra thomas, a Jamaican–American graduate acting student (who spells her name in all lowercase), and I decided to run a free summer theater project for local high school girls. We had access to Columbia's rehearsal and performance spaces. We stapled pink flyers to telephone poles on 125th Street and called all our peers, colleagues, and friends who worked with high school students. Eight Black and Latinx teenage girls showed up at our "tryouts/" info session nervous, giggly, and determined. We welcomed and accepted them all. After nearly 100 hours of rehearsal over eight weeks, we presented "Say It How It Is," an original show with every word written and performed by these eight teenagers. The text, a somewhat messy and disjointed collage of poetry, flamenco dance, monologues, and scenes, dealt with peer and parent pressure, body image, racism, and divorce. The girls wrote poetry about ideals of "beauty," created intricate step dance routines to introduce themselves to the audience, constructed dramatic and suspenseful scenes with realistic dialogue, and spoke emotional monologues about events in their lives.

The audience included the girls' families, friends, and a few teachers as well as theater artists interested in young people's voices. Their response was enthusiastic and wildly encouraging. "I know a wonderful young woman for your next project!" "My niece would just love this program! When do you start again?", and from the girls: "When we do our next show, I want to write a scene about …" Though nervous and unsure about how we would secure the funds or find more girls to repeat this process, chandra and I, buoyed by the community's support, continued. viBe Theater Experience was born.

At the time, viBe's stated mission was to "to empower underserved teenage girls to write and perform original theater, video, and music about the real-life issues they face daily."[3] As the founding executive director, I led viBe from 2002 to 2012, and in those exhausting and inspiring years produced and directed or co-directed all of our more than 60 original productions, written and performed by girls. chandra, who also worked extensively as a professional actor and producer, used her dazzling teaching artist and administrative skills to step into the role of director of programming. From 2012 to 2019, I continued to work as a guest director, collaborating with girls on a new show almost every year. chandra and I conceived a specific curriculum that fused theater training activities involving acting, directing, movement, voice, and creative writing with activities that build the security necessary for a supportive girls' group such as trust games, daily check-ins, and community rituals. To catalyze creative writing about issues that are important to them, we were constantly questioning the girls with,

> What do you believe are the biggest challenges about being a teenage girl in New York City today? When you look in the mirror, who do you see? What is important to you? Why? Who needs to hear your stories? Why?

and on and on and on. The girls were treated as artists and collaborators from the first day of rehearsal. We met in theater studio spaces, not in public high schools to enhance the "professional theater" experience.

viBe's programs introduced young women to elements of writing, acting, directing, dancing, singing, and songwriting through collaboration as well as solo work. The girls crafted the structure of their shows collaboratively as they integrated their words and ideas into a cohesive narrative. The issues they addressed included gun violence, sexual violence, body image, depression, teen pregnancy, street harassment, racism, sexism, misogynoir, youth rights, friendship, peer pressure, homophobia, cultural pride, abortion, the AIDS epidemic, and family pressure. The fully designed performances were always held free of charge at professional theaters and were open to friends, family, and all members of the community. Our process invited girls to articulate personal issues related to their identity and lived experiences, then write and perform within their constructions, sometimes fictionalizing or poeticizing some details to blur the real story.

As the years bled into more years, I heard the same stories repeated again and again. A song about surviving sexual assault. Another monologue about the stress and fears related to incessant street harassment. A poem about the impact of fat-shaming. Tears would flow freely in rehearsals as girls shared personal stories of trauma. And then performed them. I noticed patterns emerging. On the one hand, sharing their stories was liberating. It built confidence, fostered community, and contributed to their healing. Through articulating their dreams and struggles on stages, re-embodying their lived experiences and performing their own words for an audience, girls would begin to counteract the lack of confidence, poor body image, and the disenfranchisement of young, "unlistened–to" women (Winn, 2011; Brown, R. N. 2009; Myers, 2009; Hatton, 2003). But on the other hand, there was an inadvertent perpetuating of stereotypes related to race, class, and gender taking place as too often, it was the sensational stories of abuse, sexual violence, attempted suicide, pain, and trauma that brought girls so much attention, and consistent applause. Holding hands with these positive outcomes of strength and empowerment, and absent from the literature that celebrates girls' agency, are the gripes and dangers inherent in inviting (and sometimes inadvertently pushing) girls to write and perform uncensored, thinly veiled stories about their personal, often painful, experiences.

I reached a turning point. I was back in graduate school again and working on my doctoral dissertation, a research study where I had the space and support to analyze the impact performing their own words was having on the girls I was collaborating with. Through in-depth one-on-one interviews with more than 30 girls over the course of two years, I could take time outside of our collaborative rehearsal process to really listen to their personal stories and the ways they made sense of our theater process. I saw how the performance of trauma can be dangerous. My research findings (Edell, 2010, 2013) revealed that when girls are given the space, as so often is called for, this gift can inadvertently be like the wedding dress Medea gives her husband Jason's mistress in Euripides's version of this Greek myth. The moment this gloriously beautiful lace is zipped on, it explodes into flames, blazes into the bride's flesh, and destroys her.

Sometimes the very space that is, on the one hand, a gift, a positive site for empowerment and resistance, can ignite into destruction as girls speak their truths about trauma, struggles, and survival. Audiences file into the theater and assume they are hearing uncensored, "real" stories from the voices of their peers, their daughters, their students, and their sisters. Through my in-depth interview-based analysis of more than 30 girls, I saw that girls were heavily influenced by and saturated in race and gender stereotypes. In their devising of new stories and re-defining of their own best and worst experiences, girls kept the patriarchal, white supremacist wheels spinning as they added fuel to the engines by repeating and re-embodying stories of oppression. Audiences, often dazzled by the strength and courage it takes for girls to perform personal stories on stage in public, reward them with lavish applause, cheers, and further validation that these are the "real" and important stories to keep telling. I witnessed firsthand how the more that audiences give standing ovations after each girl's expression of violence, racism, homophobia, then the more girls will repeat these stories. And the wheels keep spinning.

After ten dizzying years of absorbing these stories, I began to wonder: What if instead of using the performance space as a site for girls to heal from the trauma of violence, we worked to end the violence in the first place? What if our performances were not just calls to empathize, but calls to action?

I never stopped believing in the power of theatermaking to help increase girls' self-confidence, build trust, foster community among girls, and allow audiences to see and respect girls' creativity, intellect, hard work, and accomplishments and to learn about the issues they face by hearing them share their stories. But I had reached my own breaking/turning point where I couldn't continue to produce the kind of work that seemed to accept – and broadcast – that girls' lives were filled with never-ending pain and trauma. As a key part of this burgeoning awareness, I was also struggling with what it meant to be a white woman directing productions with girls of color and felt I was perpetuating a white supremacist leadership model and to some degree profiting from the traumas of girls of color.

For every empowering monologue about suffering from racism that I helped girls stage for performance, I would internally cringe that somehow I could be doing more. I sometimes felt that my very presence in the room might prevent girls from being able to explore issues related to racism and white supremacy because they didn't want to offend or alienate me. I felt a pull to shift my focus towards working to challenge the structures, institutions, and corporations that allowed toxic sexist and racist messaging to poison our culture and society. I took a step away from girls' theater and moved towards girls' activism.

In 2012, I started my new job as executive director of SPARK Movement co-founded by developmental psychologists Lyn Mikel Brown and Deborah Tolman. SPARK is a girl-fueled, intergenerational activist organization working to ignite and foster an antiracist gender justice movement to end violence against women and girls and promote girls' healthy sexuality, self-empowerment, and well-being.[4] I worked with a phenomenal team of girl-identified activists with diverse racial, ethnic, national, religious, and gender identities, ages 13–22, from throughout North America, Europe, and Asia. Together, we launched a series of actions and campaigns that engaged girls as central to the solutions, instead of protecting them from the problems they face. Through online and on-the-ground activist trainings and collaborations, SPARK provided training, spaces, and platforms for girls and women to share and enact strategies for change that address urgent feminist issues, such as sexualization of women in the media, gender-based violence, sexism and discrimination, racism and homophobia (among others), from their respective experiences.

A few of our highest-profile and most impactful campaigns and projects included working with the National Federation of High Schools Association to create and distribute sexual violence and consent education resources to one million public middle and high school coaches who worked with young athletes. Our intergenerational team also successfully pressured *Seventeen Magazine* to publicly promise to never digitally alter images of girls and to commit to racial, ethnic, and body size diversity in their pages. One of my favorite campaigns was when we published our girl-compiled and analyzed research tracking the history of Google's homepage "Doodles" honoring people from history and identified the number of white women, women of color, and men of color compared to white men. The *Wall Street Journal* published our research along with an interview with one of our girl activists and me on their digital home page. That led to Google reaching out to us and collaborating to create "Women on the Map," a phone app that used Google Maps technology to alert users whenever they were approaching a location where a woman had contributed to history.

As part of our goal to amplify girls' voices, we also booked girl advocates on television programs such as Fox & Friends, NBC Nightly News, Good Morning America and as experts on issues that affect girls in the *New York Times*, *Wall Street Journal*, and *Huffington Post* among dozens of other local, national, and global media outlets.

Though none of these actions or campaigns was explicitly theater-based, almost all of them used a performance technique or strategy as one of their tactics. For example, as part of one campaign to demand H&M use mannequins that matched the diverse body sizes of their customers, girls in the US and the UK staged performance art where they dressed in the exact outfits of H&M mannequins and photographed themselves, standing next to the mannequins in the same poses, drawing attention to the disconnect between the real girl and the unrealistic plastic form. And yet, by my second year with SPARK, I was achingly missing the intensive, creative process of devising, creating, and producing live theater with girls. I hadn't given up on my belief that theatermaking with girls is a powerful and useful endeavor. I needed this time away to recognize that I wanted to incorporate more performance into activism and more activism into performance.

And so, I approach this next phase of my life: activist performance with girls.

This shift might not have seemed so drastic to outsiders. I was still creating and directing theater, written and performed by girls. But the core intention of the work shifted from a primary goal of impacting individual girls' lives, towards a broader community-based goal of igniting personal, political, and/ or social change. In practice, this meant my process focused more deliberately on girls identifying the issues that impacted their lives and the lives of the people they loved, and then, using the performance space as a site to offer realistic strategies for addressing, overcoming, ending or challenging these issues.

Before every viBe performance, we used to decorate the theater's lobby with brochures and applications for girls to join our programs and sell the CDs or downloads of music and published scripts that the girls created. But before SPARK performances, we invited local activist organizations to set up tables in the lobby of the theater with information about the issues they were fighting for, how people could support their cause, sign a petition or letter to elected officials, donate money, or volunteer.

Every SPARK production needed to include a "Call to Action," at least one moment of direct interaction with the audience where the audience was invited/instructed to take action related to the topics the girls brought up in the play. One show that the girls created, based on the question, "What's the difference between feeling sexy and feeling sexualized?" included a pause in the production when the girls broke the "fourth wall" of the theater to directly speak to the audience and engage in a dialogue about the role of women's and teen magazines in perpetuating highly sexualized images of girls and limited representations of "beauty." Then they distributed paper, pens, and envelopes and asked the audience to write letters to the editors of these magazines, or to people in their lives whom they felt needed to hear the messages the girls in the show were spouting. We then stamped and sent these letters.

Though the financial structures of SPARK shifted and the core organization unraveled in the years around 2016 and 2017, I continued collaborating with girls to create activist productions into 2020 until once again, the world as I knew it, ruptured. And I pivoted. As the Covid-19 pandemic blazes through communities around the world, killing (as of April 2021) more than three million people worldwide, including nearly 600,000 in the US, disproportionately taking Black, Indigenous, and Latinx people, I left Brooklyn. I lasted two months with my one- and four-year-old sons, and as a single mother unwilling to risk our health or the health of a babysitter, I had no option for childcare. Trying to write and work full time with a toddler bouncing on my lap and a four-year-old painting the walls and climbing up the furniture was not sustainable. We moved in with my parents in the house I grew up in Wilmington, Delaware with so much more indoor space for my boys, a luscious backyard wilderness to explore, and the generous help of my parents to share childcare duties. We are the lucky ones. And so, I have come full circle, back to the segregated hometown I thought I'd left forever as a teenager. The irony of writing this book while sitting at the same wood kitchen table where I wrote many a high school essay as a teenager is not lost on me. The sounds of the crickets and the smells of the pine trees too easily transport me back to my adolescence. As I imagine building a new life here as an adult, I am drawn to creating something both familiar and new. I feel called to create theater that I wished I could have engaged in as a white teenage girl in Wilmington. I am in the process of launching theater projects with white girls through the local Jewish community and using the performance space to explore internalized white supremacy, to address white privilege, and to write and perform stories that offer strategies and solutions for young white folks to be useful co-conspirators in the racial justice movement. I will listen to the voices of girls here, and let them guide us.

Teenagers are ready and eager to address all the messes that older generations left them. At the end of the second decade of the twenty-first century, most girls look around them and see sexual violence escalating, climate-changing, reproductive rights withering, racism exploding, police murdering, schools failing, and gun control flailing. These issues are impacting them and their friends. Activism doesn't seem so much an extracurricular activity for the hippies, "crazy feminists," and angry militants. Activism feels more like, as one Black teenage girl told me in an interview, "survival."

So, does it work? Did our theatermaking change the girls? Did it change the world? Were these girls using theater to prevent violence? To end racism? To shift policy? Did creating theater coded and named as "activist" have a different impact on girls than if they were just "creating theater?" This book is my attempt to answer these questions, and more. Within these pages, I rip apart my own process and my work with girls like an overripe peach, breaking the soft skin to expose the sticky sweet flesh, and eventually the rough, hard pit. I don't coat it in sugar and I am as invested in revealing the pitfalls, challenges, traumas, and failures as I am in celebrating our victories and boasting of the successes. This book invites you into not just the details of the work I did and refer to here, but also to meet other artists and activists and see the scope and scale of this growing and urgent field.

In 2007, as part of my doctoral dissertation research, I began interviewing the girls I was collaborating with. Because I learned so much from these interviews and because I quickly saw how the process of an interview brought us closer and deepened my connection with each girl as I listened to her stories, I never really stopped interviewing. Between 2007 and 2020, I interviewed more than 50 girls. These qualitative interviews were semi-structured and followed various formats including an interview method I developed where I gave each girl a tape recorder (this was pre-cellphone app recording!) and a list of questions such as,

> What kinds of stories do you write for the theater? Why do you write about these things? How do you feel after you write? Who do you want to hear them? Why? What do you hope will happen if you share these stories? Why? Who don't you want to hear them? Why?

Then, she returns her cassette to me and I listen to her responses, recorded in her own time and space, without the pressure of my gaze or prompts. I then record a response cassette for her with follow-up questions, and she records another and we go on and on like a slow-motion interview, unfolding over weeks or months (Edell, 2015). Other interviews were more traditional, in a quiet space together where I ask and she responds to questions. For this book, I interviewed several girls years after we had collaborated, in order to learn about what they are doing now and how their theater experiences as teenagers might or might not have impacted their current adult lives. I also interviewed leaders and personal heroes in the field of girls activism and girls performance.

In addition to the interviews, I have 2 decades, dozens of productions, hundreds of rehearsals, and thousands of hours of field observations of my own work with girls creating and producing theater. The title of every chapter is borrowed from the title of one of the plays I collaborated with girls to create. Their voices and stories frame and underlie all the work.

Chapter 1 – "Under construction": girls, performance, and activism

I present the historical and theoretical framework that provides the context for the productions and analysis throughout the book. I articulate the history of girls' scholarship and the introduction of the field of both Girls Studies and Black Girls Studies, then include definitions of activism and the recent burst of individual girl activists as well as girls' activist organizations. I conclude with a section about youth activist theater with a focus on girls' activist performance.

Chapter 2 – "This is not a safe space": principles of theatermaking with girls

I offer the core seven principles that inform my own activist work with girls and weave in examples from my work and insights from interviews with girls and with adult leaders in the field in order to provide a framework and guidance for other educators, directors, and activists who work with teenagers. The title "This Is Not a Safe Space" was the name of a site-specific performance created by girls outside in a Brooklyn neighborhood, addressing street harassment and sexual violence. It is meant to also problematize the ways many adults say on the first day of a youth program, "This is a safe space." We need to acknowledge the impossibility of ensuring everyone's physical and emotional safety at all moments, while also making every effort to do just that. The seven principles include:

- negotiating intergenerational power
- operating with antiracist, intersectional, and feminist lenses
- creating the highest quality, culturally responsive theater
- educating through critical thinking and liberatory pedagogy practices
- facilitating with a trauma-informed practice
- cultivating uncensored, unadulterated storytelling
- choosing an abundance of joy, play, and love whenever possible

Chapter 3 – "Real im(PERFECT)ions": performing confidence, expressing agency

I share the core issue that girls write about and the leading outcome theater organizations profess to achieve: building confidence. The playful title of this chapter and the show it refers to expresses the tensions between what is "real" and what has been coded by society, culture, and the media as "perfect," with a nod to the impossibilities of both realness as well as perfection. Within this chapter, I write about several examples from my own work with girls related to the complicated benefits and drawbacks of using theater as a site for fostering confidence, a deconstruction of how girls use theater to problematize "ideals of beauty," the challenges of girls' negotiations between feeling "sexy" and feeling "sexualized," and offer examples for what the performance space offers girls with disabilities and how girls use the stage as a space to explore their sexuality.

Chapter 4 – "Held momentarily": for an audience of one … plus

Through sharing detailed stories about how girls focus their performances on a desire to change one person in their lives, they find a specificity in their story-telling and performance process that in turn, can resonate with and impact the larger audience. The title "Held momentarily" was from one of our plays where a group of girls was stuck in a subway car, trapped underground, and forced to deal with each other. Any New York City subway rider would immediately know how to complete this all-too-common subway announcement while they waited for the "train's dispatcher" and experiencing an "unavoidable delay." This chapter evokes that same situation of audience members being "held momentarily" in their seats for the duration of the theater production and the ways girls use (and abuse) this contained space.

Chapter 5 – "Shut up and listen!": performance in public spaces

In this chapter, I look at the creation and impact of public performances including marches, rallies, and protests through the streets and in public parks, a site-specific outdoor performance through one neighborhood, and teenagers' use of TikTok as a digital, interactive public performance space.

Chapter 6 – "Finally someone hears us": considering our audiences

This chapter identifies very specific audiences and how the impact of the performance shifts for both the audience and the performers based on the demographics of who is in the audience. I analyze a performance created by girls and performed at the Boys Club of New York, a performance at the United Nations, at a conference for educators, in a Zoom chat, a specific public performance for the media, and one that critiques funders as audience members.

Conclusion – ripples of change

I offer insight about the limitations of claiming theater changes audience members and performers/creators while also holding space for celebrating the ways it does both.

Notes

1 The unpublished performance texts shared throughout this book were all written by the teenage girls in the activist theater projects I co-directed with the organizations SPARK Movement (www.sparkmovement.org) and/or viBe Theater Experience (www.viBeTheater.org). Printed here with their consent.
2 Throughout this book, I use the word "girls" when referring to any teenager who identifies as a "girl" regardless of the sex they were assigned at birth. This includes cisgender girls, transgender girls, gender expansive youth, gender non-conforming, and genderqueer teens who choose to participate in programs created for "girls." When I write about specific young people, I use the gender identities and pronouns that they request.
3 www.viBeTheater.org, 2019.
4 SPARKmovement.org, 2019.

1 "Under construction"

Girls, performance, and activism

Investigating the who, the how, the why, the where, and the what of girls' activist performance triply demands an interdisciplinary approach. I use the word "girl" to refer to the teenagers that I have been collaborating with since the mid-1990s when I was myself a "girl." This is the word they use to identify themselves. I could call them female youth or young women, but as cultural anthropologist Aimee Meredith Cox quotes one of the 16-year-old girls she writes about in *Shapeshifters: Black Girls and the Choreography of Citizenship*, her astounding ethnography, "*young women* suggests that you are trying to be polite and official, but it sounds like you have done something wrong or are in trouble with authority figures" (Cox, 2015, p. 243). When I ask the girls in our projects how they want to be identified, they have resoundingly agreed and claim the word, "girl." When I began my work, my gender vocabulary was limited as the world was still too unsafe for young people to claim their authentic and expansive gender identities. In recent years I have included the phrase "girl-identified teenagers, gender-expansive young people, and nonbinary youth and any others who want to join a project created with and for girls."

This book is for the activists who work with girls and want to understand how to incorporate performance into their campaigns. It's for the youth theater artists whose girls and gender non-conforming young people have been demanding that their shows address social justice issues. It's for the scholars and program staff and teachers and therapists and parents who lie awake at night worried about girls today. And it's for everyone else seeking to understand this current phenomenon of girls using performance tactics to chip away at the structures that attempt to silence or simply ignore them. This chapter is a thick, curly braid. Through it, I wrap the history and theory of Girls Studies then twist with a thick strand of Girls' Activism and wind in Theater and Performance. Though each strand might stand-alone, this work would unravel without an understanding of each of them.

Part I: surveying the field

Girls' Studies

After more than half a century of empirical research on children, which focused mostly on middle-class white boys and the assumed generalization of this population to all young people, the 1990s ushered in a new interdisciplinary field, now generally referred to as "Girls Studies" (Aapola et al., 2005; Brown & Gilligan, 1992; Harris, 2004; Gonick, 2003; Leadbeater & Way, 1996, 2007; Lipkin, 2009; Ginsberg & Johnson, 2016). Early groundbreaking studies, including developmental psychologists Lyn Mikel Brown and Carol Gilligan's *Meeting at the Crossroads: Women's Psychology and Girls' Development* (1992), provided evidence for the ways in which girls fear that speaking their truths could lead to emotional ruptures and broken relationships. Though these researchers were predominantly white women, they made efforts to ensure their participant pool included girls of color. This body of research showed how, in middle school, girls begin to question what they know and silence themselves. Preadolescent girl children are often seen *and* heard fearlessly swinging from monkey bars at the playground, splashing up to their skinned knees in muddy puddles and confidently demanding to be heard and listened to. But then, as they begin to pull tight the curtain of their childhood and tiptoe onto the stage of adolescence, they often leave the echoes of their loud voices offstage. In her book about girls and anger, Brown penetrated the silence of girls by digging more deeply into what holds their tongues and why:

> Girls' experiences, strong feelings, and opinions come up against a relational impasse that constrains possibilities and shuts down loud voices, a wall of "shoulds" in which approval is associated with silence, love with selflessness, relationship with subordination and lack of conflict, and anger or strong feelings with danger and disruption.
>
> (Brown, 1998, p. 109)

Brown's work outlines a crisis in adolescence for girls when they construct a chasm between what they know, and what they feel they can express. They start to see the subtle ways that girls get punished for speaking out, and get rewarded for being quiet, deferential, and demure. They notice that the toys marketed to them are the pretty princesses, the baby dolls, and the pink plastic vacuums, while the boys are encouraged to build towers, launch rockets, and fight dragons.

The timing of this influx of research related to girls makes sense. The second wave of the white feminist movement had ushered massive changes in the United States workforce for white women, including in higher education. By the 1990s, the number of women scholars and professors had increased and many of these women, influenced by the women's rights movement, saw the need for speaking out against gender injustice where they saw it. And they saw it in the research. Additionally, young researchers who came of age in the 1980s were studying with this new generation of women professors and committing themselves to following the paths the previous generation of feminist scholars had painstakingly paved.

But yet. Even though the 1970s had brought consciousness about the hierarchical gender divide (particularly for white women), the basic paradigm hadn't shifted. Most girls took for granted the most significant victories of the women's movement. They assumed abortion had been and always would be their legally protected choice (though racial and economic injustices often led to decreased access to safe and affordable abortions for lower-income white girls and girls of color); they couldn't imagine not being able to open a bank account without the "permission" of a husband or father; or that sexual harassment in the workplace was legal, expected, and omnipresent. Despite much progress, girls still notice that adult women often silence themselves and adhere to the unspoken laws that the invisible "gender police" enforce. They absorb media messages perpetuating narratives that women are meant to be desired, that being thin and pretty is the greatest aspiration, while fully clothed men in suits are the ones with the power. They hear their mothers and older sisters complain about their bodies and they witness the lengths women go to please and appease men. They internalize that one of the realities of being a woman in the world is to passively accept a second-class status.

The American Association of University Women's study *How Schools Shortchange Girls* (1992), added timber to these flames by providing evidence for links between girls' self-esteem, achievement, and career aspirations. In 2007, the American Psychological Association released the *Report of the APA Task Force on the Sexualization*[1] *of Girls*, that reviewed hundreds of empirical research studies going back decades that showed the negative impact sexualization has on girls in terms of their physical and mental health, education, relationships, and aspirations for their future. The report has been downloaded more than one million times making it the most popular report in the 130-year history of the organization. *Girlhood Studies: An Interdisciplinary Journal* published its first peer-reviewed issue in Fall 2008, and describes its mission to "provide a forum for the critical discussion of girlhood from a variety of disciplinary perspectives, and for the dissemination of current research and reflections on girls' lives …" (Mitchell et al., 2008).

Studies with more diverse samples including a majority of girls of color document similar evidence of this chasm between what girls feel, what girls say, and how far too many of the adults in their communities ignore their voices (Robinson & Ward, 1991; M. W. Morris, 2016, 2019; E. W. Morris, 2007; Crenshaw, 2015). In reaction, Black girls are either punished for speaking out, or they withdraw into silence. Anthropologist Signithia Fordham (1993) spent a year researching Black students at a public high school in Washington, DC and writes:

> I noted that silence for the African-American female is not to be interpreted as acquiescence. Rather, … silence among the high-achieving females at

the school is an act of defiance, a refusal on the part of the high-achieving females to consume the image of "nothingness" (see Christian 1990) so essential to the conception of African-American women. This intentional silence is also critical to the rejection and deflection of the attendant downward expectations so pervasive among school officials.

(p. 10)

These works look at diverse groups of girls and conclude that young women, especially those at risk of being pushed out of high school or at risk of getting pregnant, are torn between two destructive realities: they can speak out and risk getting in trouble or they can keep quiet and risk disappearing.

As abundant evidence, collected mostly by Black women researchers, has proven, when they do demand attention, Black girls, more often than white girls, are punished or treated negatively than responded to with support and encouragement. In schools, Black girls are often perceived to be taking up "too much space" and are disproportionately punished for "acting out." Critical race theorist and legal scholar Kimberlé W. Crenshaw presents, in her impactful study of girls in Boston and New York, *Black Girls Matter: Pushed Out, Overpoliced, and Underprotected* (2015), documentation that Black girls are expelled from school based on their behavior ten times more often than white girls (20). She notes that this likely stems from the way Black girls are viewed by school staff:

Researchers have sought to measure the possibility that Black girls may be subject to harsher disciplinary interventions because they are perceived to be unruly, loud, and unmanageable. One study revealed that teachers sometimes exercised disciplinary measures against Black girls to encourage them to adopt more "acceptable" qualities of femininity, such as being quieter and more passive.

(p. 24)

It is this perception of Black girls, forced to deal with the intersecting injustices related to racism and sexism (Crenshaw, 1991), who are often reprimanded as "unruly," when they are just laughing, talking, and chilling with their friends, leading to punishment or harassment. Because their contributions to public discourse are rarely listened to with the respect they deserve, they are often treated as "nuisances." When the "choice" is between speaking out in public spaces and getting in trouble, or staying silent and risking invisibility, girls have no real options. Scholar Monique W. Morris who writes about Black girls in education, asks the crucial question, "What does it mean to adopt a pedagogical practice that rejects the notion that loud or 'sassy' girls are disorderly, defiant, and disposable?" (Morris, 2019, pp. 10–11). Tracy Robinson and Janie Ward (1991), developmental psychologists, who focus their research on the experiences of African-American girls, suggest a need for girls to build internal and external resources and develop more than "resistance for survival" which includes short-term survival strategies and move towards a "resistance for liberation" (p. 89) that offers opportunities to dismantle the systems of power and racism that hold them back. They write:

> Adolescent African-American women can be helped to build upon this indigenous source of strength by learning to trust their own voices and perspectives and to develop what bell hooks calls the black women's "oppositional gaze": a way to observe the social world critically and to oppose those ideas and ways of being that are disempowering to the self.
>
> (p. 97)

Additionally, developmental psychologists Niobe Way and Bonnie Leadbeater (1996, 2007), two white women, published *Urban Girls*,[2] two volumes of edited research written by a racially diverse group of researchers that explores the strengths and resistance to failure that girls of color possess. These collections encourage their readers to look beyond stereotypes, questioning how adolescent girl identity has been shaped throughout the twentieth century, and how this image has been destructive. In their attempts and successes at painting a multicultural, inter-class, comprehensive portrait of girls of color, these works made the case that further research needed to be done to address the deep-rooted problems of poverty, sexism, and racism that still poison the waters that young women must drink in order to survive in cities. As anti-racist, white women researchers, their access to resources and tenured positions at research universities allowed them to publish and promote this work. These early texts by both Black and white scholars highlighted the need for more research about girls of color and began to pave the way for the upcoming Black, Indigenous, Latinx, and Asian American scholars to analyze the experiences of a more racially and socioeconomically diverse subset of girls.

In the next decade, the Girls Studies field was making progress in representing the actual demographics of girls in the US and further illuminating the ways in which race and class affected girls' lives by welcoming the emerging sub-field of Black Girlhood Studies. The first pioneering texts of this interdisciplinary field focused on the role of the arts, particularly performance in the lives of Black girls. Black feminist scholars Kyra D. Gaunt and Ruth Nicole Brown literally and figuratively set the stage in their works, Gaunt's *The Games Black Girls Play: Learning the Ropes from Double Dutch to Hip-Hop* (2006) and Brown's *Black Girlhood Celebration: Toward A Hip-Hop Feminist Pedagogy* (2008). As Owens et al. wrote in their article, "Towards an Interdisciplinary Field of Black Girlhood Studies":

> Ruth Nicole Brown dared to believe not only that Black girls were worthy of our intellectual artistic, and political labor, but also that they had something in turn to teach us – that they could, if we listened, change the world.
>
> (2017, p. 117)

This new generation of girls' researchers shared powerful research showing the specific challenges girls of color faced and the unique resilience they possessed. Black women created a new framework for understanding the lives of Black girls and actualized it as "Hip-Hop feminist pedagogy." Ruth Nicole Brown and Chamara Jewel Kwakye (2012, p. 4) define this practice as one that:

(1) Appreciates creative production expressed through language, art, or activism, (2) privileges the in-betweenness of black girl epistemology or a black feminist standpoint, (3) values and cares about the shared knowledge produced by black women's and black girls' presence, (4) interrogates the limitations and possibilities of Hip-Hop feminism, and pedagogy and is, therefore, self-adjusting, (5) stages the political through performance-based cultural criticism, (6) and is located and interpreted through the community (or communities) in which it is immersed.

(Brown, 2008; Durham, 2011)

As a white researcher, I express immeasurable gratitude to the Black women whose scholarly, cultural, creative, and activist work has paved a path through the field of academia that has historically privileged white, male voices, and research. I benefit from the professional and personal risks they have taken to articulate new and valuable theories and processes for doing research with and about girls of color.

Girls' activism

In 1991, lawyer Anita Hill testified at the Supreme Court hearing to confirm Justice Clarence Thomas. She publicly shared that he had made lewd, inappropriate, sexual comments to her and asked the Congressional committee, comprising white men not to confirm him as he had created a hostile and uncomfortable work environment. They confirmed him. For girls and young women watching on television, her testimony and its abrupt dismissal was a wake-up call that women, despite much progress of the Women's Movement of the 1970s, still had much work to do before there was true gender equity.

Rebecca Walker, a young, Black, feminist activist wrote in an article in *Ms. Magazine*, "Becoming the Third Wave" (1992):

So, I write this as a plea to all women, especially women of my generation: Let Thomas' confirmation serve to remind you, as it did me, that the fight is far from over. Let this dismissal of a woman's experience move you to anger. Turn that outrage into political power. Do not vote for them unless they work for us … I am not a post-feminism feminist. I am the Third Wave.

The anger that Walker wrote about was already coursing through this generation and became visible as the Riot Grrrl movement (Kearney, 2006). When pushed to rage, some girls will "do it themselves" and forge their own activism. "Revolution Girl Style Now!" was the rallying cry from this collective, surging mass of savvy (mostly white) girls who spread their creative resistance to sexism, misogyny, and homophobia through punk music and self-published 'zines, among other arts-based activist forms (Kearney, 2006). This growing surge of girl activists denounced patriarchal constructions of femininity, subverted the rules of mainstream media by lying to reporters and journalists, printed and distributed thousands of independent, copy-shop-homemade 'zines, and used their loud, electric guitar-amplified voices to express their desires for social change (Garrison, 2000).

Printed on an undated flyer for the all-women punk band Bikini Kill in response to the question, What is Riot Grrrl?:

> BECAUSE a safe space needs to be created for girls where we can open our eyes and reach out to each other without being threatened by this sexist society and our day to day bullshit. ... BECAUSE we girls want to create mediums that speak to US. We are tired of boy band after boy band, boy zine after boy zine, boy punk after boy punk after boy …
>
> (Hanna, undated, in Darms, 2014)

At this same time that rage against sexism was activating masses of predominantly white girls and young women, hip-hop was ushering in a new generation of bold, sexually confident, politically charged young women of color, led in part by the music of Salt-N-Pepa, Lauryn Hill, Queen Latifah, Lil' Kim, and Missy Elliot, among other groundbreaking female singers and rappers. Their music was smart, political, critically acclaimed, as well as chart-topping. Within a music genre where men dominated the mainstream, and often sang explicit lyrics that sexualized and objectified women, the women who pushed back were fierce in their opposition to this norm. They confronted the sexist stereotypes and exemplified a new face of female success and celebrity.

The publication of Joan Morgan's *When Chickenheads Come Home to Roost: My Life as a Hip Hop Feminist* in 1999 exemplified a common dilemma for many of the young Black women who loved and followed hip-hop. They were passionate about the music, but were enraged by the misogynistic lyrics and sexualizing music videos. The few female recording artists who pushed back gained a huge following and inspired girls that they can use music and performance to articulate gender justice themes.

In the United Kingdom, pop music had a different flavor, all sugar and a dump of saccharine spice, super sweet without much depth. The Spice Girls, formed in 1994, were telling us what they really, really want – and it was this sugar watered down version of Riot Grrrl. It was bold, sexy, and confident, while not actually challenging anything about the status quo, and their 85 million records sold made them the best-selling female group of all time. The marketing genius that propelled them to superstardom was their understanding that branding "girl power" as an inspirational, aspirational, materialistic concept would appeal to girls who wanted to express power while still remaining comfortably within the confines of patriarchy's demands that their "power" exists within a system where they will never actually approach or surpass boys' dominance.

Additionally, the gendering of this issue cannot be ignored. Though social ideals of masculinity have done significant harm to developing boys, often by perpetuating an opposite trope: that boys are and must be strong, secure, confident, and autonomous. The thought of a "Boy Power" campaign is unimaginable, though we are moving toward deliberate and public actions for a necessary "Boys Care" campaign that encourages boys to express their more vulnerable feelings (Way, 2011).

The early 2000s brought a co-option and marketing of "Girl Power" (Lamb & Brown, 2006; Harris, 2004; Taft, 2004), and the corporate rebranding of "feminism lite" as baby doll t-shirts with female Venus symbols have served to distract from and placate the rage that had been bubbling under the strawberry flavored lip gloss. "… [T]he beginning of a genuine movement to give girls more power and more choice got co-opted and turned into a marketing scheme that reinforced age-old stereotypes," (p. 1) developmental psychologists Sharon Lamb and Lyn Mikel Brown write in the introduction to their comprehensive analysis of the ways in which clothing, books, films, television, and toys have been selling girls a watered-down, dangerous, and misleading brew of power, sexuality, and passivity. Girls Studies scholar Jessica Taft (2004) also writes about the ways in which popular culture has created barriers to girls' agency and activism and suggests that "girls' programs need to develop even more ways of challenging the depoliticizing meanings of Girl Power and further encourage girls as agents of social change" (p. 77).

Coinciding with the research about girls and the pop culture's interest in "Girl Power," activists and youth service providers stepped in and created new programs for girls that seemed to fill these needs. Though the framing of "Power" for girls never actually meant that girls would learn or practice wielding any form of power in the outside world. This new focus and resource allocation for girls' development led to a generation of girls growing up in the United States – who had access to girls-only programs – who were told they could "do anything." Mantras of these programs trickled over to girls of diverse backgrounds who found the texts printed in glitter on clothing ("Girl Boss" and "Fight Like a Girl!") sold at Walmart, Kmart, and other reduced-price clothing stores ensuring that these messages became part of the cultural norm for American girls.

Though girls today are certainly not lacking in activist energy (Rich & Sagramola, 2018; Renold, 2018; Brown, 2016; Taft, 2011), there remains a simmering belief that "third wave feminism" has crashed ashore, leaving a calm sea. In her study of 75 girl activists across the Americas, Jessica Taft found that feminist discussions were missing from most of the youth activist groups she encountered (2011). When girls realize that they and their girlfriends are earning better grades, more leadership positions, and greater college acceptances than their male peers many believe the battles their mothers fought are dusty victories (Rosin, 2012). However, these advances serve to obscure the ways in which girls are also still embedded within larger social contexts and cultural discourses that continue to position them as sexualized commodities (Gill, 2008), and lesser than boys. As girls encounter actual injustices, they are shocked to realize they cannot actually "do anything," that they have been nurtured in tinted bubbles where they can't see the reality of the world outside where sexism is rampant and gender-based violence abounds.

We are at a unique moment in history where the generation of girls born after 2000 has learned the language of empowerment, has been trained to be leaders, and yet still witnesses and experiences firsthand the limitations and traumas women still face.

When looking at the marketing of the "Girl Power" movement, it is clear that the girls presumed to be "empowered," are also overwhelmingly white. The blending of pink miniskirts with combat boots refers to Disney princesses and fairy tales and other Eurocentric aesthetics of girlhood as a site for purity and innocence which has been coded as white for centuries. Girls of color, though often marginalized and treated unjustly because of both race and gender, were excluded from the mainstream girls' empowerment movement for the same underlying issues of systemic racism that hindered Black women in the feminist movements (hooks, 1999).

Despite being left – or pushed – out of opportunities and programs created to "empower" girls, according to education scholar Charlotte Jacobs's report for Girls Leadership, *Ready to Lead: Leadership Supports and Barriers for Black and Latinx Girls* (2020), 48 percent of Black girls agree with the statement, "I am a leader," compared to 31 percent of white girls. Her report continues to show the ways that Black and Latinx girls have the ambitions, passion, and drive to advocate for social justice and serve as leaders in their communities. What they lack are the resources to support them and enough mainstream role models to normalize Black and Brown leadership to pave the way for the next generation. Toya Lillard, viBe Theater Experience Executive Director, in a podcast interview with Arts Management and Technology Lab (2020), frames the findings this way:

> [Black girls] show up to school as leaders because that's how they see themselves, and they're speaking up and out and they're told to be quiet. They're told that they're being disruptive. They're told that they're being distracting to boys. So eventually that takes its toll and girls either drop out, there's a huge school push-out problem, or they just shrink.

From the dearth of female representation in government and among corporate leadership, the imbalance of women (and girl) protagonists in film and television and the outpouring of stories of sexual harassment and violence shared through the #MeToo movement, a multiracial and diverse generation of girls are clamoring to fight back and take action. Girls recognize that they cannot always trust the adults and that the issues that impact them most, need to be addressed by them and their peers.

Brazilian educator and activist Paolo Freire articulated his theory of who needs to be at the forefront of movements for social justice and liberation in *Pedagogy of the Oppressed* (1970):

> Who are better prepared than the oppressed to understand the terrible significance of an oppressive society? Who suffer the effects of oppression more than the oppressed? Who can better understand the necessity of liberation? They will not gain this liberation by chance but through the praxis of their quest for it, through their recognition of the necessity to fight for it.
>
> (p. 45)

But just because they (and some of their adult allies) understand the need for them to be at the forefront of movements that focus on the struggles they face, girls are still not systematically welcomed as activist leaders. Youth activism scholar Hava Gordon (2010) provides some reasons why young people are rarely fully considered or trusted to lead action campaigns or projects:

> Age is an axis of inequality and not just a socially constructed difference ... Central to the construction of adolescents as a subordinated group and of age as a system of inequality is the maintenance of what I call "citizen-ship-in-the-making": a model of ambiguous social belonging where young people's political participation can be imagined, but only in terms of their adult eventuality.
>
> (pp. 7–8)

As Gordon writes, young people and especially girls are often not taken seriously as agents of change and their voices are frequently silenced – or at least the volume turned down – in many activist movements. Studies reveal how even within programs focused on civic engagement and activism, systems of gender differentially impact girls and boys as activist movements that are perceived to be gendered as "feminine" lack the legitimacy of more "masculine" movements (Einwohner, Hollander, & Olson, 2000).

A proliferation of girls' programs and organizations erupting in the early 2000s through the present, touting missions of "empowering girls" created the illusion that "Girl Power" was alive and well and that suddenly girls were actually wielding real power and taking on serious responsibilities. Though a closer look at some of these programs shows that it is more often the adults who are fully in power. They design and run programs that give girls the illusion that they are taking action or making a social impact and sometimes this manipulation and false sense of autonomy can backfire and further disenfranchise girls or mislead them into unrealistic assumptions of their potential power. Gordon writes how adult power and sexism intersect to produce girls' political subordination (2007) and subvert girls' political motivations and activities (2010). Girl activists report that they do not feel sufficiently supported by adults, who see them as cute, incapable, and in need of adult guidance (Taft, 2011).

For example, according to the ambitious mission statement of the United Nations Foundation's Girl Up program:

> When girls stand up for girls in need, they empower each other and trans-form our world. As the United Nations Foundation's adolescent girl cam-paign, Girl Up engages girls to take action. Led by a community of nearly half a million passionate advocates raising awareness and funds, our efforts help the hardest to reach girls living in places where it is hardest to be a girl.
> (girlup.org/about/)

What's missing from this inspiring, and yes "empowering" description, are the facts and structures beneath the surface. Though incredibly popular among girls in the US (boasting more than 450,000 members) and often their first foray into activism,[3] Girl Up is a corporate-funded (Nike is a primary sponsor), adult-organized, "girl-serving" organization. With their primary activities "raising awareness and funds," girls are led to believe that girls activism is mostly about providing resources for *other* girls in *other* less privileged countries than the US. The Girl Up website includes a 22-page "Brand Guidelines[4]" that outlines in detail the language and images girls can use when advocating as representatives of Girl Up, ensuring that girls do not go rogue and create their own fliers, posters, and digital memes, but that the Girl Up logo is prominent and clear on all materials.

Girl Up's organizing model evidences adult saturation and relies on tugging on the heartstrings of privileged girls in the US to raise money locally and then send it around the world to "save" girls living in poverty or without access to education. As Girls Studies scholar and former Co-Chair of the Working Group on Girls at the United Nations, Emily Bent (2013) writes:

> [T]he missionary girl power logic works to mediate the discursive relation-ship between Western and Third World girls – solidifying colonized images of Western benevolence and Third World oppression, and embedding them within notions of normalcy, difference, and liberation … instead solidi-fies the assumed differences between Western and Third World girls and in doing so, limits the forms and possibilities for their political subjectivity and agency.
> (pp. 15–16)

Bent's analysis illuminates the seductiveness of this model for some girls themselves, especially girls new to activism. The commodification and neo-liberalization of "Grrrl power" is translated into Girl Up up-type programs and this acts as a set-up of sorts – all this posturing and branding and false advertising, that leads everyone (especially girls) to believe girls have enormous power to act alone if we just give them the chance, a platform. This false story enhances their desire to lead, or rather to be seen as leading actions. And too many well-meaning adults are happy to oblige and create the structures and safety nets so girls can appear – to themselves and to the world – to be in charge.

For every dozen girls' activist organizations like Girl Up, there are smaller, more community-based and highly successful organizations that do provide the training and spaces for girls to understand how to use their power, and actually make an impact. The mighty Girls for Gender Equity (GGE), founded in New York City in 2002 by Joanne Smith, a Black social worker and activist, is "an intergenerational organization committed to the physical, psychological, social, and economic development of girls and women. Through education, organizing and physical fitness, GGE encourages communities to remove barriers and create opportunities for girls and women to live self-determined lives" (ggenyc.org). I appreciate the rare transparency apparent in their naming their work as "intergenerational" and acknowledging the labor, expertise, and leadership of their adult staff. Naming these intergenerational partnerships does not lessen the work the girls do, but provides more realistic expectations for what is possible for teenage activists. GGE's social justice curriculum educates young people to understand the history of racial and gender-based oppression and provides tools for fighting it. Their youth have partnered with their staff to co-design and participate in successful campaigns to advocate for ending sexual harassment in public schools and ending school "push out" for girls of color.

Another girls' activist organizations with strong, girl-driven models include the national chapter-based Girls Learn International (girlslearn.org), an initiative of the Feminist Majority Foundation where girls form in-school chapters and identify activist projects they wish to tackle in their communities, nationally and globally. The girls often meet weekly with a faculty advisor and follow a loosely structured curriculum to identify issues and strategize how to create and launch campaigns. Many of their projects include advocating for girls' education in less developed countries or joining national Feminist Majority Foundation action campaigns such as protesting gun violence and advocating for reproductive rights. Additionally, Black women-led activist organizations such as A Long Walk Home in Chicago and SOUL Sisters Leadership Collective in Miami and New York City offer girls leadership training programs that use an arts-based, healing centered approach to activism training and opportunities.

By the 2010s, activists and some Girls Studies scholars were recognizing the ambiguity of the very term, "girls." Trans young people, genderqueer, gender expansive, nonbinary, and gender non-conforming teenagers began expressing their gender identities at the highest rates we have ever seen. According to a 2017 study by the Human Rights Campaign and the University of Connecticut, of the 10,000 self-identified LGBTQI+ youth surveyed, 34 percent identified as trans, nonbinary, genderqueer or somewhere off the gender binary that assumes people are either girls or boys. Actor Laverne Cox and writer Janet Mock, two adult trans women, and teenage writer and television star Jazz emerged as the first wave of transmedia celebrities and began to speak out, contributing to a slowly growing normalization of trans experiences. Television shows such as Transparent, Pose and Euphoria feature trans characters. By the time actor Elliot Page came out as trans in 2020 with an Instagram post that included the line, "I love that I am trans," alongside staggering statistics about the murders and violence against trans people, the mainstream media's coverage had improved tremendously. While not perfect, nearly every article seemed to use the correct pronouns and avoid objectifying and invasive questions. Though before we jump to any false conclusions that transphobia has ended, we must also remember that 2020 was the year with the most murders of trans people in the US since 1998, tragically illuminating how dangerous the world still remains for people marginalized by gender identity.

Keeping up with this culture shift, girls' programs began to change their mission statements and marketing to accept "girl-identified young people," or "teenagers marginalized by gender," or another description akin to the comprehensive definition from Alliance for Girls: "Girls refers to gender expansive youth, cis girls, trans girls, nonbinary youth, gender non-conforming youth, gender queer youth and any girl-identified youth" (alliance4girls.org). Organizations have recognized that the category of "girl" needed to evolve, embrace the new inclusive gender vocabulary and make space for the young people who don't experience the male privilege that a cisgender boy identity can bestow.

Around the mid-2010s, activism in general and youth-based activism in particular spread across the youth programming world, as girls started demanding spaces to talk about social justice issues and opportunities to fight back. Social media had exploded with sites and spaces for young people to educate themselves about issues such as on Tumblr blogs and Twitter feeds. Girls suddenly had easy access to a digital community of others eager to join and build a movement and provided ample and inspiring examples of girls taking action – and gaining global attention for it. Teenage Pakistani education rights activist Malala Yousafzai seemed to be everywhere: speaking out at the United Nations, celebrating her bestselling autobiography, and at 17 becoming the youngest winner ever of the Nobel Peace Prize. When a shooter killed 17 people at a high school in Parkland, Florida on Valentine's Day 2018, its students took action and coordinated massive rallies and marches, and spoke out widely in the media. Girls heard teenage Emma Gonzales' shaky, tear-stained voice shout out from podiums and marches as she demanded gun control policies. Sixteen-year-old Greta Thunberg captivated the world by speaking out with rage and passion at the United Nations' Global Climate Action Summit. Teenage celebrities from Zendaya to Emma Watson to Amandla Steinberg all proclaimed their feminist status and spoke out about sexism and racism – and were celebrated for it. Activism was trending and teenage girls wanted to join the movement.

Buoyed by a tsunami of media attention paired with the 2016 presidential election of Donald Trump in the US and the Brexit vote in the UK, these young celeb-activists inspired many other enraged teenagers to take action. In response, the publishing industry churned out a slew of new books to serve as guides for young people, and girls in particular: Kaelyn Rich and Guilia Sagramola's *Girls Resist! A Guide to Activism, Leadership, and Starting a Revolution* (2018), Caroline Paul and Lauren Tamaki's *You Are Mighty: A Guide to Changing the World* (2018), Maureen Johnson's *How I Resist: Activism and Hope for a New Generation* (2018), Joanna Spathis and Kerri Kennedy's *Wake, Rise, Resist! The Progressive Teen's Guide to Fighting Tyrants and A*sholes* (2017), Jamia Wilson and Andrea Pippins's *Step Into Your Power* (2019) and Emma Gray' *A Girl's Guide to Joining the Resistance: A Feminist Handbook for Fighting for Good* (2018) are but one heaping handful of resources for teenagers trying to make a difference. They all follow similar structures with a hearty acknowledgment of the current troubled times, an inspiring nod to young people from history who have successfully made a difference in the world, a toolkit with advice and guidance to launch action campaigns and finally a gentle reminder to practice self-care. What is missing though from the media's obsession with these lone wolf activists is the partnership with adults and participation in community-based organizations. As Lyn Mikel Brown (2016) writes in *Powered by Girl: A Field Guide for Supporting Youth Activists* (my personal favorite book about what it really takes to do activist work with teenagers):

> Young activists don't just pop up fully formed and informed. They are brave, passionate, and wide awake, yes, but they don't possess unique activist genes. They have been the beneficiaries of supportive environments, raised or educated or scaffolded by people with deep skills. They have been enabled by socially conscious and committed adults who know how the system works, who have shared their knowledge and resources, their time and their connections.
>
> (p. 12)

For girls passionate and eager to make a difference, the local and national organizations have expanded or created programs to support them. Even the Girl Scouts, founded in 1912, jumped on the activist bandwagon and launched a new initiative in 2017 called "The G.I.R.L. Agenda," to inspire and promote activism and civic engagement. "Many people, including girls, want to become active in public policy and learn how to advocate for positive change, but they don't know where to start," said Girl Scouts CEO Sylvia Acevedo.

> Through the G.I.R.L. (Go-getter, Innovator, Risk-taker, Leader) Agenda and our proven civic-engagement programming, Girl Scouts serves as a nonpartisan resource for girls – and those who care about them – to learn concrete steps they can take to stand up for what they believe in.

In fact, a Girl Scout Research Institute poll found that just 38 percent of girls stated that their teachers encouraged them to pursue politics and community leadership (Girl Scouts of the USA, 2017).

This proliferation of activism within girls' programs makes sense through both a marketing as well as a youth development lens. Girls seem to be craving experiences where they can have an impact on the world and push back against the injustices that they witness every day. And the research is slowly building to show that these experiences are good for girls. Education scholar Monique W. Morris (2019) describes an anti-disciplinary approach for girls at a predominantly Black public middle school in Columbus, Ohio who might have a "bad attitude." As an alternative to punishment and suspension that often serves as a pipeline for Black girls from school into the juvenile justice system, the principal implemented a multipronged approach to addressing issues that would previously have resulted in disciplinary action:

> Girls in the school are encouraged to engage in advocacy and activism as part of their healing process … She gave an example of a group of girls who used their [in-school suspension] assignment to research resource disparities among district public schools and craft a letter to educational policy makers demanding change.
>
> (p. 19)

What researchers and activists are finding is that activism is both good for the community, and good for the girls themselves. As the executive director of SPARK Movement since 2012, I saw firsthand both the desire for and impact of activist experiences on girls. SPARK was initially launched[5] as a response to the American Psychological Association's "Report of the APA Task Force on the Sexualization of Girls." Along with co-founders, developmental psychologists, Lyn Mikel Brown and Deborah L. Tolman, we linked the fight against sexualization of girls in the media to the need for "enabling conditions" for young women's healthy sexuality, a condition that could only be created out of the shared passion and momentum of an explicitly intergenerational action-based movement. As the founding adults, we were not interested in creating yet another organization that runs activism programs *for* girls, but we aimed to create an intergenerational space where girls and women work together toward change. As Black Girls Studies scholar and artist Ruth Nicole Brown quotes State Senator Nia Gill (D-NJ) at the 2004 National Hip-Hop Political Convention, "Young people need power, not programs" (Brown, 2008, p. 26). Brown continues:

> Programming for programming's sake attempts to manage young people's lives. Programming for programming's sake defines young people as the problem. For example, although girl empowerment is the professed goal of many gender-specific programs, power is rarely considered, and when left to function without question, many program processes marginalize some of the same young people they claim to be "empowering."
>
> (26)

Another example of this shift from power to programs is SPARK. Brown's words reflected our desire to launch SPARK in resistance to traditional, hierarchical programs that "serve girls." Instead of protecting girls from gender-based violence and injustice, we wanted to include them as key to the solution and as agents, not objects of change. This model, core to classic community organizing where the people most impacted by an issue needed to be key and proactive in solving it, was still somewhat foreign in the youth activism world.

Significantly, the language we use to describe the work we are doing has an impact on who shows up and what their expectations are. Branding the work as "activist" can be both a lure and a deterrent for girls, depending on their definitions and understanding of what that word means to them. Sasha, a 23-year-old woman whom I interviewed about her experiences as a teenage activist, told me that for her, activism is, "A move, a decision, a push in a new direction" (interview). Annie, at 16, was a little more blunt. Their definition of an activist included, "someone who's actively not taking part in society's bullshit. You know is actively working again it … Activism is anything you do that helps creates change" (interview). My own definition is informed by the wisdom from girls: *An activist is a person who is taking personal or public action to ignite change that they believe will improve their own life and/or the lives of others.*

For many of the women who are doing some of the best work I've seen with girls, they are focusing on constructing frames where girls have agency and spaces to express themselves; they are amplifying girls' voices, stories, and ideas; they are supporting girls to trust and transform themselves; and they are changing assumptions about what girls are capable of. But they do not always explicitly label it as "activist." viBe Theater Experience Executive Director Toya Lillard told me in an interview:

> Activism in my life constitutes the everyday actions that I must take in order to save my own life. As a Black woman – what some folk call "activism," which is something that we're socialized to think one opts into or not, right, like an elective, that it's something that you can choose to do or not. "I think I'll do a little activism today. No, no, maybe not." That for a lot of us it's non-negotiable that we must be what you call "activists" and I use air quotes. You can put that in the book, too. I don't have a picket sign or a t-shirt or a pink hat. But you better believe this is true of our girls that every day, I am taking great risks and standing up in ways for myself and others in order to save my own life in order to prolong my life so that I may live longer than my mother. So that my daughter may live longer than both of us so that what we have popularized as "activism," that is being at a protest or a march with some sort of costume on with a picket sign is a byproduct of our need to package and commodify things and make them palatable. That for much of the population, that's activism and why they don't necessarily call themselves "activists."

Concurrently, Ruth Nicole Brown describes her own work creating SOLHOT (Saving Our Lives Hear Our Truths), as "a space where Black girls could express, create and make space to be free" (solhot.com). When I asked her in an interview if she saw her work as "activist," she responded:

> I'm as resistant to the role of activist as I am with other categories of identity. Like, that is so slippery. I think given how that word circulates, particularly with girls, I'm not sure if I don't want to be so easily understood. I think when you work with girls, it seems like it can become an easy trope in the sense that that is what success looks like after this. In that role-playing, like, at the podium, with the microphone. And I'm all for that, I'm just not *only* for that only. Because the power is with the individual and I think it is with the people always. So, in the sense that we are *all* activists, yes. But in the sense that, success is – I'm playing this *role* of activist, no. Like, that's not, that's not how I define success.
>
> (interview)

Exquisitely and poetically articulated, whether they brand it with the label of activism or not, the Black girls of SOLHOT offer their truths about their impact on the world, posted on their website:

> We want you to know and remember that Black girls are geniuses. We create knowledge, spaces, bonds, trends, language, movements, music, and art no one else can. We have similar cultures, experiences, and ways of being, but no one can put us in a box. We individually add to the diverse definition of what it means to be a Black girl. We are quiet, loud, sassy, laid-back, strong, and delicate. We defy your stereotypes and exceed your expectations everyday. Despite what's thrown at us, we still shine.
>
> (solhot.com/know-and-remember)

Considering SOLHOT's practice as a transformative and creative space, I turn my attention to the next intersection – girls and the performing arts. Though not often described as "activist," a site that is inherently and deliberately about amplifying girls' voices is the performance space.

Girls and performance

When writing about girls and performance, I use a broad definition of performance. According to performance studies scholar Richard Schechner (2013), "The underlying notion is that any action that is framed, enacted, presented, highlighted or displayed is a performance" (p. 2). While I am not quite so liberal in my definition, I borrow from his acknowledgment that performance is a field that exists beyond the walls of a traditional theater or what we would call a play. Within my work and the scope of this book, I understand performance to be an intentional, live event that includes one or many people, the performers, who act, speak and/or move their bodies for the purpose of impacting another person or group of people, the audience. Theater and performance workshops that use performance-based activities are included within my definition. In these spaces, "audience" is not necessarily an outside group of people viewing a final product, but other participants within the space engaging in the performance techniques with and for each other and themselves. In addition to more traditional forms of performance such as plays performed in theaters or performance workshops in community spaces, I include pieces that include spoken word poetry performances, dance, live music, stand-up comedy, protest speeches, and rallies. Additionally, I apply a performance lens to actions girls have taken toward political ends.

Emma Gonzalez, a survivor of the shooting at Parkland High School stood silently at the podium of the March for Our Lives in Washington, DC for six minutes and 20 seconds marking the exact amount of time the shooter was firing his gun. This is performance.

Alice Brown Otter, a 12-year-old activist, ran 1,519 miles from her Standing Rock Sioux Reservation to Washington, D.C. to protest the Dakota Access Pipeline. This is performance.

Belissa Escoloedo and Rhiannon McGavin speak their choreographed poetic duet, "Rape Joke," at the Brave New Voices Teen Poetry Slam. This is performance.

Girls who use their voices and bodies in public spaces in order to educate, entertain, inspire, and ignite change are activist performers.

Teenage girls, at a developmental moment where their hormones are roller coasters of swelling emotions, yearn for spaces and relationships where they can express their feelings and find outlets for their rage and joy. In their study of 658 young adults, developmental psychologists found that they had higher "activated positive affect," or "happiness" on days when they had engaged in a creative activity (Conner, DeYoung, & Silvia, 2016). When teenagers' daily experiences escalate and plummet like melodrama, many of them find performance – or performance finds them. Through creating and performing, they discover a way to channel their desires to connect, to be heard and to have an impact on their communities. For girls yearning to tell their own stories or the stories of girls like them, spaces that foster original playmaking or performance can be a life jacket tossed in a turbulent sea. In live performance, the writer/performer is actively, in-the-moment engaged in dialogue with the audience. Her rhythms, beats, emphases, and intensity are dictated in part by the energy that the audience is feeding her. Her experience is heightened through the audience's reactions as she learns instantly how her words are heard.

Applied theatre researchers Jenny Hughes and Karen Wilson's 2004 study, "Playing a Part: The Impact of Youth Theatre on Young People's Personal and Social Development" surveyed 700 youth theaters throughout England and found that, "Channeling feelings, energy and anxiety through performance helps young people learn how to cope with and control their feelings and express themselves more effectively in a range of contexts" (p. 66). This outlet for expression is often a space where girls, once in touch with their feelings of rage, passion, and hope, yearn to share these heightened feelings with each other and with audiences.

Though there is a robust field of research documenting the impact of youth theater experiences for young people regardless of gender (Cahill, 2008; Gallagher, 2000; Nelson, 2011; Woodson, 2015; Woodson & Underiner, 2018; Brenner, Ceraso, & Cruz, 2021) there is a more slowly growing literature and research that looks at the live, physical act of teenage girls performing and the potential impact – on them and on the audience – it might have for them to speak aloud on a stage with an active audience responding in the moment (Gallagher, 2000; Hatton, 2003; Myers, 2009; Winn, 2011).

According to social justice and education scholar Maisha T. Winn's inspiring and applicable study that celebrates theater's effects on teenage girls impacted by incarceration who write and perform plays (2011):

> By creating characters, developing dialogue, and seeking resolution in complex lives, formerly incarcerated girls who participate in Girl Time, have an opportunity to reintroduce themselves through the medium of playwriting and performance.
>
> (p. 3)

As Winn's work shows, marginalized girls use the performance space to shift audience members' perceptions of what they are capable of, and literally reveal their strengths in a new light.

Nearly every girls' theater company's website includes similarly gushing tributes and quotations from girl alumnae of the programs and/or parents waxing on and on about the positive impact that the performance experience had on the girls.[6] Though websites are obviously promotional spaces used for recruitment and fundraising purposes, the collective lovefest of girls' voices crediting these organizations and performance project for their "confidence," new friendships, public speaking, and writing skills, cannot be easily dismissed as brochure language fluff. These performance experiences, to varying degrees, have self-described transformative impact on the girls.

In the years after chandra and I co-founded viBe Theater Experience, there were a few other girls' theater companies launching in New York City, with overlapping but unique origin stories.

In 2008, Ash Marinaccio, a young, creative visionary, was invited to write and direct a play with teenage girls as part of a women's theater festival. At 21, she was barely much older than the girls performing. Quickly realizing that the girls were the best authors of their own experiences, she shifted to a devising process whereby the girls co-created the text through a process that included conversations about social justice, sharing personal stories as well as interviewing people in their community. Their first performance, aptly titled "Girl Power," was a collage of scenes and monologues addressing all the issues the girls wanted to talk about. It was incredibly successful and ran at the New York International Fringe Festival.

"We wanted to make teen girl theater forever. This is just amazing, working with young women in such a fearless space" Ash told me in an interview, her eyes shining with pride as she remembered those early performances. "There was a trust there. The work was good. We were able to challenge each other intellectually, but also creatively. The group was talented … We talked about race. We talked about class. We talked about gender." I still remember seeing some of their early performances and being dazzled by the energy, passion, creative choreography, singing, and earnest and heartfelt story sharing. She eventually branded this work Project Girl Performance Collective (currently known as Girl Be Heard), and went on to produce new shows every year that addressed issues such as sex trafficking and gun violence and included performances at the White House, the United Nations, and tours to nine countries including Taiwan, Bosnia-Herzegovina, Bermuda, and Trinidad among others.

When I asked Ash if girls joined the project because they wanted to be in a girls' group, wanted to create theater or were interested in activism, she replied:

> It was about being in a girl's theater group and the activism was in part because it was a group of girls coming together, like "here we are! We're a group of women of young women artists coming together and making work," and that was the politics of it. And that was also the aesthetic, but the purpose was to make good theater.

Ash is also a professional theater director with a dance background, and while she served as the Artistic Director, they were making aesthetically bold productions with skilled performers and an excellent design team. Take a moment to check out the video of their powerful and passionate production *9mm America*.[7]

In addition to these more traditional theater experiences, spoken word poetry, a performing art form that goes back thousands of years from the epic poems of Homer to African oral folk traditions, is also a highly popular form for girls today. Every year, Urban Word, a youth poetry organization in New York City hosts the NYC Poetry Slam at the historic Apollo Theater in Harlem. In 2019, all of the five winners were girls. In that year's competition, girls wrote and performed poems addressing street harassment, sexual assault, poverty, racism, and climate change. They composed creative lyrics and spat them in rhythms and beats that led the audience to snap, hoot, holler, hum along, and cheer in solidarity.

Though these girl–created performances may have a strong impact on girls and their communities, girls don't need to write their own material to benefit from performance experiences. Several theater companies and most single-sex high schools for girls produce classic and contemporary plays with all-girl ensembles. According to their website, The Viola Project, founded in 2004 in

Chicago, Illinois uses Shakespeare's texts as the foundation for a social justice education. They advertise:

> The Viola Project celebrates play and performance in young people while creating a foundation for young women to stand up, advocate for themselves, and demand inclusion: inclusion in the classroom, in the workspace, in the world and on the stage. Our students have the unique opportunity to examine critical issues through creative play, interdisciplinary workshops, and, of course, Shakespeare. Why? Shakespeare's characters are determined to get what they need, to be understood, to be listened to. There is no better teacher for how to use language to make your voice heard than William Shakespeare.
>
> (violaproject.org/mission)

Other companies either by choice, such as The AMY Project (theamyproject. com) that offers free performing arts training programs serving young women and nonbinary youth in Toronto, Ontario, Canada, or by default such as at the hundreds of all-girls schools that produce plays where the entire cast comprises girls and nonbinary young people. From writing personal monologues to performing as Richard III, from composing poetry set to music beats to collaboratively writing new fictional narratives, girls and other young people marginalized by gender are using the tools of performance to collectively and unabashedly be seen and heard.

Girls enacting theater for change

Though this book is most definitely not a comprehensive theater history text, I want to nod to the legacy of performance as a civic engagement tool that extends back thousands of years across every continent. We know that ancient Africa and Asia and the Indigenous people of Australia, North America, and South America all had robust performance traditions that included ritual, oral poetry, and music traditions that were often used to foster community, educate about local issues and transmit the moral values of the culture (Zarrilli, Williams, & Sorgenfrei, 2006; Banham, 2004). Due to European colonialism and the violence and destruction in its name, nearly all written documentation from these cultures has been destroyed, leaving and celebrating the texts and artwork of Ancient Greece which then gets credited, as Columbus's "discovery" of the already inhabited "New World," for "discovering" theater. As an undergraduate Ancient Greek major myself, I acknowledge the dangers of assuming they were the first to produce theater, and yet I can still note and celebrate their impressive contributions to the art form. Though Euripides, Aeschylus, Sophocles, and Aristophanes usually get the credit and glory for their brilliant plays and the ways they used theater as a political tool in their nascent democracy, it is Phrynichus who I want to shout out. Writing in the fifth and sixth centuries BCE, he was the first known and recorded playwright to do two significant and oft-forgotten things that changed the course of the European-based tradition of theater to what we know it to be today. One, amidst a patriarchal and misogynist culture, he wrote female characters (though performed by male actors) in his plays, acknowledging that women's contributions to the community are important. And two, he strayed from previous playwrights who only wrote about mythology and he wrote a play about current events as they impacted the Athenians in the audience. Shortly after the Athenian army was defeated at Miletus, he wrote the play, *Capture at Miletus*, and was punished and according to Herodotus, was fined, "for reminding them of their own troubles." These two actions are the core of my work: centering the experiences of women and using theater to make sense of, raise awareness about, and take actions related to our current social and political climate. Obviously, much has evolved since Phrynichus's "crime," and the work of girls today is a faint echo from the structure of an Ancient Greek tragedy, yet these methods are still subversive.

Fast forward 2500 years to girls today, particularly girls of color Performing their own words live on a stage in front of their community is an expression of defiance to a culture that often still dismisses them. The content does not always need to include politically charged issues, though I have found girls will naturally gravitate towards them. When asked what they want to tell their audiences, stories of injustice and demands to be taken seriously often float to the top of the scripts. Because they are so often silenced, or not taken seriously, just speaking their truths can be a radical act.

The 2019 New York City Youth Poet Laureate was Camryn Bruno, a teenage girl who won this competitive title by performing, "Politics Bite," her poem about voting rights. In an interview with Queens.com, she spoke about her experience performing spoken-word poetry:

> I think it's more about getting the social issues out there, and that's where I started off, writing about teenage pregnancy and the school-to-prison pipeline … It's really about finding social issues and finding a new way to speak about them.
>
> (Bagcal, 2018)

It is no wonder that activist organizations often use performance as a tactic to get out their message. Theater can lure the audience into the content with emotional urgency and share stories in an engaging way so people do not easily forget what they have seen. SOUL Sisters Leadership Collective, whose mission is to,

> mobilize systems-involved girls, femmes, and TGNC[8] youth of color – Black, Brown, and Indigenous – to interrupt cycles of state violence, poverty, and oppression. Our four pillars are leadership, healing, social justice, and the arts.
>
> (soulsistersleadership.org)

Within their model, performance is used to both amplify the girls' activist messages *and* as a community-building tool that offers a fun, creative, collaborative process and gives girls the confidence to speak up and speak out. Theater is not the core of the organization's work, and yet without it, girls might not stay as engaged. According to the results of an outside assessment of their program, 100 percent of the girls in their program, Sisterhood Academy expressed that they "are more able to speak up for what they believed in, even if it is unpopular to do so," and "100 percent showed an increase in motivation to fight for social justice."

As even the design of this survey tool shows, success for this activist organization is measured primarily in the leadership and activist development of the girls, not in the social justice impact of their campaigns. These organizations are playing the long game. Their current priorities lay in training young people who then could use their newly honed creativity and leadership skills in a lifelong fight for freedom and justice.

As core to their successful leadership training, executive director Wakumi Douglas described the connection between the artmaking process and the leadership development process:

> I think that the artists, the artwork is really important for leadership development and that it supports young people to see the material manifestations of their ideas. It's really important to be able to be like, "I have an idea. Oh, and now it's like a thing." Yeah, that's what organizing is too, we have an idea or a dream or vision for what the world should be like, and then we work together and then in an ideal world, the thing happens and it's a very similar process to me as an artistic process. And so, I think there's parallel for that with young people.
>
> (interview)

As part of a Black Girls Matter Coalition Summit in Miami, Florida, they produced a haunting and powerful performance that I had the opportunity to see on video. Instead of just telling their story or talking about their upcoming campaigns, a group of Black girls created a performance. In a large convention hall, three teen girls step onto the stage and speak boldly and confidently about themselves until another girl comes on stage, silences them by taping their mouths, hands one a sign stating, "Sweet Thing," crosses over to a podium and begins to bark as an auctioneer, asking the audience to bid on her body. When she is "sold" to the highest bidder, she introduces the next girls, "Wifey will cook your food and clean your house," and "Submissive, She doesn't have a name, she doesn't have an identity!" The "auctioneer" continues to rally up the audience into a frenzy and demands they bid on the girls. They use humor and energy to get the audience worked up until, they pause. The performers all start clapping, and shouting, "Wake up! Wake up! Wake up!" as they move through the audience. The purpose of the piece was, as Executive Director Wakumi Douglas shared:

To tell the story of what it's like to be Black and a girl, the sort of intersectionality of that experience is often misunderstood and there's a really important component: They're organizing. How can they win any campaigns on their behalf if people don't understand just the very basics of the issues they face and also understand the historical legacy of those issues? So, the young people created that piece really with a clear understanding of history. Like the fact that it was an auction block, you know, like with a very clear understanding of the historical legacy of the issues facing them.

(interview)

Through using historical research, playwriting and performance as organizing tactics, SOUL Sisters reaches both their young activists and the communities they are trying to change. When given a microphone, girls will often use it to preach about what they see as unjust in their world, and why we all need to try to fix it, as well as share personal stories about the often-untold experiences they live through. This is nothing new. Historically silenced populations have often turned to live performance to forge their place within their community's dialogues. Applied theatre scholar Jan Cohen-Cruz writes that, "the very act of speaking one's story publicly is a move toward subjecthood, toward agency, with political implications" (2006, p. 104). Her research, along with many other community-based theater scholars and practitioners, documents the processes, transformations, and community's responses to performances created through personal and communal storytelling (Cohen-Cruz, 2005, 2006; Nicholson, 2005; Taylor, 2003; Thompson, 2003).

Drama educator and scholar Kathleen Gallagher (2000) writes about her experience teaching drama at an all-girls school and her recognition that girls gravitate to issues of social weight:

From my classroom teaching, I have found that adolescents are often grappling with representations of authority and with conflicts that address the difficult questions of "right and wrong," "truth and fiction," "poverty and wealth," "self and other." The "social issues" of some urgency to adolescents often include questions of "freedom," "oppression," and "relationships." They are also drawn to situations that ask them to explore their identity and individuality. As a teacher, I am looking for sources that provide some context for investigation of these complex concerns.

(p. 45)

For girls passionate about making a difference in their community, but with varying degrees of experience in or exposure to theater, *The Vagina Monologues* VDAY project has consistently been a gateway drug to feminist activism. With thousands of productions on college campuses and high schools around the world raising more than $130 million for organizations and activist working to end gender-based violence, *The Vagina Monologues*, is arguably the most effective piece of feminist activist theater. Ever. The brilliance of its playwright and creator V (formerly Eve Ensler) has been her foresight and ability to use this single play as a tool for not just raising awareness about gender-based violence, but actually mobilizing millions of young people to take action. Every February since 1998, she has offered her play, royalty-free, to any group who wants to produce it as long as they commit to donating a percentage of their proceeds to organizations working to end violence against women. The play itself serves to raise awareness about some of the issues, and serves as an organizing tool to young activists with a detailed toolkit and production guide for untrained theatermakers. Productions could range from simple readings with performers sitting on stools on a stage and reading the script from a music stand before them. Other productions have been fully staged with live music, choreography, costumes, lighting, and set designs. Though written in 1994, years before my current students were born, I am always taken aback by its still-relevance for my undergraduate students when we read it each year in my New York University Theater & Activism course.

Not without controversy, the play has historically been seen as problematic in its treatment of transgender identity (namely that having a vagina means you are a woman), statutory rape (celebrating a story about a 24-year-old woman who seduces a 16-year-old girl with alcohol and sex), and the othering of violence in countries such as Afghanistan and the Democratic Republic of Congo. Yet despite – and sometimes because of – its vast flaws, it remains a lightning rod for action. Productions have been censored or banned at campuses throughout the United States and around the world, which often ignited more rage and action specifically *because* of the controversy. In 2020, Daphne Eleftheriadou and Mara Halpern, two high school girls in Berkeley, California who had been involved in their school's annual production for a couple of years decided to do something different. Frustrated by the transphobia and "white savior" aspect of the original "outdated" and "problematic" script (Orenstein, 2020), they decided to make their own. Inspired by the form and themes more than the specific content of the play, they invited students at their school to write "Our Monologues," about their own true stories. Their new play included pieces about "immigrating to the U.S. from Mexico, crossing the border without their mother," a piece about gun violence in schools, another about sexual harassment and assault in the Berkeley High community. They used the structure of *The Vagina Monologues* play and the strategy of the VDAY movement by donating proceeds to Bay Area Women Against Rape in order to produce a youth-driven, locally relevant performance project.

Whether girls are creating their own performance narratives, or engaging with previously produced or published texts, the content and intention of their work most often defaults to investigations of social justice themes or explorations of identity.

Notes

1 According to the APA report, sexualization occurs

> when a person's value comes from his or her sexual appeal or behavior, to the exclusion of other characteristics; a person is held to a standard that equates physical attractiveness (narrowly defined) with being sexy; a person is sexually objectified – that is made into a thing for others' sexual use, rather than seen as a person with the capacity for independent action and decision making; and/ or sexuality is inappropriately imposed upon a person.
>
> (2007, p. 2)

2 Starting in the 1990s, the word "Urban" has been used as a code for Black and Brown girls, mostly low income. In the attempt to label respectfully, words and phrases such as "at-risk," "disadvantaged," and "marginalized" were seen to be labels of what the girls *lacked* as opposed to an assets-based language. "Urban" is also misleading as it rarely is meant literally as it almost never includes rich, white girls who live in cities.

3 Between 2011 and 2015, when I was reading hundreds of applications from girls hoping to join SPARK team of girl activists, I noticed approximately 15 percent of the total applications included stories from girls saying that their experience as members of Girl Up was formative and inspired them to want to do more activist work.

4 https://girlup.org/wp-content/uploads/2014/10/Girl-Up-Branding-Guidelines.pdf

5 For a more detailed history of SPARK Movement, visit www.SPARKmovement.org

6 girlbeheard.org, viBeTheater.org, acompanyofgirls.org, actlikeagrrrl.org

7 www.ashmarinaccio.com/9mm-america

8 TGNC is an acronym for Trans & Gender Non-Conforming.

2 "This is not a safe space"

Principles of theatermaking with girls

A proposed framework for facilitators, educators, activists, and mentors

Though every project has its own unique set of values, goals, and processes, there are particular underlying principles and methodologies that I have experienced and witnessed as most effective in my own activist theater work with girls. Based on more than two decades of experience, what follows are the specific principles that I have developed – often in collaboration with my co-directors – that inform my girl-driven activist theater projects, honed from my work with Inside/Out Performing Arts (co-created with Katie Eastburn), viBe Theater Experience (co-created with chandra thomas and later, Toya Lillard), SPARK Movement (co-created with Lyn Mikel Brown and Deb Tolman) and my newest initiative, The ART (Anti-Racism Theater) Project (co-created with Andrea Jacobs) at the JCC.

Seven leading principles have informed the diverse works that I have facilitated and co-facilitated. They are relevant whether it be three-week intensive projects where a group of girls creates a collaborative choreopoem performance to six-month-long projects, such as song-making experiences where girls write, produce, and perform a full-length album of original music. Though each project might include different activities, processes, and performance structures, all share these core unifying and interlocking principles that have become the foundation for my work:

- negotiating intergenerational power
- operating with antiracist, intersectional, and feminist lenses
- creating the highest quality, culturally responsive theater
- educating through critical thinking and liberatory pedagogy practices
- facilitating with a trauma-informed practice
- cultivating uncensored, unadulterated storytelling
- choosing an abundance of joy, play, and love whenever possible

I have sometimes been lured away from one or more of these core principles but found myself returning to them, as they are my North Star. Whenever

I feel stuck or challenged in the midst of a process, I look to them for a strategy or solution. I do not argue that my process or framework is the best or that it will be effective in every community or can be replicated exactly by any director or facilitator, but I do believe my principles cut through different ways of working. Some of the principles demand a lengthier definition, with varied examples of the principle in action. Others hopefully can be understood more simply. I hope that my detailed articulation and reflection will help people find their own way and be a source of meaning and guidance for their work.[1]

Principle # 1: negotiating intergenerational power

Mostly unspoken power structures exist in all intergenerational work. Teenagers live in the transition between childhood, where most decisions are made for them, and adulthood, where they are expected to be responsible for themselves. Almost all of their theater experiences, after-school activities or summer camps at this point in their lives will have been in programs or projects created, directed, and led by adults. This "in between" status as described by anthropologists in rites of passage studies (Van Gennep, 1960; Blumenkrantz, 2016; Turner, 1967) is usually orchestrated by adults who are legally and ethically responsible for young people's safety and survival. And yet adolescence is also the time when teenage girls are pushing against these boundaries, simultaneously and contradictorily seeking both connection *and* autonomy in a world that privileges independence (Brown & Gilligan, 1992).

Typically, girls are supported and enabled by passionate and committed adults working within organizations and communities who have shared their resources, their time, and invested their energy. Too often we simply applaud organizations that claim to "empower girls" without a nuanced understanding of the real differences and intersectional, intergenerational tensions between girls' lives and adults' desires and experiences.

When I spoke with Monique Letamendi, the current artistic director of viBe Theater Experience, she described a frustrating, and all-too-common experience she had when she was working at a different organization that was ostensibly "serving youth." She told me:

> In my other job, we have these program taskforce situations and it's literally a room of adults coming together, talking about, "how can we serve the youth better?" And it's like, well, why aren't they here? Your first problem is — these meetings start at 7 PM. Like, let's talk about it. I remember I was like, "Hey, I think that's the first thing we need to think about is like, why are we having these conversations without them here?" And then we had a conversation about how they were using the word, "underrepresented" and they were having the conversation, the discourse of like, "Well, what should we call them?" And I was like, "Have y'all asked *them*?"

Sadly this simple, "Have you ever asked young people what they want?" is missing from too many projects that purport to "serve" teenagers or to offer young people leadership opportunities. Adults are so afraid that if we let go of our power, chaos will ensue. What that actually just shows is how little adults authentically trust young people.

As Natasha Blanchet-Cohen and Brian Rainbow (2006) argue, "Working in partnership with children requires that adults leave aside the role that society has often prescribed to them of being the teacher with all the answers. We are partners seeking answers to creating a better world" (p. 122). In her analysis of intergenerational dialogue in the Peruvian child labor movement, Jessica Taft (2015) writes,

> There is an ongoing and unresolved tension between the idea that the movement belongs entirely to kids, where their voices are primary, and the idea that the movement is a space of intergenerational dialogue, where the voices of kids and adults are each valued for their different contributions.
>
> (p. 465)

Though I question whether referring to teenagers as "children" or "kids" offers due respect, I agree with these concepts that adults need to truly partner with young people.

Developmental psychologist and girls activist Lyn Mikel Brown writes extensively about the intergenerational dynamics between adults and girls. She challenges the notion that programs for girls should focus on adults' attempts to "fix" girls' problems and finds through her decades of experience and research that supporting and training girls to collaborate with adults to take action is actually more transformative for girls and for our world. She writes:

> We are accountable, then, not for fixing girls and young women, but for providing them with opportunities to understand, engage with, and potentially transform what limits and harms them. Providing a girl with what she needs to persist in the face of oppression means connecting her with opportunities to be a catalyst, to participate in the transformation of her environment.
>
> (2016, p. 41)

Powersharing occurs at multiple sites throughout my work with young people. Just as important as it is to defer to girls throughout the process of a project, I also make attempts to collaborate with young people when I write about and publish research about our work together. In 2016, I co-wrote a piece with Lyn and Celeste Montano, a 21-year-old Latinx woman who had collaborated with Lyn and me in SPARK since she was a teenager. Celeste's voice was vital to our article about intergenerational partnerships. Her insights included:

It's hard for anyone to call out a figure of authority, particularly regarding stuff like race, but younger girls especially are used to just ignoring their own discomfort and listening to what adults say. Because their relationship with adults in school and at home is largely about respect and not challenging authority, they're much less likely to speak up if something feels wrong – if they even realize it's the adult's actions that make them uncomfortable. Often girls tend to think they're the ones in the wrong.

(p. 704)

Understanding the depths and dangers of adultist frameworks is the first step towards creating an activist girls' performance project. I name my biased assumption and language addressing the readers of this book as adults who desire to/or already do work with girls, as opposed to assuming that you, dear reader, might be a girl reading this book in order to design and launch or better understand your own activist theater work. The reality is that more often than not, adults have more of the resources, power, funds, relationships, networks, experience, structured time, education, training, confidence, and skills to do the work. And girls, as full-time high school students, living with adult guardians or parents, do not. And so, how do we best partner in ways that celebrate our unique contributions without the usual mistrust that zigzags back and forth between generations?

I asked Annie,[2] a Black, 16-year-old who describes themself as "a queer person. I don't really subscribe to any pronouns, so anything's fine cuz I just feel like gender's a social construct. I'm pretty gay and I do have a uterus." Annie had been participating in viBe's programs for more than three years. When I asked what advice they would give to adults who want to work with teenagers, they told me:

Well, you have to listen more than you speak, right? Because once you're not a teenager anymore, I feel like you never understand what a teenager is again. You have to sit there and really listen to what we have to say. Because, as a teenager, like, we're not gonna let you know when we like something or when we don't like something. We're just not gonna come again. So, you have to sit there and really listen to what we have to say and actively participate in the things that we wanna do and help us, you know? And not really try and push your agenda but try and understand ours.

(interview)

I heed Annie's wisdom, and also add that it is often the adults who provide the frame and the structure for the programs, campaigns or projects, but it is fully in the power of the young people to control the content and direction. Adults have the resources to pay for and book the rehearsal and performance spaces and hire additional teaching artists and designers, but the young people should be the ones naming what they want, collaborating with the artists to imagine the design for the show, editing their scripts and having veto power over elements of the process or production that are not working for them. Megan Alrutz and Lynn Hoare, co-authors of *Devising Critically Engaged Theatre with Youth* (2020) offer the following in their book's section on "Shared Power":

> Although [Performing Justice Project] facilitators and teaching artists create partnership models, identify program goals, and plan sessions, they also create opportunities for young people to shape the performance, influence decisions in the room, and offer feedback to peers and adults in the project.
>
> (p. 57)

They then add community-based performance scholar and youth educator Stephani Etheridge Woodson's words:

> Adult facilitators walk into the studio with specific knowledge of benefit to the ensemble, but everyone in the room holds knowledge and ability – capital – no matter their age.
>
> (2015, p. 85)

"It's really a dance," is how Ruth Nicole Brown describes the collaboration between the adults or the "homegirls" as they are known in SOLHOT and the girls:

> It's hard to pinpoint when something is girl led and when something is initiated by the homegirls. I guess we always, it always comes back to this certain kind of, like, everybody has their hands on this before we might consider it a finished thing … So maybe it's also process-oriented and I'm still so clear that the structures demand certain kinds of resources that usually adults have.
>
> (interview)

Another aspect to building trust across differing power statuses is to embrace radical honesty and transparency. It might sound obvious, but when a girl bravely asks a question, we must answer with the truth to the best of our knowledge and experience. I see too many instances where adults try to protect girls by keeping information from them or faking confidence. Teenagers are the best bullshit detectors and they see through the games adults play and then pull away. I'll share an example from SPARK Movement that might be "taking things too far" for some adults who want to hold onto their power. By the third year of our activist work with girls, as executive director, I felt a need to engage in the radical transparency I had been advocating for. I chose to share the organization's budget with the girls and to invite them to weigh in on how and where we should allocate our meager funds, including my own and their salaries, and then implement their suggestions and demands. This is radical transparency and offers girls real power in the organization.

As part of her research, social justice and education scholar Maisha T. Winn interviewed teaching artists who facilitated performing arts workshops with girls in prison. I was struck and disappointed to read the words of Anne, a white teaching artist with a self-described privileged background. She said, "My biggest fear is the girls are going to know my secret, which is that I haven't had a hard life … What right do I have really? I don't know their life and they're going to know that'" (2011, p. 43).

As a white, middle-class woman, I have shared Anne's feelings. Early in my work with girls, I (guiltily admit now) also kept quiet when girls shared stories of struggle as I felt ashamed of my privilege and feared that if they knew I had not experienced similar hardship, they would never trust me. It took me years to learn that the opposite was true. The more I kept quiet, the more they sensed I was hiding something, and retreated. Sharing parts of my life with them was part of building authentic relationships with them. It meant more to me – and to them – that they knew I had grown up in a wealthy white suburb, attended private schools my whole life, *and* chose to commit my work to collaborating with girls to make theater. It felt more condescending to them to assume that they would never connect with me just because I come from a different socio-logical, racial, and class background.

Every word you use gives girls clues about power. For example, in the marketing and recruitment or other calls for participation, if you post, "Audition!," you are signaling that there will be someone (almost always perceived to be the adult running the program/project) who will decide if they are "accepted" or "good enough" to join the project. Consider other ways to invite girls in. Our flyers would often include a series of questions such as, "Do you want to create an original show with a group of other girls? What are the issues most important to you? Do you want to change the world through theater?" And then, we would invite any possible artists to "Join us for an infor-mation share where you can get to know us, and we can get to know you." This strategy starts to dismantle power structures by articulating to girls that they are also able to interrogate *you* about the project, that they have power when they can choose whether they want to join the project, or not. Additionally, I recom-mend inviting other teenagers to join this "selection committee," so that they are weighing in about who might gain the most from and contribute to the project and that from the very first interaction, prospective artists see their peers in positions of shared power with adults.

My last naming of power is to offer a meta-analysis of my own power as a researcher and writer of this book. As its sole author, I have the ultimate control over whose stories I include, whose voices are amplified and how I choose to ana-lyze the experiences of the girls with whom I have collaborated. I heed the words that anthropologist Aimee Meredith Cox (2015) writes at the end of her stunning ethnography of Black girls at Fresh Start Homeless Shelter in Detroit. She writes:

> I fully realize that I owe my career to Janice [the girl whose experiences she centers in the book], the Brown family, and all the other young women at Fresh Start. This is an important point to make, I believe, as we (the researchers, practitioners, activists, and educators invested in the lives and

livelihood of vulnerable young people of color) often build names and gain visibility from the cultural and intellectual labor of incredibly brave and incisive young people with the most to lose.

(pp. 238–239)

She continues to ask us to consider how the young people we write about might benefit from their participation in our research and in these pages. My hope is that this book is useful for practitioners and that the insights I learned from the girls I write about will, in turn, ensure that their sisters, peers, cousins, and friends across the country and around the world will benefit from stronger, more mutually beneficial activist performance projects. But what does that provide Annie and the other young people who have collaborated with me and agreed to be interviewed for this book? When possible, I paid young people stipends for their time during the interview, sent gifts of appreciation or made monetary donations to the activist or theater organizations they participate in. I shared versions of this manuscript with them to approve so that they felt confident that their words and stories were represented in a way they felt good about. I have also made efforts, when writing about the work we do together, to co-author those texts with girls, like Lyn and I did with Celeste as mentioned above. To date, I have co-published four additional articles and book chapters with teenage girls (Edell, Allicock, & Duran, 2021; Edell, Christophe, & Shawlin, 2018; Edell, Brown, & Montano, 2016; Brown, Edell, Jones, Luckhurst, & Percentile, 2016) and I have co-presented at more than a dozen academic conferences with girls, my colleagues. These are not just tokenistic performances of shared power, but acknowledgments that the contributions of girls to the academic literature and discussions about youth, activism, and performance, are necessary. Their voices matter.

Principle #2: operating with intersectional, antiracist and feminist lenses as the white facilitator of mostly Black and Brown ensembles of girls

As Black feminist theorist bell hooks defined it, "Feminism is a movement to end sexism, sexist exploitation and oppression" (hooks, 1984, 2000). She offers this both in her *Feminist Theory: From Margin to Center* and then additionally felt the need to re-articulate it in *Feminism is for Everybody*, her 2000 book whose professed goal was to provide an answer to the frequently asked-of-her-question, "What is feminism?" that is rooted neither in fear or fantasy (p. xii). This idea that people (mis)understand feminism through either a lens of fear or fantasy has been very present in my work with young people. As a white woman who first started thinking about feminism in high school in the 1990s, my introduction was mainly through reading about it in books predominantly written by and for white women. I was a subscriber to *Bust*, *Bitch*, and *Sassy* magazines. I read all the writings of Rebecca Walker, Amy Richards, and Jennifer Baumgartner and saw myself reflected in their stories of struggle and injustice as young women not being taken seriously. I fell into the white supremacist funnel that seemed to churn out stories that mostly impacted other white women, yet branded it as "all women." I have grown up with the word "feminist" whispered guiltily, barked angrily or dismissed sarcastically, always careful of how and where and with whom I spoke it or attempted to claim it. I have learned about the ways Black, Indigenous, and Latinx women were always integral to the different movements fighting for gender justice in the US, though were too often relegated to the shadows or sidelines while the white women received and accepted most of the mainstream attention, by focusing on issues most prevalent in white communities (hooks, 2000).

As I collaborate with primarily Black and Brown girls, I often ask them what the word "feminist" means to them and whether, why, and how they might or might not identify with it and whether it is a useful framework to use for our work together. Kimberlé Crenshaw's legal scholarship (1991) identifying the intersections of racial, class, and gender oppression and the ways each cannot be extracted from the other, proved the ultimate burden Black women face as they are often marginalized by their multiple identities.

Kuenique, a 16-year-old Black girl asked in one of her monologues, "Feminism is about achieving equality of the sexes, but what about equality of races, even with the same gender?" Black feminist scholars such as Patricia Hill Collins (2000) have expressed the need to distance themselves from feminist theory that did not include their unique struggles and began to articulate a "Black feminism" or a "Womanism" that more specifically detailed the experiences of Black women. When I use the word "feminism" while working with girls, I attempt to frame it in all its problematic histories. I offer a definition in the simplest of words as hooks has provided, though am also careful to not negate the violent erasure that people who are not white, straight, and cisgendered have experienced at every step in its lifespan. By asking young people to express what the words "feminism" and "feminist" means to *them*, how it tastes in their mouth, whether they want to attach it to their bodies, can be a movement towards understanding how it can – or can't – function in their lives. Reorienting the theory to serve the girl can allow her to decide whether it might be a window that helps her see the world more clearly or whether it's just broken shards of glass to cut her.

Every one of the more than 70 theater productions I have co-directed or directed has been in collaborations where more than 97 percent of the girls in the ensemble were Black, Brown, Indigenous, and/or other people of color.[3] I am a white cisgender non-disabled woman. As part of my life's social justice mission to use my privilege and power in my work to dismantle the interlocking systems of white supremacy and patriarchy, I have chosen to use my resources and time to offer creative and activist experiences to people who have systematically been pushed out of easy access to such human rights. To this end, I have consistently collaborated with young people marginalized by age, gender identity, race, sexuality, nationality, immigration status, and socio-economic class. My life's goal is to make sure I am using my racial, gender, and class privilege to support the rights, safety, freedom, and creativity of those who, through systemic, institutional, racial, and social oppression, do not share these same privileges. I hold an understanding and commitment to considering the ways race, class, gender identity, ability, sexuality, and other identities intersect. As Crenshaw (1991) wrote, "the intersection of racism and sexism factors into Black women's lives in ways that cannot be captured wholly by looking at the race or gender dimensions of those experiences separately" (p. 43). Identities are not towering and isolated monoliths. I cannot write about the sexism girls endure without recognizing the ways that their race, class, and other identities intersect to impact their lives.

I remember during a talkback after one of our performances when the issue of my race came up and I was haunted by the response. The girls had just performed an energetic show that addressed many issues; including sharing stories about the racism they had faced in their lives. They were glowing, sweaty, beaming, and proud and sitting with me in chairs on the stage as we invited the audience, as we do after every show, to comment on the performance they just witnessed and ask any questions. One audience member asked, "What was it like for all of you girls to work with a white woman as one of the directors?" Without skipping a beat, Rae, a Black 17-year-old raised her eyebrows, dropped her jaw in mock outrage, skootched herself back in her chair and exclaimed, "You mean, Dana is white?!!" As the room laughed, a gnawing nausea in my gut whispered to me, "You failed."

Though I know she had been joking and seemed to be sweetly acknowledging that she saw me as different from other white people in her life, the deeper implication behind her statement was problematic to me as an antiracist activist. In my work, I absolutely and intentionally understand that the girls I am collaborating with are Black, Brown, and Indigenous and that their race matters. If white folks pretend we don't see race, that we are "colorblind," we are doomed to ignore the impact of racism (DiAngelo, 2018). I name myself as a white woman on the first day of rehearsals, lest there be any confusion about my background as I have dark curly hair, dark eyes, thick black eyebrows and have sometimes been mistaken as possibly biracial, Middle Eastern or Latinx. My ancestors were Jews from Eastern Europe and Russia and though they faced ethnic and religious persecution, violence and oppression, my family immigrated to the United States in the late nineteenth and early twentieth century and is now considered white by every current definition of race in America and we reap all the benefits that whiteness bestows (Brodkin, 1998). I acknowledge race as a social construct whose boundaries and labels might shift over time, but always hold real implications.

There are many ways that I acknowledge my whiteness in our process. First, I make every attempt to partner with a co-director who is a Black woman and this has been the norm for more than 85 percent of the productions I work on. White leadership reinforces patterns of white supremacy that have hurt young people and communities of color since enslaved African people were stolen from their homes, kidnapped and forced to come to the United States

(Emdin, 2016). I have not always had the resources to make sure I was sharing leadership with a Black woman, but it has always been beyond worth the effort. It is important that girls of color – and white girls – see models of interracial leadership and the ways that the white person is not always "in charge." In all our detailed rehearsal outlines, we specifically mark and alternate who leads which activity or warm-up to ensure our voices and leadership are balanced in the room. When I would co-direct viBe shows with our original co-founder, chandra, she almost always led the choreography and singing rehearsals as those were her strengths, while I often led the staging and design. We alternated leadership through the writing and scripting process. Additionally, co-leadership models a deliberate breakdown of hierarchies of power. In activist spaces focused on dismantled power structures, single movement leaders send a contradictory message about power in the hands of one person. It is significant to its impact and image that the Black Lives Matter movement was co-founded by Alicia Garza, Patrisse Cullors, and Opal Tometi, a trio of Black women, and remains a decentralized global movement without one person in charge.

As Inaugural Chair of African American and African Studies at Michigan State University, Ruth Nicole Brown tells an interviewer that she co-wrote the welcome letter to incoming students with Founding Associate Professor Tamura Lomax:

> Because I value collectivity and know from previous experience that to create beyond a collaboration, often times, rethinking our relation to hierarchy is necessary. You have to show the people how you meant togetherness, as a radical act and demonstration of other ways of relating. It seems to me elitist representations of expertise can be undone by the presence of more than one. And ideally, by the showing up of all involved.
>
> (Brown & Lomax, 2020)

Co-directing has always been important for me personally, as I have always learned from the Black women I partnered with. I am able to see more clearly the spaces where our lives overlap as women and also to better recognize the sharp edges where they diverge because of race and recognize when, if, and where my presence is useful. For example, there were times in our rehearsal process when the girls were talking about personal stories related to racism and I would step out of the room in order for them to have a deeper conversation about racism that often isn't possible under a white gaze.

That said, I also advocate for the need for white adults whom youth of color trust and who can use their racial privilege to advocate for them in spaces where they are rarely invited. As Kuenique told me in an interview about why she wanted white people in the audience for her show, "We can't just be performing for Black people. They already know about racism. We need to change the minds and hearts of white people."

I also encourage white adults to not assume that the lives of Black and Brown teenagers are filled with stories of trauma, and to accept that they may never want to share their stories with you – or with anyone publicly – and that's ok. Annie responded to my question, "What do you want white folks who work with teenagers of color to know?":

> Don't put yourself in there as some sort of white savior going in to fix, like, the youth, "the troubled youth" ...You have to really listen and not push your agenda and not – and oh! And not let your implicit biases show too. So, on top of like, listening and trying to understand what we're saying, don't be, you know, unintentionally racist. Like it sounds crazy, but it happens all the time. It happens all the time. Really think about what you're gonna say and how this has a lasting impact on this youth. Because, you know, generational trauma, you know, we're not gonna trust you immediately. And you have to be okay with that. Because there's generations upon generations of damage. And you have to be okay with a little animosity between you two.
>
> (interview)

I concur with everything Annie said, and I want to add my thoughts about the significance of their last part. A little tension is to be expected while trust is being built. Too many white folks bristle, get defensive or quit when they are challenged by teenagers of color or questioned about their intentions. For every one of them, racism has been a part of their lives either from microaggressions they've experienced, perpetrated by "well-intentioned" white people, violent acts of racism, police injustice, shopkeepers' mistrusting eyes or the systemic racism that has segregated them into less resourced schools and neighborhoods. White people need to work deliberately and diligently to earn their trust.

In 2019, we performed at the annual American Alliance for Theater Education conference for an audience of predominantly white theater educators. Following our performance, we had a lively discussion about the opportunities and limitations for white directors and teachers who do theater work with Black and Brown youth. I remember one compassionate teacher, a white man who was directing a show with mostly Black girls in the cast. He wanted the costumes to accurately show the time period of the show, but the Black girls told him their hair would never "fit" into the styles he envisioned. So, he asked the girls how *they* wanted their hair and was prepared to follow whatever they said. They told him they wanted to wear wigs which, as an outsider to Black girl culture, he hadn't even considered. He allocated enough money from the budget for them to go wig shopping and buy wigs that would fit them and their characters. I include this story to encourage all educators to follow his example by asking the girls you partner with what they want and need at every step of the theater process, and then providing enough resources to actually fulfill their requests.

Actively dismantling white supremacy culture

As activists who partner with young people, often marginalized by any combination of race, gender identity, age, socioeconomic class, and sexuality, we need to be aware of how our own positionality, power, privilege, and identity shows up in the ways we organize and strategize for social change. Poet scholar Audre Lorde's immortalized words are helpful here as we consider the ways we inadvertently and unintentionally reinforce white supremacy in our work:

> For the master's tools will never dismantle the master's house. They may allow us to temporarily beat him at his own game, but they will never enable us to bring about genuine change. Racism and homophobia are real conditions of all our lives in this place and time. I urge each one of us here to reach down into that deep place of knowledge inside herself and touch that terror and loathing of any difference that lives here. See whose face it wears. Then the personal as the political can begin to illuminate all our choices.
>
> (Lorde, 1984, p. 2)

Simply based on replicating education models and performance theories we experienced in our training and communities, white people and others with power or privilege over teenage girls often inadvertently employ tools and processes more aligned with a "respectability culture" (Higginbotham, 1993) or one that upholds core tenants of white supremacy culture than with theories of social justice. According to Aysa Gray at the Stanford Social Innovation Review (2019), white supremacy culture is:

> the systemic, institutionalized centering of whiteness. In the workplace, white supremacy culture explicitly and implicitly privileges whiteness and discriminates against non-Western and non-white professionalism standards related to dress code, speech, work style, and timeliness.
>
> (ssir.org)

When collaborating with young activists, consider the ways you might be subscribing to these standards and ideals. For example, how do you address lateness among girls in your process? White supremacy culture would argue that promptness is a sign of personal responsibility and is strictly enforced so as not to waste time in rehearsal.[4] Another way of looking at timeliness is with respect for other cultural understandings of time, relationships, and productivity. As Gray writes, "Polychronic cultures, while still able to get tasks completed, prioritize socialization and familial connections over economic labor."[5]

I admit with transparency that this learning has been challenging for me, having grown up in a culture that centers whiteness, with a focus on perfectionism and overachievement. I know so many other youth programs run by white people that would kick young people out if they were consistently late or absent. On one hand, I am deeply frustrated when I get to rehearsal early and wait for up to an hour until all the girls arrive. I have to reimagine the goals for the day, let go of certain activities I had planned on and restructure our time together to best make use of a group of three, then four, then six, then eight as girls trickle in. There were many attempts in my first decade of collaborating with girls to try to reverse this trend and we would create initiatives such as "take a minute, give a minute," where if a girl was 15 minutes late, she then "owed" the ensemble 15 minutes back. This could mean coming early to the next rehearsal to make up writing, help with out-of-rehearsal labor for the show such as picking up costumes or props or making copies of scripts. But after years, this began to feel punitive and wasn't actually "fixing" the "problem." I shifted my thinking on this issue and leaned into one of our other core values of "choosing joy." What if, instead of reprimanding girls for being late or showing disappointment, we just celebrated them whenever they managed to arrive and made sure that our time together was so rich and enjoyable that she would make every effort to be there, and not stress her out that she would "get in trouble"? If she missed the rehearsal because she was checking out or wasn't interested, I took their action to mean that they did not want to be in our space and that I had extra work to do to create a space they would enthusiastically return to. But more often, I learned from the girls that they missed the rehearsal because they had to babysit a younger sibling, stay after school to get extra help from a teacher, or needed to run home to get subway fare. By respecting her circumstances and efforts, we were respecting *her.* Was it still frustrating for me to rarely have a full group in rehearsal? Yes. Did it compromise our productivity? Depends on how you define, "productivity." By trusting that the girls were engaged to the best of their efforts and abilities, we were very productive in building a community of trust and mutual respect.

When I was considering people to interview about their work with girls, Ruth Nicole Brown was at the top of my wish list as someone who tirelessly throughout her life and career, advocates for, celebrates, and amplifies the voices of Black girls. I remember visiting her in Champagne, Illinois in 2008 to experience SOLHOT (Saving Our Lives Hear Our Truths), her work in action. As I sat in a community recreation room at the local public library, I witnessed clusters of girls singing along to a song, a group writing poetry at a table, another taping pieces of a collage together. Girls were wandering in and out, were shouting loudly or sitting quietly yet there was no sense of urgency (another tenant of white supremacy culture) or frustration from Dr. Brown. I can best describe it as a joyful chaos. She swirled through the room, her three-year-old daughter dancing with a pair of graduate students, dropping in on different groups. After a period of time, she stood in the center of the room and gradually most of the girls joined her and they all engaged in an interactive, call and response dance cypher where each girl had a chance to dance solo in the center while the girls in the circle shouted and clapped and danced with her. There was so much laughter and so little tension. I remain deeply inspired by her trust and acceptance of Black girls to be unapologetically who they are and her refusal to discipline their bodies, ask them to sit down, be still, be "on time" or be quiet (Brown, 2009, 2013).

You can also learn a lot about a process and the values of the people running the project by paying attention to how the public performances begin. Does a white adult stand on stage before the play starts to welcome the audience? Does she thank the rich people and the foundations who gave money to support the project? Does *she* describe the process of how the show was created? I write these questions with a gulp in my throat because I used to do all of this. Looking back now, I see how these announcements reinforce white leadership. And yes, funders often want to be thanked publicly, but consider the message it sends before the show to give them the recognition and power before the performance even starts. Instead, consider thanking the community partners, the girls who created the work, the parents and teachers who supported them. What might it look like to shift power and gratitude from the corporations and foundations back to the changemakers? Who are you truly accountable to? I am not naïve enough to say that the funders are not important partners but be aware of the messages your audiences hear before and during the performance. You can thank the funders in printed programs, on your website or write them personal letters.

Imagine if one of the performers stands before the audience to welcome them and hype them up, encourage them to cheer and talk back, and to take photos and videos and post them to social media as the show is unfolding. To speak for herself and her collaborators, in her voice, according to her cultural traditions.

Principle #3: making the highest quality, culturally responsive theater

As a passionate, life-long theatergoer and artist myself, I am committed to doing everything in my creative power to collaborate with the girls to make the very best quality performances we can, so that they feel genuine pride and faith in their abilities as artists. I often say, "The only thing we censor is 'bad theater.'" Though within this goal and principle, I acknowledge the impossibility of ever defining what might make one piece of theater "bad" and another "great." I use this principle to guide me in the rigor I expect from the creative process – the importance of rewriting and workshopping poetry until we all agree a piece is the best it can be. I believe that in order to best communicate the messages of the play, the performance needs to be engaging and innovative.

In all the projects I have worked on, when we are inviting girls to join, we are never looking for the most "talented" girls or girls who have extensive performance training and experience. As activist projects, the focus is on the stories that need to be told and the anticipated impact of the production, not necessarily the aesthetics. Therefore, as we move through the rehearsal process, there often comes a time when we struggle with our attempts to create a visually interesting, rhythmically entertaining, well-paced, high-energy and "good" performance. We tend to rely on the authentic power of girls performing the stories closest to them. As community-based performance scholar Jan Cohen-Cruz (2005) writes: "The commitment of people who've lived through the circumstances performed is the pleasure [community-based performance] offers in place of virtuosity" (p. 107).

Yet here, I warn about the ways that racism and classism show up in a theater creation process. Many girls come to activist theater processes with little or no experience creating, and oftentimes even seeing, live theater. Their cultural context of performance might include music videos by their favorite R&B or hip-hop stars, singing in church, TikTok dance challenges, and reality television. Because its ticket prices are so high and unaffordable for most people, attending live theater is rare for most American teenagers outside of the infrequent school trip to a matinee performance. At the same time, many, primarily white adult theater activists who are directing the shows with girls, graduated from liberal arts universities, sometimes with advanced degrees in theater, where they studied theater history through a European lens and were taught that theater "started" in Ancient Greece and evolved throughout Western Europe and was exported to America. I remember an elective course when I was a theater major at Brown called, "Non-Western Performance," taught by a white man. In courses such as these, framed in contrast to "Western" theater and rarely even required for theater majors, offered an opportunity for interested students to learn about the ancient roots of performance throughout Africa and Asia and created by Indigenous people in pre-colonial times in Australia, New Zealand, North and South America. We know there was a rich history of community-engaged theater and performance rituals in these parts of the world, predating and likely inspiring European contributions. The archival and documentation prowess of European countries and the colonial violence that destroyed these records in other parts of the world, ensured that the plays, mostly written by white men, acting techniques and performance theories, articulated by white men, inside theater buildings designed by white men, survived.

White men such as Euripides, Shakespeare, and Stanislavski were brilliant artists and writers who have contributed enormously to the art form of theater, yet naming their experiences and texts as "universal" disregards the vast cultural differences between their worlds and the worlds of teenage girls of color today. Though it might, assuming that the performance styles of these men and others throughout history will resonate with girls does not allow for girls themselves to choose a dramaturgical and performance style that speaks to them – and that they feel confident they can excel within. That said, there is a lot to borrow and adapt from history.

Today's professional theater has more diverse influences, though the lineage often still extends back through Europe. Political theater in the US today owes a great deal of its aesthetics and theories of addressing social and political change to the writings of German theater theorist, playwright, and director, Bertolt Brecht, writing in the first half of the twentieth century (Willett, 1977). In terms of playwriting, American theater was dominated throughout the twentieth century by white men such as Eugene O'Neill, Arthur Miller, Sam Shepard, and Tony Kushner who wrote plays, often with strong male protagonists who struggled as individuals against various systems of oppression. At the same time, there were African American playwrights whose work had a significant impact. August Wilson's plays blended a more lyrical and poetic language and focused more on family and community than on individuals' journeys. He also addressed the power of community and the injustices faced by African American families. He publicly expressed that he did not approve of white directors directing his plays as he felt they did not have the cultural vocabulary, aesthetic or experience to understand his characters and his work (Bryer & Hartig, 2006).

When exploring performance styles and forms more aligned with the cultural experiences of girls of color, I have always been deeply influenced and inspired by Ntotzake Shange's work. A poet and playwright, Shange created the award-winning and groundbreaking theater piece, *for colored girls who have considered suicide/ when the rainbow is enuf* that appeared on Broadway in 1975 and coined a new word for her lusciously unique blend of poetry, music, dance, and theater that doesn't follow linear narrative structures: the choreopoem.

As an example of a project that deeply adheres to the logic, creativity, and energy of Black girls, I asked Ruth Nicole Brown how she would describe the kind of performances the girls created in SOLHOT. She responded, "It's DIY, our aesthetics. It is so organic, it is so self-taught and collectively made, I love it. We work primarily in the tradition of the choreopoem theatrically" (interview). In her book *Black Girlhood Celebration*, Brown also referred to the influence of games and songs Black girls played and performed as children including Double Dutch jump rope skipping and hand-clapping songs. These "self-taught" and "collectively made" performances are too often dismissed as amateur and therefore lacking a more "polished" aesthetic, yet for generations of Black girls, they have been the foundation of their performance aesthetic and have deeply influenced contemporary popular music and dance forms. Kyra Gaunt, an ethnomusicologist who focuses her research on the extraordinary – and unacknowledged and undervalued – contributions Black girls make to contemporary music culture, writes:

> Everyday, black girls generate and pass on a unique repertoire of chants and embodied rhythms in their play that both reflects and inspires the principles of black popular music-making … Listen in on girls' daily broadcasts from the playground and you'll hear more than "nonsense." You'll hear a sophisticated approach to nonverbal syllables that mirror the melodic and linguistic approaches found in jive talk, scatting, and the verbal freestyling of hip-hop. Watch their daily routines, which mix colloquial gestures and verbal expressions, and you'll be hooked on their fascinating rhythms, their use of call-and-response from word to body, and their rap-like manipulation of phonics and rhymes just for the fun of it.
>
> (Gaunt, 2006, p. 1)

In line with the aesthetics of SOLHOT and Shange's work, performance scholar Cristal Chanelle Truscott developed SoulWork, based on the contradictions and tensions she felt as a Black artist trained as an actor using European acting methods that focused on psychological realism, in opposition to the performance styles she had grown up with through communal singing in the Black church and engaging in call and response. She describes SoulWork as:

> A philosophy of theatre-making based on African American performance traditions and aesthetics that shifts actors' focus away from "me" and onto "we"; it relocates the directors' ownership from "mine" to "ours" and rescues the audience relationship from "them" to "all of us."
>
> (p. 39)

As part of a tradition of collaboration and devised work, the aesthetics of antiracist theater need to respect the meaningful contributions Black artists and theorists have made to the form and content of theater. This section is not a denunciation of work created within a European theater tradition, but an invitation to acknowledge these roots, where they come from, why they have dominated the aesthetics of theater, whose aesthetics have been ignored and dismissed, and why. Engaging with the girls about theater form and style with a nod to the colonizing history of the art form is part of an antiracist process.

This plays out also during public performances as we guide our audiences in how to respond to our work. Anyone who has been in the audience of a Broadway or other professional theater show is familiar with the pre-show announcement that usually includes some version of, "Unwrap your candies now so you don't make any sounds during the show! Silence your phones! No talking or whispering! If you have to leave your seat, don't expect to be able to come back!" And audiences at symphony performances are often reminded not to clap until the end of a piece of music. These demands for audiences to sit still in silence and pretend to be invisible are in opposition to the cultural norms of people who grew up in Black churches or in communities with thriving call and response cultures that celebrate speaking up, offering verbal support as well as finger snaps, claps, feet stomping, and shouting out.

Principle #4: educating through critical thinking and liberatory pedagogy practices

How do you train and support young social justice activists? Personal stories and experiences of oppression and injustice can form the foundation for girls' awakening to a desire to take action. But in addition to the lived experiences, I advocate for the rehearsal process to also be a site for education and critical consciousness-raising about the root causes for the issues girls face, and the possibility for liberation. My practice as an educator is deeply grounded in Brazilian education activist Paolo Freire's theory of a liberatory pedagogy that he outlines in his seminal *Pedagogy of the Oppressed* (1970). His core theory involves a dismantling of the ever-present model of "banking education" where teachers deposit "knowledge" directly into students' heads without engagement or critical thinking about the information. This would be akin to a theater director telling the girls exactly what to write about, where to stand on stage and how to speak their lines. A Freirian process of engagement includes a co-intentional structure where the students and teachers are working together to learn about the issues, identify and map the "oppressors" or the power players who are operating unjustly and co-strategize tactics for liberation. Iris Young describes this process in her chapter in the book of collected essays, *Oppression, Privilege and Resistance* (2004):

> The only way to fight against powerlessness and the Culture of Silence is to gain a greater consciousness. Oppressed people throughout history have gained a greater understanding and consciousness of themselves and others through education, literacy, and self-reflection. It is through the act of using their voice and gaining a critical perspective of their oppressors that the oppressed are able to free themselves of Indoctrination and (eventually) free their bodies from oppression as well. Freire calls this process of gaining critical consciousness … Conscientization.
>
> (p. 3)

We begin our activist theater process with exploratory discussions and activities that guide us to identify and understand the core issues girls are facing, and why. Instead of focusing on ranting and fuming about injustices such as racism, misogyny, and the intersections between them, we also problem pose about why these injustices exist. When a girl brings up an issue of unfairness she has experienced at school, we read Kimberlé Crenshaw's report, "Black Girls Matter: Pushed Out, Overpoliced, and Underprotected" (Crenshaw, Ocen, & Nanda, 2015) about the discrimination Black girls endure in public schools. And we discuss the research. We ask the girls questions about their experiences in their schools. Why are almost all the students in your public school Black or Latinx? Why are most of your teachers white women? What do your answers tell us about why our communities are structured along race lines? What has been done to change this? What can *we* do to change this? We talk about the root causes of racism and sexism. We talk about slavery. We talk about red lining, Jim Crow laws, school segregation. We ask how to fix this. We ask: Who is a leader? What does a leader look like? Who is an activist? What does an activist look like? Girls strike poses, make gestures, feel the power course through their bodies. How does this feel? Do you see yourself in this image? Why not? Why? Why? Why? What would it look like if you were in charge? Why? Why? Why? The constant questioning, answering, questioning becomes a web of content for the show.

Freire writes that a problem-posing model of education, "bases itself on creativity and stimulates true reflection and action upon reality, thereby responding to the vocation of persons as beings who are authentic only when engaged in inquiry and creative transformation" (1970, p. 65). Taking his theories and applying them to a theater process, Brazilian theater director and political activist Augusto Boal developed an arsenal of participatory theater techniques that he called *Theater of the Oppressed* (Boal, 1979). Boal's games and activities were a frequent part of our warm-ups and a thread through the rehearsal process as his methods offer excellent on-your-feet strategies for understanding and mapping power and using the form of theater itself for creative problem-solving.

Here is an example of a step-by-step script for how I might facilitate an example of Boal's classic Image Theater process:

1) In groups of four, discuss your experiences of injustice within a specific site: school, family, neighborhood.
2) Choose one story and create a frozen image of the moment where the injustice peaked. A silent and non-moving snapshot.
3) Let's witness this image in the school. Walk around and observe every detail. What do you see? Who has the most power? *A teacher with a hand on her hip looking angry and pointing at a girl.* What gives her power? *Her job. Her age. Maybe she's white.* Where does her power come from? *The principal. The district. The structure of school.* What might she do with this power? *She makes the girl feel ashamed, feel sad, feel angry. She can have the girl suspended or expelled.* Who has the least amount of power? *The girl seeming to shrink away and pull up the strap of her shirt.* Why doesn't she have power? *She's younger. She's a student. She's vulnerable.* What makes her vulnerable? *Her clothing. She's getting in trouble for not following "dress code."* How do you know? *She's holding the strap of her shirt.* Who else is in this image? *Another student laughing at her. Another student walking past looking at her own shirt.*
4) OK. Let's pause. What is the story of this image? *A girl is getting in trouble for violating the dress code, while a boy student walks past.* Is this an example of oppression? Why or why not? *Yeah, she's wearing the same thing as other girls, but because of her body size — maybe also her race — she's getting in trouble. She's being treated unfairly.*
5) Let's discuss. Who relates to this issue? *Me! Yup. Me, too. This happens ALL the time at my school. Mine too! They say you can't show cleavage but on really hot days, with no AC in our building, if I wear any teeshirt that I'm comfortable in, I might show a little. Girls with big chests get violations if their shirt is "too tight" or "too revealing" when we don't have any other options.* Is this fair? *No!* Why do you think this system exists? *They say it's "distracting to boys!" Well, it's distracting to MY education to be sent home once a week to change my clothes. And boys should be able to focus on their schoolwork no matter what girls are wearing!* Think deeper. Is this really just about the dress code? *No. It's about policing Black girls' bodies. It's about sexualizing girls. It's about blaming girls for boys acting mad dumb.* Who has the power to make a change here? *The teacher. No, actually, she's probably following the rules from the principal. The principal following the district.*

6) What would be the ideal solution for this? How could this moment be resolved? Go back in your group and create your "ideal image," with everyone still playing the same character

7) Let's witness this new image. What do you see? *The teacher sitting in a chair looking up at the students. The girls standing together at a (mimed) board and pointing at what looks like a piece of paper and referring to another girl standing confidently and touching her shoulders.* Who has the power in this new image? *The three students. They are standing and the teacher is looking at them.* What's going on in this new image? *It looks like the students are presenting a paper that they created to the teacher.* How do they feel about the paper? *They're happy. She's smiling.*

8) Let's hear from the folks in the image. When I hold my hand over your head, speak your inner thoughts. Let's start with the girl holding the paper. *I'm so proud of the new dress code guidelines we wrote together!* Now let's listen to "the teacher." *I suppose these new guidelines are clearer and don't give me any space to say one girl is violating the code for the same reason that another is not. I can also see how the previous code wasn't fair for bigger girls.*

9) Do we agree that this ideal image is the best we can do? Does this solve the problem for the girl? Does it solve the problem forever? Does anyone want to create another "Ideal Image?" *(Girls create different versions of what the "Ideal" could be that include: free school uniforms; a team of girls ripping up a "dress code policy" paper; students going on strike and the principal leaving, presumably fired;* Let's discuss each new image. What did we gain? What did we lose? Is this a realistic solution? Why? Why not? What would we need to get there? Let's choose the "Ideal Image" we feel would have the greatest impact *and* be possible to achieve.

10) Let's see the original image again *[they move back into the first image].* Let's discuss. How can we get from the first image to the ideal image? Who needs to initiate the change? What needs to happen? What are the obstacles? How do you overcome these obstacles? Can the change happen with just these people within the image? Who else needs to be involved? *The principal. The girl's mom. More students to stand in solidarity with the girl.* Take 20 seconds, and let's see the transition from this first image to the ideal image, without using words. Now, let's activate the transition with improvised text.

This process in rehearsal could go on and on until we reach a consensus space where the girls feel they discover a realistic strategy. There are other techniques Boal created that might also be useful in articulating solutions to this issue. In Forum Theatre, the group could stage a scene between the original student (the protagonist), the teacher (the antagonist) who is reprimanding her for a "dress code violation" and any bystanders. Once they perform the unresolved scene for the audience of the other girls in rehearsal, they repeat it from the beginning. At any point, any girl can call out "Stop" and freeze the action, then she can step in for the protagonist or bystander and re-start the scene offering a strategy for fixing this problem. We would then discuss whether this strategy was realistic, possible and if it could be successful.

Boal wrote,

> It is not the place of the theatre to show the correct path, but only to offer the means by which all possible paths may be examined. Maybe the theatre in itself is not revolutionary, but have no doubts, it is a rehearsal of revolution.
>
> (1985, p. 141)

These interactive, performance-based strategies offer girls real tools to unpack the issues, understand how power plays out in their lives and utilizes the unique art form of theater to guide them to work together to find solutions.

Principle #5: practicing a trauma-informed process

When I use the word, "trauma," I refer to any experience of emotional or physical pain that has interrupted and ruptured a person's life and continues to haunt and torment that person. Experiences of racism can be trauma. Violence can be trauma. Humiliation can be trauma. Neglect can be trauma. I avoid clinical definitions because I believe trauma is defined by the survivor, not the textbook.

A girl stands on stage, hands clasped tightly in front of her in the pose often referred to as the "Eve" representing the first lady's awkward, insecure, shame-filled covering of her genitals. Her eyes laser into the floor before her. Her toes turn inward. Her voice starts with a meek squeak as she starts to tell a story, her story. A story of violence. A story of pain. A story of shame. A story of trauma. As the narrative unfolds, her volume builds. As she feels the audience lean in to her, she straightens. As her story reaches its climax, her body opens up and her voice spills with energy into the room. As she rises, audience members' tears fall. With her final word, the audience leaps to their feet, wipes their eyes and cheers. Moments like these, repeated and repeated and repeated in youth theater programs again and again and again are often hailed as celebratory. As evidence for claims that theater is healing, empowering, therapeutic. That the roar of approval from the audience validates the girl's survival, and that bravely sharing her story will somehow release her from the pain the memory inflicts upon her.

A certain unspoken assumption permeates the field of devised youth theater that encouraging young people to share their stories on stage is "good," is healing, is useful – for them and for the audiences. I believe this comes from a misguided trust in Freud's psychoanalytic theories that date to the late-nineteenth century that then infiltrated our cultural understanding of how to recover from emotional pain and trauma. In simplified terms, his "talk therapy" invited patients to tell their therapists the details of their painful memories as a way to release them into the air in order to exorcise them from their psyche and help them let go of the pain. For many people over the past generations, paying a trained, experienced, and certified professional to listen and respond in a private and protected setting, this was effective.

Though psychiatrist and trauma studies expert Bessel van der Kolk is skeptical of this process. He writes in his impactful 2014 book, *The Body Keeps the Score: Brain, Mind, and the Body in the Healing of Trauma:*

> Traumatic memories are fundamentally different from the stories we tell about the past. They are dissociated: The different sensations that entered the brain at the time of the trauma are not properly assembled into a story, a piece of autobiography. Perhaps the most important finding in our study was that remembering the trauma with all its associated affects, does not, as Breuer and Freud claimed back in 1893, necessarily resolve it. Our research did not support the idea that language can substitute for action. Most of our study participants could tell a coherent story and also experience the pain associated with those stories, but they kept being haunted by unbearable images and physical sensations.
>
> (p. 196)

And yet, despite clinical evidence to the contrary, young people in theater programs, particularly programs that profess to make work addressing "social justice" are often asked to share and then perform their stories of trauma under a false assumption that this will be "good" or healing for them or that it will ignite audiences to empathize with (or pity) the young people and then somehow work towards change. For example, in describing *I Dream*, a national youth applied theatre project created by artist and activist Daniel Beaty, facilitators Joshua Rashon Streeter and Nicole Olusanya write, "*I Dream's* goal is for young people to recognize the causes of oppression by unpacking their own stories of hardship or struggle" (2021). Though facilitators often overlook the fact that rehearsal and performance spaces are obviously so different from therapy. These spaces are public, communal, filled with others (director, other young people, audience) who listen and respond to the stories without the training or resources psychology professionals have earned.

What theater can offer trauma survivors, especially young people who want to create performances *about* their trauma as part of their activist vision to end the violence or injustice that caused it, is a space to explore around the issues, a space to investigate the root causes and articulate strategies for change and healing, based on their own research or lived experiences. As part of operating within a trauma-informed practice, I am extremely wary of girls who want to perform the details of their personal stories. It often seems like a brave idea and they almost always get support from their peers and audiences and yet, I question how healthy and healing this is for them vs the potential for their own retraumatization by asking them to keep repeating the story in rehearsals and performance and re-experiencing those painful memories. In these moments, I suggest collaborating with the performer to find new, poetic ways to communicate elements of the story without the need for specifics, to find the aesthetic distance that puts a barrier between the story, and the survivor. Additionally, hearing such raw and often unprocessed stories of trauma can trigger painful responses in audiences unprepared to confront such content. Instead, I might invite them to share examples from their healing, focusing on moments when they were reclaiming control and making choices for their wellness that could potentially help other survivors.

Later in his book, van der Kolk writes about his research exploring the impact of theater interventions on trauma survivors and he offers several examples of organizations that have found ways to use theater as a successful form of trauma therapy. He describes programs with teenagers in the Boston juvenile justice system, young people living in foster care in New York City and military veterans in treatment for post-traumatic stress disorder. His examples significantly all include performances of fictional or devised texts, not testimonies of specific experiences from survivors.

He writes about how a theater process can help survivors restore their lost sense of control, ignited by trauma, by going beyond the simple act of telling their story:

> Simply exposing someone to the old trauma does not integrate the memory into the overall context of their lives, and it rarely restores them to the level of joyful engagement with people and pursuits they had prior to the trauma … In contrast, [other treatments including] theater – focus not only on regulating the intense memories activated by trauma but also on restoring a sense of agency, engagement, and commitment through ownership of body and mind.
>
> (p. 258)

Van der Kolk's research on theater programs and trauma shows how the process of rehearsals, the connections survivors make between their story and stories from fiction or other participants and the community trust built through collaboration allow people a path toward recovery where they reclaim ownership of their memory and can lessen its continued power to haunt them. But to be clear, just telling your own story on stage is very different from finding solace in your connection to the emotional language of Shakespeare's war general or Sophocles's tragic hero.

Additionally, Helen Cahill (2008), deputy director of the Australian Youth Research Center, writes about the dangers of young people seeing their lives as defined by their own worst moments. Encouraging teenagers to share their specific stories of trauma, reinforces that this story is integral to their identity. She writes,

> [W]e can think critically about the practice in some arts-based interventions whereby youth "at-risk" are invited to play out their defining story. We can

question whether it is necessarily therapeutic to play and replay a victim story, as this may reinforce the story as defining one's identity.

(p. 23)

When we consider how and when and if to share personal stories in our process, there are many different activities that can help foster the trust needed to even think about such invitations. In "Tree Falling in the Forest," a popular trust game, a teenager stands with her eyes closed, arms folded protectively across her chest in the middle of a circle of her peers who stand with their hands up facing her, elbows cocked and flexible to straighten or bend if needed. She falls backwards into the circle of hands who catch her and gently push her back in the opposite direction where she is caught by the girls on the other side of the circle. She sways, her feet grounded to the floor, her body swirling around the circle as hands catch and toss, catch and toss her. If there were a hole or gap between girls around the edge of the circle, she would fall. The more hands at the periphery, the softer and safer the fall. This game provides an apt metaphor for a solution to girls' personal and vulnerable storytelling about traumatic events or memories. The presence and support of the other girls cushion her fall and provide a web of care. We – and she – trust that with a gentle cushion of loving support, she will survive.

During a Zoom interview with Wakumi Douglas, Executive Director of S.O.U.L. Sisters Leadership Collective in Miami, she shared a creative and deeply inspiring arts-based activity her teaching artists led with the young activists. They played an R&B remix of the song, "Favorite Things" from *The Sound of Music* and then:

> They took the lyrics apart and asked the young people some critical questions to help build their self awareness around the way they show up. So they pulled the lyrics out, "When the dog bites," and asked, how do you respond when confronted with a challenge? They pulled out, "when the bee stings." And asked, Name some of the things that, you know, things that can uplift you when you experience negative emotions and they took the young people through each of the questions. And they talk through it. This develops deep self awareness and sisterhood. They see other people, they see themselves and others. They are able to talk about strategies that they don't forget, and learn new strategies through other people's strategy.

(interview)

Though not specifically performance-based, this beautiful activity exemplifies how we can use arts-based strategies for addressing trauma in our processes. By providing supportive, collaborative spaces and gentle prompts to grant young people the choice to talk about how to heal from trauma, we are modeling effective alternative, community-based strategies for recovery that do not demand the retelling of the trauma itself.

Another tactic of a trauma-informed process is to take time before any writing or movement prompt to ask the girls to take a moment and think about what they might want to create and the memory it stems from. Using a trauma-informed lens demands that we anticipate a response related to trauma at every moment. Trauma and its triggers are unpredictable. For example, a writing prompt such as, "Tell the story about a time you were brave," could both inspire one girl to recall an inspiring story that brings her pride and happiness while another might be paralyzed by a memory of pushing back during a sexual assault. Before the girls begin to write anything, try asking,

> When you think about this memory, what feelings come up? Where are those feelings in your body? Check in from your toes up to your head and assess any pain, nausea, pleasure that you might be experiencing. Breathe through these feelings. Feelings are natural and have no judgments attached. We can't help or predict what we feel but we can change the way we act and what we choose to do with those feelings. What do you want to *do* with these feelings? If you are experiencing a feeling that hurts or makes you uncomfortable in a way you do not want to explore, choose a different memory. If you want to breathe through the feeling and sit with it until you're ready to write, that's ok too. You are in control now of what you write and what you share and who gets to hear it.

"You are in control, here." This reminder is core to all parts of our process. Girls must trust that their stories will not be co-opted. That if they need to take a break, they can go. If they feel pain, they can stop. If they need to talk, we will listen. If they want to be quiet, we won't pry. Too often, programs are run according to tight schedules, curricula, and agendas dictated by adults and accountable to rigid theater production schedules or school calendars. Without building in the flexibility to follow the girls' lead, disengagement and distrust will likely occur.

Trauma expert and social worker Resmaa Menakem offers an extraordinary gift in his provocative, groundbreaking and immensely useful book, *My Grandmother's Hands: Racialized Trauma and the Pathway to Mending Our Hearts and Bodies* (2017), that is filled with his personal journey understanding the impact of intergenerational racial trauma as a Black man, and providing guides, meditations and activities for both white folks and folks of color to engage with and heal from our traumas. He leads readers through tactics to both "settle" and "activate" bodies as he writes, "A calm, settled body is the foundation for health, for healing, for helping others, and for changing the world," (p. 164).

In addition to actively engaging with the ways trauma shows up throughout the process and performance of theater, viBe Theater Experience Executive Director Toya Lillard shared the ways that she has built in a culture of care to her organization for both the girls and the adults who work with them. She offers a free yoga and movement series to girls and "Caretaker Take Care" series for "BIPOC youth and cultural workers, teachers, teaching artists, artist "artivists," arts educators, cultural leaders, arts administrators and interns."[6] As she often states, "You can't *run* program if you *need* program." She names and honors the labor that adult women do on behalf of the girls they work with, and the cost it takes to do it. She continues:

> How are you going to help somebody else get free when you don't even know what that feels like? So, I owe it to our practitioners. We owe it to our folks that are on the ground, touching these people that we say we're serving, we owe it to them. To make it a non-negotiable thing that their freedom, too, is a part of our mission ... And I'm doing my own internal work, understanding how important it was for folks, for artists to be able to do the same, that it is abusive to ask someone to be vulnerable through their art and not offer them healing spaces and that's what the nonprofit industrial complex encourages us to do. To abandon people. And as soon as we extract all the juice of their story – "Thank you so much!" and we assume that by them unloading their trauma that they are better for it because they told us. And it's not true, it's the opposite. So yeah, so therapy and yoga and movement and whatever else we can dream up or they can dream up is just as important as the shows that we create.
>
> (interview)

Thank you, Toya! Her words are worth repeating and absorbing: You can't run a program with and for young people, if you still need programs for your own healing and growth. Too often, the adults have our own backgrounds of trauma and pain and if we're not also cultivating healing spaces for ourselves, either on our own or alongside the girls, we are modeling dangerous behaviors.

Principle #6: "Saying it how it is": on the rejection of censorship

Developmental psychologists Lyn Mikel Brown and Carol Gilligan (1992) observed how adolescent girls notice the ways adult women in their lives silence themselves, and in turn, distrust their own knowledge and experience of relationships. As a white, middle-class woman raised in the suburbs, I was definitely taught that, "If you don't have anything nice to say, don't say anything at all." This generational modeling of "good girls" and "good women" silencing themselves presumably in order to avoid conflict arguably instead created a norm that speaking your mind was not only impolite, but totally unacceptable. In our goal to raise activists, it was core to our values that girls never feel silenced in our process and that when they expressed their thoughts, opinions, and feelings, they would be heard and valued.

During our interview, I asked 16-year-old Shanique what she would like to say to adults who attempt to censor teenagers during a theatermaking process or tell them they can't use certain language or tell certain kinds of stories. She said:

> You have an open mind to what the teenagers are trying to say, or else they feel like they're being judged and they'll immediately shut themselves down from saying anything. And that's when it gets bad, because once that teen just shuts down, they won't want to really be compassionate with any other person inside that program because they feel like, "Oh, I was judged from the first hand, so what's the point of continuing to allow myself to be here and really develop myself?" … So just be really open minded about what they're saying and don't place any filters on those teens because there are things that need to be said, but sometimes there's certain ways of saying it that society, quote-unquote, doesn't deem correct. But in reality, there's no other way to say it. Or they don't know another way to say it.
>
> (interview)

In many ways, dealing with the censorship of words and language can be a straightforward process. Just don't do it. But there have been times, girls have used language that has been offensive to me and I have struggled with how to respond. In these situations, the girls have not shared my view that certain words or phrases were violent or offensive. With frequent listening and usage, many words that once had edges of fire, to them have been dulled into invisibility.

An example of how language can dissolve into numbness is the horrific (to me) naming of white, ribbed, cotton sleeveless shirts as "wife beaters." The history of this epithet is extremely problematic to me. Historically, these shirts were sold and worn as undershirts by men. The "wife beater" image comes from stereotypical images of men who sit around in their undershirts, drink beer, and beat up their wives. Prominent examples of abusive men from Hollywood movies are of Robert DeNiro in *Raging Bull*, Marlon Brando in *A Streetcar Named Desire*, and Gianni Russo in *The Godfather*. The phrase is so tightly linked to the apparel that most of the teenagers who use it rarely think about the connotations, history or literal and metaphoric meaning. Because these shirts were extremely popular and fashionable in the first decades of the twenty-first century, especially among teenage girls, the name is tossed around so frequently that the girls believe it simply means: ribbed white sleeveless shirt. A participant in a 2008 viBe show wrote and performed the following lyrics:

> K to the A to the Y to the A
> I represent Darren & Niara all day
> Some say I'm kinda conceited
> But I say that I'm convinced
> So full of many jokes
> And lots of intelligence
> I consider me a leader

With my cool wife beater
I promise that I can make it worth your while
And PLEEZE oh PLEEZE
RESPECT MY STYLE!

When I ask Kaya what she means by "wife beater," she looks at me with total confusion and a hint of annoyed condescension. She points to the white ribbed tank top she's wearing that day and says, "you know, 'a wife beater.'" I ask her why she calls it that and there is an awkward silence where it seems she is actually thinking about it for the first time, a word she has probably spoken hundreds of times. The moment erupts into a brief dialogue among the rest of the girls about whether it is an issue that this phrase bothers me because it is obvious that all the other girls know what she means. It is a moment when I feel them pushing me into the cliched category of "old, white feminist with no sense of humor." In the end, Kaya does change the line, but I'll never know if that was because she eventually understood why the phrase was problematic, or if she just didn't want to talk about it with me anymore. It was a moment when my authority and power caused her to alter the text she would have performed if I had not interrupted her.

This example shows how complicated the issue of censorship might become when a young artist creates a piece that she had not considered offensive in the least. As part of our commitment to trusting girls, we do not censor anything or change any grammar, spelling or language in the texts that the girls construct. But sometimes granting such boundless freedoms can create ethically challenging struggles and frustrations for us. As the previous example shows, through dialogue with the girls, we can encourage them to make changes, but these changes might be to appease the adults and avoid conflict, which is also antithetical to my first principle of negotiating power. Sometimes censoring is silencing and sometimes censoring is encouraging an edit in order not to offend or turn off an audience member.

Another more recent example of me trying to nudge a girl to change her text occurred in our 2018 production. Annie, at 16, wrote a witty and engaging monologue that began with the line, "Dear Caucasian people," and continued into a brilliant rant about a series of microaggressions white people had done to her and her fellow Black friends and called out the very real issues of gentrification in her Brooklyn neighborhood, cultural appropriation and other racist behaviors they had encountered. As a white person, I was offended by the use of the term "Caucasian" to describe all white people. Since race is a social construction, not a biological or regional identifier, I asked them if they would consider changing the first line to "Dear white people." Their response was that people of color were always misidentified by race, so they were fine if white people felt offended by this word. They did not change it. And I totally supported them. This was an example of my own overstepping because of my personal discomfort, which in some ways was exactly the purpose of Annie's monologue – to hold white people accountable for the damages we have done to folks in the global majority. It was, in fact, quite brilliant of them. I was asked to consider how my race was being defined and when I said I did not like this classification, I was dismissed.

An important strategy is to leave space for the participants to identify the issues the performance will address and the dramaturgical structure of the piece, allowing them to have necessary ownership over the process and content, while also making sure they have access to research and engage in discussions about the issue. Oftentimes due to funding cycles or grant requirements, adult leaders need to plan far in advance and include some of these details. For example, an environmental justice foundation might fund a performance where girls would make a play about climate change. In such a situation, be transparent with the girls about why and how this was determined to be the topic of the production, make ample time and space for the girls to research the issue and discover how it impacts their own lives, and always leave space for them to adapt it, question it or reject it, even if it means letting go of that specific funding. If you try to force them to make a show about something they are not interested in, the project will likely backfire.

Principle #7: embracing pleasure, joy, humor, and play

It is no wonder that at the end of every one of the how-to-be-an-activist books for girls, there is a section about "self-care" filled with suggestions for bubble baths, cookie dough, and Netflix bingeing in acknowledgment of the heaviness and possible triggers for past trauma that can ignite when spending time fighting for social justice (Rich & Sagramola, 2018; Paul & Tamaki, 2018). So far in this chapter, I have also done my part in leading you to believe that most, if not all, activist performance processes are filled with gloom and horrors. There is often an assumption that activism is all about focusing on the ruptures and negativity in the world. When inviting girls to write and create performances, they frequently do write about these weightier topics.

When asked about her writing process, 16-year-old Izzy reveals a lens through which to understand girls' gravitation towards darker material:

DANA: Do you write when you're happy?
IZZY: Sometimes, but not as much. When I'm happy it's just like, "Weeee! I'm happy! I'm happy! I'm happy!" And then I get down on myself and I'm like, "Damn! I'm mad," then I'll write something. It's like I get – I'm more creative when I'm pissed – like you see it in my writing. Most of [my poems] are very morbid and very angry.

(interview)

Because girls often grab a pen when their hand clenches into a fist, the writing that explodes from these emotions is tinged with the anger, rage, loneliness or fear that consumes them. Developmental psychologist Carol Gilligan (2004) reflects about her experiences with an all-woman theater troupe:

I observed that the hardest place for women to go was joy. Much easier to tell a tragic story. Because to go back to joy or pleasure in your relationship with your mother or whomever means to stand in a place where loss is in front of you rather than behind you. It means to risk what we often say we'll never risk again. So instead, we tell a tragic story.

(p. 145)

Though Izzy states that when she is happy, she is celebrating her joy and there is no time or need to document it or write about it, Gilligan's theory suggests that at a certain level, Izzy resists the memories of joy. Arts therapists have found that when the emotion is negative, writing can be a powerful outlet, and safer than other methods such as drugs or risky behavior, to release the intensity of emotion (National Research Council & Institute of Medicine, 2002; Jones, 1996).

Activist performance does not always need to encourage writing about lurid stories of injustice and violence. For some girls, boldly stating their desires, pleasures, accomplishments, and dreams in a world that often silences or rejects them, is an example of activism.

"Pleasure is a measure of freedom," writes activist adrienne marie brown (2019, p. 2). She continues, "Pleasure activism is the work we do to reclaim our whole, happy, and satisfiable selves from the impacts, delusions, and limitations of oppression and/or supremacy" (p. 2). Expressing joy and taking pleasure in life is part of the necessary human experience of survival. When asked about the core identity of SOLHOT, "a space where Black girls could express, create and make space to be free,"[7] founder and visionary Dr. Ruth Nicole Brown told me during our interview, "If girls are not laughing, it's not really SOLHOT."

Talking about injustice, racism, violence, and so many of the other broken parts of our world that need fixing, can easily bring you down. Our core organizing principles have always included finding the balance between rage and struggle with also exploring the joy, hope, love, and fun in our process and productions. If we can't imagine positive solutions, then we will never achieve them. Incorporating play into our activist work is strategic and intentional. As video game designer and activist Mattie Brice defined in her TEDx talk, "Creating play is manipulating environments, bodies, and social systems to reveal new possibilities" (Brice, 2017). Through the creative practice of playing together and laughing together, we deepen our connections and feel bolder in our risk taking.

If we can't start making the world we want to live in, we might never see it. I believe wholeheartedly in the necessity for incorporating playfulness and celebration into our rehearsals and in naming and acknowledging that choosing love, fun, and connection is a valid organizing strategy. Artist and activist Benjamin Shepard writes about the power of playfulness in activist movements. He describes the work of Reclaim the Streets (RTS), an activist collective that produces celebratory and performative street parties as a way to raise awareness about and protest the privatization of public space.

For RTS, the best way to accomplish this is with a buoyant cultural activism, which relies on street parties rather than pamphlets, lectures, or boring speakers. RTS favors a Groucho-Marxist approach closer in style to the Situationists and other pranksters. The point is to use culture – music and performance – to involve people in playing and building community, rather than telling them to do so … As activists, they understood that little in life does more to help folks get by than a good laugh. As such, they built on this spirit of irony, play, joy, pranks, and humor to create a new approach to political performance as cultural mobilization.

(Shepard, 2005, pp. 53–55)

We sprinkle playful games throughout the rehearsal process that bring a spirited energy of fun into the room. We'll play versions of Simon Says, Musical Chairs or Follow the Leader as a way to get everybody moving, being creative and also erupting in giggles when anyone "messes up." In our scene work and story circles, we'll intentionally guide girls towards creating humorous sketches, playfully and carefully exaggerating certain stereotypes for comic effect or sharing stories about "embarrassing moments" to infuse lightness and laughter into the space.

In addition to the need for incorporating play and laughter into the rehearsal process, we also find ways to include humor in our productions. Kuenique reflected in an interview about the importance of fun in a theater production:

I want there to be theater about what's happening now. This is the struggle that we're going through – I want there to be theater that teaches people but, at the same time, they have fun. And so they remember it, you know? You don't want to just listen to the theater just go on, and on, and on about our struggles, but I want it to be fun! You want to cry, but you also want to laugh.

In a performance I co-directed, with spoken word artist and Africana Studies professor Crystal Endsley, as part of the Girls Speak Out at the United Nations on the 2018 International Day of the Girl, produced by the Working Group on Girls, we created a show that wove creative and personal writing from girls from more than 20 countries with speeches from girl activists about their work on the ground in their homelands. As part of the performance, Leo and Aniaha, two teenagers in New York City, wrote and performed a comical piece about their periods:

LEO: Everyone needs to relax so I can explain what REALLY goes on in a girl's life through one of the most awkward topics no one seems to want to cover *[pause]*. My period *[smiles]*.

ANAIS [as host]:   Ignore her.

ANIAHA: Don't be so rude, give us our time. This is a serious topic we need to cover.

ANAIS [as host]:   That can only be done by someone … mature.

ANIAHA: We ARE mature!

[*ANIAHA & LEO stick their tongues out at ANAIS*]

LEO: Exactly. Anyways, back to my period. I get it 12 times a year.

ANIAHA: For a week.

LEO: For 168 hours.

ANIAHA: For 10,080 minutes.

LEO: For 604,800 seconds, approximately. But, of course anyone who doesn't have it would think, "Oh, how bad could it be to bleed for an entire week?"

ANIAHA: Oh, how bad? Would YOU like to bleed for a week? With the possibility that every single one of those 604,800 seconds a singular drop of blood on any shade of pants that isn't black would ruin your day?

LEO: That in all those seconds, you basically have a child inside you over how uncomfortable and bloated you feel? Oh, and the pains? Don't get me started.

ANIAHA: The feeling is exactly how it'd be to have a needle constantly poking you a million times while being punched in the gut. Trust me, not fun.

LEO: So please don't tell me it's nothing or look at me like an idiot when I say I don't want to go out.

The audience of mostly teenage girls laughed in recognition and solidarity as they related to the cramps, pains, and embarrassments of getting your period as a teenage girl. Playwrights have been using humor to address political issues at least since Aristophanes in Ancient Greece. Stand-up comedians have always understood the power you have once you can get audiences to laugh. Following the laughter from the previous sketch, the next scene included one of the girl activists giving a more serious speech about girls in Kenya who stopped attending school because they lacked access to menstrual products. The juxtaposition of the two scenes showed both the near-universal experience of cisgender girls,' trans boys, and nonbinary teens' menstrual cycles and the wide range of anxieties, injustices, and even violence it can cause across cultures. The first scene encourages the girls in the audience to giggle about the biological "injustice" of suffering each month, but the next scene adds to those feelings by sharing a more dangerous impact of the same issue that girls in other parts of the world face. For millions of girls around the world, their monthly period is not just uncomfortable, but can endanger their educations and their lives.

Porshe Garner, Dominique Hill, Jessica Robinson and Durrell Callier, Black girlhood scholars and SOLHOT homegirls, write: "Pleasure, as we know it to be experienced and expressed through our organizing work with SOLHOT, is produced when we dismantle systems of power that seek to infringe on our ability to be our whole selves. Black girlhood pleasure as a method of anti-respectability, then, must move us away from dominant desires to only know Black girls through deficit frames or to name Black girls' vulnerabilities due to their social locations within a society that has never cared for or about Black girls. To do so, we argue, requires a rootedness in Black girls' aesthetics of love, reliability, funk, and performance," (2019, p. 191).

Because their experiences outside might be fraught with tension, with violence, with a hostile world that rarely celebrates young people marginalized by race and gender, we must always push harder to cultivate internal spaces of love, laughter, joy, and celebration. Ruth Nicole Brown shared the following story about the spiritual depths of girls' connection to these spaces:

> [On the first day of SOLHOT,] I asked, "Do you all know why you're here?" And it was one of those rhetorical questions, right? But to my surprise (laughing) To my surprise, this girl raises her hand, she's like, "Oh, I know exactly why you all are here." And she proceeds to tell this beautiful story about how, she's like, "I know why you guys are here," she said, "You guys are here because my dad sent you all." She's like, "My dad passed and right before he passed, he told me to always choose love. To always be love." She was like, "That's what I hear you all telling us to do and because you're telling us that in the same way my dad did, I know you're here because he sent you." Choose to love, yeah. Always choose love. And I was like, it had nothing to do with SOLHOT. We're not here because of what happened in SOLHOT in 2006. We're not here because of that great grant funding that they gave us … I was thinking, you know what, that's exactly why we're here and to think that we're, you know, it expanded my imagination. Like, if we said we're here as a part of some girls ancestral – I don't know – continuity.
>
> (interview)

Though I definitely cannot match that specific experience of a girl signing on to a project specifically because of the deathbed wish of a loved one, I relate to the experience that this work can often connect with girls in a sparkling, nonverbal, mystical way. Through focusing on celebration, creating rituals, and inviting girls to "choose love," we make room for a space to explore magical possibility.

These principles are not a blueprint where you have to follow every step or your structure will collapse, though if any one of them is entirely missing, I might warn you that your foundation might wobble. In the following chapters, I offer a collection of stories of these principles in action as they are both the lighting that illuminates my process and the scaffolding that supports the creation of the theater worlds.

Notes

1 For readers looking for a practical step-by-step "how-to" guide for creating activist theater with young people, I also suggest a few excellent books that outline specific processes that could be of value to readers. Megan Alrutz and Lynn Hoare generously share their entire process in their comprehensive book, *Devising Critically Engaged Theatre with Youth: The Performing Justice Project* (2020) about creating work with young people that addresses racial and gender justice. Jo Beth Gonzales's *Temporary*

Stages II: Critically Oriented Drama Education (2013) offers excellent resources and lesson plans for high school theater teachers, and Kathleen Gallagher has published widely and brilliantly about her work with girls and with co-ed groups in schools (2000, 2007, 2014).

2 All names of the young people have been changed to pseudonyms of their choosing. When they did not select a pseudonym, I used the character name they created in the performance pieces they wrote.

3 In my most serious attempt to describe the racial identities of the young people I work with, I am choosing to be as specific as possible and to use the words that they use to describe themselves. Of the nearly 1,000 girls referred to in some way in this book, approximately 750 described themselves as Black or African American; 220 identified as Latinx, Latina, Brown, or Hispanic; five claimed part-Native American or Indigenous heritage; five were South Asian, Bangladeshi, Indian, or Pakistani; and approximately 15 were white. Though the term "BIPOC" (Black, Indigenous and People of Color) has recently gained momentum in scholarly and popular publications, it is still somewhat controversial, and in consultation with many of the girls interviewed in this book, none of them felt connected to it. They preferred the phrases "Black and Brown" and "girls of color" when describing themselves and their friends, or asked that I use a more specific identifier of their choosing when discussing individual girls. I am aware that these labels and words change and evolve over time, but as I am writing today in 2021, I defer to the girls.

4 See also Tema Okun's writing at www.dismantlingracism.org

5 ssir.org

6 viBeTheater.org

7 solhot.com

3 "Real im(PERFECT)ions"
Performing confidence, expressing agency

Perhaps surprising to many, teenage girls' most pressing issues are not parallel to what an adult-controlled political party might include on their policy platform. Though systemic and legislative issues have a substantial impact on girls' lives, their core lived experiences revolve around their home, neighborhood, and school and they are often most concerned about the daily stresses related to their own development, their exploration of identity, often as it relates to race, their friendships and relationships and how they measure up to their peers, and their stressful and often oppressive interactions with teachers and administrators at under-resourced schools.

"Teenage girls have no self-esteem"

I wanted to start this chapter with an offering of one of the key issues that girls often choose to write about when asked what feels most urgent and important to them. I wanted to share heartfelt quotes from interviews with girls about how this issue rips through their lives and prevents them from achieving their greatest potential. I wanted to post poetic excerpts from their writing to show you readers how they frame it, speak it and attempt to recover from it. But then my insecurity crept up from the tightening clutch in my gut to the hot reddening of my cheeks as I burned with the familiar mantra the voice in my head has been whispering to me since I was 11, "Nope, this isn't enough." Shouldn't you tell the readers that girls are working on ending world hunger or reversing climate change?

When questioned about what they felt the most important issue girls today face, nearly three-quarters of the girls I have collaborated with would name some version of self-esteem, body image or lack of confidence. In a society that reinforces unrealistic ideals of women, girls are at a developmental stage where they are testing out what it means to be a woman and often struggle as they attempt to measure up. I acknowledge that as a white woman serving as one of the directors of the projects, many girls of color might have been wary about sharing stories related to the ways racism and white supremacy impact their lives. I was almost always co-directing with a Black woman who spoke openly about race and racism, but I was still present at nearly every rehearsal as co-director. I have no doubt that racism is always a dominant issue, and you will see throughout this chapter and the rest of the book the ways it is often the cracked spine that holds other issues together.

"OK," I begin at one of our early rehearsals of a theater project. "Since you all identified: 'Teenage girls have no self-esteem,' as the issue you want to work on with your show, what are some strategies?"

"You have to love yourself," is a response given by 15-year-old Emerald. With no recipe for this epically ambiguous demand/ request/ fantasy of "loving yourself," girls are left knowing they are "supposed to" love themselves despite most messages they receive that reinforce all the ways girls are "unloveable" (i.e., too emotional, too loud, too quiet, etc. ...). When considering topics for activist productions, "girls' self-esteem" doesn't quite have the same weight and allure as addressing seemingly more important or seemingly life-threatening issues such as violence, climate change, migration, or poverty. Saliesha, a green-eyed 18-year-old Puerto Rican girl living in the Bronx who stopped going to high school halfway through her junior year, was one of the many girls who told me that "confidence and self-esteem was the biggest issue" girls like her faced. She said:

> Yeah. I don't know – if you don't have [confidence and self-esteem], then you're messed up. Like even with school, you'll just feel stupid. Like I know me, for one, in high school, I did not feel smart at all. I felt like the dumbest thing on earth. Especially when people get it and you still need a couple minutes to get it yourself. But if you feel that – if you have that confidence, like, okay, I may not get it now and other people may get it, you know, but I'm gonna get it eventually. You have to, like, think like *that*.
>
> (interview)

Saliesha outlines a common narrative about confidence and self-esteem in her response to my question. "If you don't have that, then you're messed up," she states, validating a prevalent American ideal that in order to succeed or even to survive, one must have enough faith in oneself that they can succeed. For example, in a study published by the Community College Research Center, researchers Susan Bickerstaff, Melissa Barragan, and Zawadi Rucks-Ahidiana, found that "when students are not confident, and don't expect to succeed, they are more likely to drop out" (2012). For Saliesha, the feeling of insecurity and shame about her intelligence, pushed her to leave high school, a choice that deeply compromised her potential for future work, a career, an income, and stability. These "feelings" though do not just bubble up in a vacuum. As a Puerto Rican teenager, she had likely spent much of her lifeconsuming media that rarely highlighted the intellectual contributions of people who looked like her.

In *Rock My Soul: Black People and Self-Esteem* (2003), bell hooks hypothesizes that the critical problem of racism towards the Black community will never be solved until the issue of self-esteem within that community is addressed. She outlines shame, jealousy, lowered expectations, misogyny, and fear of success as several of the factors that contribute to this self-esteem crisis. hooks advocates for a need for spaces where Black people can express their feelings, cultivate hope, and imagine a more ideal world. These three pillars are the foundations for the activist theater spaces we strive to create where girls use creative writing and performance to construct and inhabit a world they want to live in.

Seventeen-year-old Josia, a passionate, Dominican girl, told me why lack of confidence was such an urgent issue for girls to overcome:

> It's kind of like making excuses, where you see all these obstacles and you immediately give up. It's kind of like that fear holds you back from so many things especially like for example, if you don't get to say what you need to say, like you still have that in you. And so yeah, getting over that fear is a big thing.

Research has revealed a confidence gap emerging in young women at the time of adolescence (AAUW, 1992). This liminal space between childhood and adulthood can be particularly challenging for girls. As they skip, slink, or trudge through puberty, their bodies transform into unfamiliar shells that often don't match the same pace as their mental and emotional development. New breasts and hips can unwittingly deceive men in public spaces to treating them as older than they are. The catcalls and street harassment can lead to shame and fear as they move awkwardly through the world. And for young transgender people and those who identify outside the gender binary of boy/girl, adolescence can be a time when their body's physical development does not match their gender identity. Since developmental psychologists Lyn Mikel Brown and Carol Gilligan's groundbreaking 1992 study of middle schools girls' plunge from self-assured, ready-to-take-on-the-world, sprightly confidence at ages eight and nine to a more guarded, insecure, hesitant mass whose newest favorite phrase by age 13 was, "I don't know." The American Association of University Women's 1992 report "How Schools Shortchange Girls," revealed, based on research of more than 2,000 girls that their confidence levels nosedived 30 percent from middle school until the end of high school. This freefall impacted the types of courses girls would enroll in (not much math or science), how much they spoke up in class or asked for support (not enough) and their hopes and plans for the future (setting the bar too low as compared to boys who often saw themselves in leadership or executive roles). And more than 25 years later, in a 2018 survey of more than 1,000 girls from diverse backgrounds, researchers confirmed that nothing had changed – between the ages of eight and 12, girls' self-expressed confidence levels plummeted by 30 percent (Kay and Shipman). The damage this gap rips through the souls of girls can be debilitating, prevents them from achieving their greatest potential, and when paired with depression and anxiety, can sometimes even be lethal (Brown & Gilligan, 1992; Orenstein, 1995).

An entire industry has emerged in response to this documented and perceived crisis. As I wrote in the first chapter, much of the "Girl Power" industry was created to cash in on parents', teachers' and the larger society's fears that girls were in need of a marketing campaign and a plethora of products to tell them how "awesome!" they are. And we know that girls have internalized these messages as they express again and again how vital a sense of confidence is to their survival.

And yet. As I let the faces and voices of the hundreds of girls I have collaborated with scroll through my memory, I ache from our failure to do something concrete towards ending the misogynist systems and institutions that lead girls to believe it is *their* fault if they are not succeeding. That if only they, as individuals, were stronger and "more confident," if they could somehow just dismiss the negative messages they get and just love themselves more, they would be thriving at everything they set out to accomplish. By naming a lack of confidence as such a core issue in girls' lives, we, in effect, let everyone else off the hook, and blame the girls for their developmentally normal experiences.

As education and public policy scholar Sally A. Nuamah writes in *How Girls Achieve* (2019):

> When we adopt these problematic assumptions [that success could be predicated on a single factor rather than a system or set of systems], we place the source of achievement inequities on a defect in the individual (for example, low confidence) and thus contribute to the development of thin solutions based on removing the defect (for example, increasing her confidence) rather than improving the context by dismantling the patriarchal structure in which girls and women find themselves.
>
> (p. 110)

As readers will notice throughout this book, I am obsessed with the tensions between activism that advocate for a transformation within an individual girl versus activism that works to dismantle the systems of oppression that impact girls' lives. And so, as I consider which issues to begin to write about, I find myself returning back to this issue of confidence as a strong example of one core issue that impacts girls as individuals – and remains one of the most-frequently written about issue by girls – as well as serves as a lens to understand the social and political forces that affect girls' lives.

Girls of all races and ethnicities are media-trained to hate their bodies, to never feel "beautiful" enough within the limited culturally prescribed ideal of beauty. It is in the best financial interest of the beauty industry (worth over $80 billion) and the diet industry (worth $66 billion) that girls and women crave and will pay for "solutions" to the "dilemma" of physical "imperfection." Saturated with media images of airbrushed, make-up slathered, starved and implanted, white, blonde, "American" girls, many teenagers are left feeling inadequate

(McRobbie, 2008; Brumberg, 1997). Celleste, a curvy Dominican 16-year-old girl expresses the prevailing feeling of so many girls in the following monologue from one of our 2007 productions:

> What do you see when you look in the mirror? You see the defects instead of the beauty. What is the first thing that comes to mind when you see a magazine? "I wish" is that first phrase that pops to mind. We want to become something we're not.

White girls who seem, on the surface to fit the "beauty ideal," also struggle to achieve an impossible perfection. Emma, a tall and lean 18-year-old white girl with sparkling aquamarine eyes, glossy dark ringlets, and many stories of being stopped on the street and asked to model. She participated all through her high school years in viBe's theater programs and SPARK Movement's activist campaigns, and spoke out at the 2013 Girls Speak Out at the United Nations implicating the media for violence against girls by their rampant use of digitally altering women's bodies and skin and only promoting a very (literally) narrow image of "beauty." She stands at a podium and tells her story:

> I am the survivor of an eating disorder. Since fifth grade I tried everything to rid myself of my worst enemy: body fat. The models in the magazines I read and the actresses on the shows I watched all defined what it meant to be beautiful. They all were super skinny, had flawless skin, full breasts and straight, glossy hair. I didn't have any of that and I was ashamed. As high school drew near, I became drained by dieting, starving myself, failing to make myself throw up and truly hating my own body. For a long time my eating disorder was my deepest darkest secret. I was embarrassed and ashamed. In my mind, having an eating disorder made me weak, imperfect and damaged. But as I got older, thanks to organizations like SPARK and the wise, strong women in my life, I came to understand that our society and the media which permeates virtually every aspect of our lives, makes girls vulnerable to disorders like mine. After years of healing and growing, I am proud to say that I am a survivor. I am moved to do two things based on this experience. Firstly, I try to help the girls in my life, from my little sister, to the third-grader I tutor, to evade what trapped me for so long. Secondly, I fight with SPARK to change our society so all girls can love their bodies.

For Emma, speaking out about her own experiences helped her heal as well as potentially inspire girls in the audience to see through the media's messaging and try to accept the unique beauty of their own bodies. In the theater space, young audience members who watch and listen to girls on stage, can look up and see themselves mirrored back. They might muse: If she can stand so boldly and speak about overcoming the hate she used to feel for her body, perhaps I can too. Though we rarely survey the audience to learn exactly what might be buzzing through their minds (and honestly, it would be rare for girls to reveal such vulnerability in a survey form) as they watch and absorb a performance, brave girls often linger afterwards to talk with the performers or sign up for the next program, showing that to some extent, the messages of the performance were received. Speaking out seems like a good idea.

For many Black girls, a seemingly contradictory trope and stereotype impacts them: the myth of the "Strong, Black Woman" who is impervious to pain and can always be counted on to selflessly assist others. Womanist social scientist Tamara Beauboeuf-Lafontant (2009) describes these impossible pressures that Black women face:

> [M]uch of the acclaim that the concept of strength provides for Black women is undermined by what I argue is its real function: to defend and maintain a stratified social order by obscuring Black women's experiences of suffering, acts of desperation, and anger.
>
> (pp. 1–2)

For too many Black girls, an assumption of their superhuman strength can prevent their peers, teachers, and other people in their communities from recognizing when they truly need support and resources.

In a 2007 study about perceived racial discrimination and self-esteem in African American adolescents, developmental psychologists April Harris-Britt, Cecilia Valrie, Beth Kurtz-Costes and Stephanie Rowley found:

> a unique interactive effect of perceived discrimination and racial socialization on self-esteem in a sample of African American adolescents. Qualitatively, adolescents' reports of race pride messages appeared to serve as a direct buffer on this relationship, as perceptions of discrimination were associated with lower self-esteem for adolescents who reported minimal exposure to positive messages about their heritage and culture, whereas adolescents who reported more frequent exposure to race pride messages did not seem to be negatively affected by perceived discrimination.
>
> (p. 678)

Experiences where Black girls can collectively and individually express racial pride and be celebrated for their creative expressions of race, culture and ethnicity can have a positive impact on their emotional, mental and physical health.

When understanding how girls navigate the issues of "self-esteem," "confidence," and "strength," I examine how theater can build it, shatter it and re-imagine it. Many girls, in fact, credit their adolescent theater experiences with helping them gain confidence. Monique, a boisterous and dynamic 29-year-old Black woman whom I first met as a high school freshman and has since then, worked her way up to her current position as viBe Theater's Artistic Director, reflected on her own experiences as a young artist in the same company:

> I remember just being happy and, at that time, that being one of the only places that I felt like I could express myself and I felt like – as cliche as it sounds – I felt like whatever I was saying, mattered. Like, I felt like I was valued. I felt like I was being honored. I felt like a creative. I felt like an artist at 12, at 15, it was like, I'm writing a play. It was one of the very poignant moments in my mind of just feeling extremely confident in myself and feeling like I can do something.

There have been numerous studies that report how the roar of applause after a performance validates the performers' efforts and talents and contributes to their feeling a sense of accomplishment (O'Brien & Donelan, 2008; Pendzik, Emunah, & Read Johnson, 2017; Beare & Belliveau, 2007).

"Beautiful and ..."

Tension exists in the emotional space between the dual desire to both acknowledge that beauty lives in all shapes and colors, *and* the desire to convince girls that they are so much more than their appearance and that being "beautiful," no matter how it is defined is only one part of all the qualities girls possess. You are beautiful ... but, beauty doesn't matter!

In 2013, I collaborated with the New York City Mayor's Office to help design the NYC Girls Project, a city-wide billboard campaign that posted thousands of posters in subway cars, stations, and buses. The goal of the campaign was to "reach girls from about seven to 12 years old, who are at risk of negative body images that can lead to eating disorders, drinking, acting out sexually, suicide and bullying."[1] Sitting through meeting after meeting, I heard how difficult it was to use the resources to promote what was perceived to be a complicated message that girls are more than their appearance. In the end, the committee of government workers, girls' advocates, educators, marketing directors, and psychologists designed a campaign that was not as bold and inspiring as I had pushed for.

We got: A series of posters that all had a variation of an exuberant photograph of a girl or a pair of girls, adequately representing racial, ethnic, and body size diversity and ability, having fun, next to the shout-out declaration, "I'M A GIRL" in a huge bold font, with a line below it half the size but still big and bright stating, "I'M BEAUTIFUL THE WAY I AM" and then in teeny, tiny, get-real-close-so-you-can-read-it a list (different on every poster) practically whispering, "I'm sporty, curious, caring, playful, courageous, sincere and funny." The message: Sure, you can be all these great qualities but the most important is that you are "beautiful." Despite the best intentions of the team, the campaign was watered down into mixed message muddy slush.

What went wrong? In the production of a static, visual poster that was supposed to represent all the messaging the committee wanted to express to our city's girls, we fell short. In attempted compromise and collaboration, we tried to do too many things. It was important to some that we show girls that there are so many different ways to be beautiful. It was important to others to deemphasize that beauty should matter as a quality girls strive to possess.

What this poster series couldn't do, performance sometimes can. Girls can write and perform text that teases out nuances, can perform the contradictions, can include a mix of voices and experiences and allow the audience to witness the emotional tension embedded in these ideas about beauty and its relevance.

During our 2013 production, 18-year-old Monica, a conventionally pretty Black girl with a radiant smile, wrote a clever and poetic letter to her make-up in order to inspire the audience of mostly teenage girls to see the repercussions of focusing so much on attempting to alter and improve their physical appearance. She performed:

> Dear Make-up,
> Let's make love, not war.
> Work with me, not against me.
> Be a catalyst to my creativity, not a mask to what is really me.
> I think I've gotten too dependent on you. I feel needy and greedy for what you have to offer and to be real, in this relationship you're giving 80 percent while I'm throwing in 20. I'm not saying we should break up, but let's take it down a notch. We've been movin' too fast and I think I got caught up. I don't love you for the right reasons anymore and I think I've been using and abusing you. Just give me time. I just need to reflect on what I bring to the table.
> Signed,
> 'It's Not You, It's Me'

The performance space here is a site where metaphors and poetry can communicate depths of thought differently than personal and literal linear narratives. Monica uses humor to ignite critical thinking for girls in the audience about how much time, energy, and resources they are spending on their make-up products and routine. By slyly comparing her relationship to make-up as a potentially abusive romantic partnership, she illuminates how codependency can be harmful.

In a different production, Jessica plays the "Conscience" of Nevaeh and embodies the inner dialogue girls often have about their worth:

NEVAEH: Oh my gosh! Your voice is annoying.
CONSCIENCE: What do you mean? My voice is beautiful.
NEVAEH: Really? Well, it doesn't sound beautiful when all you tell me is negative things.
CONSCIENCE: They're not negative things. They're the truth. C'mon look at you. You're too tall. Your legs are some thunder thighs. Your face is pale, You dress awful, and –

NEVAEH: Shut up! You don't know what you're saying. People that love me say that I look pretty and it's the inside that counts, not the outside.

CONSCIENCE: Well they're lying to you.

NEVAEH: No. You're lying to me and I'm not taking it no more. I have to destroy you and form a new mind. I'm tired of you putting me down. I can't take it no more. Leave me alone.

CONSCIENCE: Ha! You can't get rid of me! I'm with you forever! Muahahahahaha …

[*They fight and NEVAEH defeats CONSCIENCE, pushing her to the ground and standing over her, her foot on her chest in victorious triumph*]

NEVAEH: Overcoming this voice is a challenge. Thinking over it is hard. I just have to find my strength and inner confidence, smile and move forward.

The theater space allows for Nevaeh to directly address the voice inside her head that is always telling her she is not enough as she is. The dramatic structure of dialogue provides the opportunity to explore this conflict between Nevaeh and her "conscience" and show the audience one tactic for personally confronting, challenging and overcoming her insecurities. Through performance, Nevaeh practices and shares with her audience what agency and self-efficacy can look like for girls battling with self-esteem.

And yet, this battle shows the audience potentially the wrong villain. For girls like Nevaeh, blaming themselves, or the voices in their heads for their insecurities lets the larger systems and institutions such as the corporate beauty and diet industries off the hook. Nevaeh's simple strategy to "find [her] strength and inner confidence, smile and move forward" is optimistic, but for most girls, not nearly enough. In hindsight, I wish I had encouraged Nevaeh to think more critically about the messages she was receiving about beauty, where they were coming from and how she – and her peers – could collectively challenge the companies and systems that profit from girls' insecurities. I can imagine using more rehearsal activities to guide Nevaeh to start to see where her feelings of insecurity are coming from. One strategy, I might talk the girls through in rehearsal:

Let's work together to create a scene from Nevaeh's line "People that love me say that I look pretty and it's the inside that counts, not the outside." Nevaeh, tell us more about these "people that love you." Cast them. Let's improvise this scene so Nevaeh can play in this moment of feeling loved and accepted for who she is. Now let's consider all the forces that are preventing her from believing this. What is Nevaeh seeing in magazines? On Instagram? What are the images of girls in the shows and movies she watches? What does she see being advertised on the billboards she walks past everyday? Let's create an image of Nevaeh, surrounded by the advertisements she sees. What do these messages tell her? How does Nevaeh feel when she sees them? Who has created these advertisements? Why? What are they gaining from Nevaeh feeling this way? Who is accountable? What can Nevaeh and her friends do to push back? What power does Nevaeh have? How can she and her friends use their power? What does *that* look like? On one hand, theater can be a valuable space for girls like Nevaeh, Emma, and Cellest to express how they feel about themselves and their bodies. This act of sharing these stories paints the picture for audiences of what girls go through on a daily basis and lets them see the struggle beneath the smiles. And on the other hand, I imagine a raised fist. Theater can also be the space to challenge these norms that lead girls to hate their bodies, to guide girls to see the systems and people whose actions and behaviors enact harm. Through the rehearsal and performance process, girls can start to imagine and embody their own journey toward changing the system, and changing themselves.

"Sexy or sexualized?"

Another dangerous way that girls suffer due to this unrealistic and dangerous focus on their bodies is through the process of sexualization. According to the American Psychological Association's "Task Force on the Sexualization of Girls (2007)," a person is sexualized when "made into a thing for others' sexual use, rather than seen as a person with the capacity for independent action and decision making" (p. 2). Despite significant advances in girls' educational achievement, leadership opportunities, and legal protections (Rosin, 2012), girls continue to be bombarded with negative, narrow, sexualizing, and objectifying imagery and expectations about female sexuality that are associated with negative psychological and societal outcomes (APA, 2007). They are denied access to information and discourse about their sexuality and relationships that support their growth into embodied adults (Tolman, 2002). But a simplistic assessment of an inevitable cultural imposition onto girls does not capture the complexity of real girls' engagement with sexualization (Renold, 2015).

A feminist understanding of the sexualization of girls has to address agency, while simultaneously acknowledging that, "for young women today in post-feminist cultures," as cultural theorist Rosalind Gill (2007) writes, "a 'technology of sexiness' has replaced 'innocence' or 'virtue' as the commodity that young women are required to offer in the heterosexual marketplace" (72). As popular culture promotes "sexiness" as a defining characteristic of strength and autonomy from celebrities such as Cardi B, Nicki Minaj, Beyoncé, and Kim Kardashian, girls recognize and understand that sexual desirability can also be a form of female power (Hernandez, 2020).

As an example of girls addressing sexualization through performance, I share more about the creation process of *BodyVOX!*, the play that contained Monica's make-up monologue described in the previous section. *BodyVOX* was a feminist-activist production written and performed by nine teenage girls, and co-directed by Aimee Meredith Cox, African American Studies scholar and dancer/choreographer, and me in New York City in 2013. We discovered through our process that a unified call to action addressing these issues of sexualization and agency might be as challenging, impossible (and painful) as running a marathon in six-inch heels.

We began our process responding to two statements: "I feel sexy when ..." and "I feel sexualized when ..." The text and choreography for the production erupted from the examples shared by the girls. They danced, ranted, celebrated, joked, vamped, critiqued, analyzed, and shared stories of street harassment, "duck face" poses for Snapchat, Facebook "likes," sexting, and dance club twerking. We stitched together a performance illuminating the complicated ways girls navigate the desire, pleasure, attention, and shame that their bodies communicate in their lives and relationships.

Complicated politics erupted when some girls stated their pleasure and delight in the verbal validation (aka: catcalls) they receive from men in the street when they feel they look good. Others proclaimed that unwanted, un-asked-for compliments or comments about their bodies were harassment, invaded their personal space, and led to fears about walking in public spaces. One girl's "feeling sexy" was another girl's "feeling sexualized." Simply stated, conservative politics articulate a need to "protect" girls, ban all pornography, censor advertisements, and boycott certain companies. Liberal and libertarian politics of choice and government devolvement allow for girls to express themselves any way they desire, without policing or shame (Phipps, 2014). The latter beliefs led Emma, the 18-year-old tall and slender white girl whose speech at the UN I described earlier, to celebrate her personal sense of fashion freedom and to critique the notion that a girl who dresses in sexually pro-vocative clothing should be treated disdainfully and called a "slut," a negative, misogynist, sex-shaming word. Emma wrote and performed this ode to her high heels:

> With my wedges, stilettos, pumps and platforms, I embrace the raw power which is mine ... My heels do not cripple me. They do not reduce me to weakness ... They are not an invitation – they do not speak for me. With them, there is six more inches of me present in the world.

In contrast, 15-year-old Sasha wrote and performed the following monologue while the ensemble made two lines of poses on either side of her representing their own versions of "sexy" and "slutty":

> I feel sexy in a pair of denim jeans, wedges, and a cute croptop. Not fishnet pants, a tube-top and stilettos. That to me is too revealing and slutty.

To be clear, there are important intersections of race and class that must be considered when analyzing these two speeches and understanding how these individual girls perceive which bodies are "sexy" and which are "slutty," and who can safely express these ideas.

Gender and Sexualities Studies scholar Jillian Hernandez writes about Nicki Minaj's "aesthetics of excess" in her astonishing and brilliant book of the same title. She writes about the controversial photo on the cover of Minaj's single "Anaconda:"

The image featured the artist photographed from behind in a spread-eagled squat position in a pink thong, pink bra and sneakers, with her head turned to face the camera with a steady and commanding gaze. The image drew negative backlash in the media as vulgar and hypersexual, which the artist responded to via Instagram posts that juxtaposed her image with the then-current Sports Illustrated, which featured three thin topless white women in thongs photographed from the rear at a beach. By placing the accompanying caption "Angelic. Acceptable. Lol." On her post of the young women and "UNACCEPTABLE" with the post of her "Anaconda" photo, the artist directly critiqued the double standard that sanctions white women's sexual display in mainstream spaces while vilifying that of a Black woman as inappropriate, dangerous to youth, and excessive.

(p. 166)

This analysis of Black women's bodies being "inappropriately" sexual while white women, in the same postures and clothing is branded as simply, "sexy," is a dangerous paradox that dates back to the seventeenth century when European settlers kidnapped and enslaved African people in order to build America. Townsend et al. (2010) offer a historical analysis of why the sexualization of Black female bodies has been woven through the media and cultural landscape of the United States. They theorize:

> The legacy of slavery associates the sexual exploitation of African American women with distinct dehumanizing and degrading practices. In order to justify their enslavement and incessant sexual violation, the role of primitive sex object was ascribed to women of African descent.
>
> (p. 274)

Emma is white, attends a progressive and expensive West Village private school and lives in a middle class suburb outside New York City. Sasha is Black, lives in a working class neighborhood in Brooklyn, and attends an underfunded public high school. Each girl likely navigates the public space and the neighborhoods she passes through in different ways. For Sasha, there is a very real (and highly unjust) danger to walking through her neighborhood. Though street harassment does not discriminate (or care much what the girl is wearing) and girls and women of all races report experiencing it, according to the 2014 *Stop Street Harassment* study, "Black, Hispanic and multiracial women" report more they are harassed regularly at nearly double the rate of white people (Unsafe and Harassed in Public Spaces: A National Street Harassment Report, 2014).

Collaborators on the same project are not always in total values alignment and the disconnect between different girls' experiences within one activist project was not the only chasm. After three weeks of intensive rehearsals, the day before the first performance, we did our first full run-through with costumes and music. Nine girls in their black leggings and fitted red shirts breezed both confidently and awkwardly around the stage marking all the right poses with hips and chests thrust out and bodies wiggling and jiggling. In our feminist, activist performance meant to address the issue of sexualization, Aimee and I noticed that we had in fact perpetuated the very concepts we were seeking to challenge and critique – that girls' bodies are meant to be gazed upon, stared at, and objectified. On a bare stage, in costumes that hugged every curve, we seemed to invite and demand that the girls' bodies be the center of every moment. I was horrified. I questioned whether the performance space could aptly serve as a valid site for a critique of the sexualization of girls. Although the girls were unfazed.

My personal politics differ from the message some of the girls wished to communicate about self-sexualizing and owning your sexuality. I feel that hypersexualized fashion is sometimes not so much a "choice" of the wearer, but one of few options (dictated by patriarchy) in a limited buffet of "acceptable" expressions of female beauty (Gill, 2008). As an adult collaborating with teenagers, I feel my beliefs, grounded in my own experiences and my consciousness of sexist media, allow me to suggest subtle changes to the girls' costumes and text, though always in conversation with the girls themselves. In the end, we discussed these issues together and collaboratively decided on a middle ground of presenting the uncensored content. We decided to break the action mid-play and engage with the audience in a conversation about our process, confusion, and decision-making. Instead of adhering to one political lane, our show offered a buffet of options, demanding the audience think critically about the choices they make in their own lives, and the consequences of these choices.

As part of our process for creating theater through an action lens, we included one portion of the show that involved audience interaction and demanded that the audience members actually do something beyond sitting in the darkness and witnessing the performance. Inspired by Monica's fictional and anthropomorphizing letter to her make-up, we included a scene in the show that led to the performers inviting the audience to write letters. The scene began with the girls discussing among themselves where and how they imagine change could take place:

MALIKA: Who's to blame?

XIAR: How do we freakin' change the system?

CRYSTAL: *[Holding up a magazine]* Dear *Glamour,*

XIAR: Dear *Cosmo,*

EVINEE: Dear *Seventeen,*

MIMI: Dear *Allure,*

KAIA: Loosen up a bit, will ya?!

MONICA: Girls have smiles, freckles, discolored teeth, blotchy skin, healthy bodies and zits.

MIMI   Show the diversity you've experienced, not just the smiles but the heart ache and pain.

MALIKA: Teach me how to breathe and meditate.

CRYSTAL: Teach me to self-heal, to wake up, wash my face, put on some mois-
turizer and go.

XIAR: Teach me and most importantly yourself how to keep it real. Love,

ALL: My self-esteem

ALL: Dear Fellow Teenagers,

KAIA: I'm constantly trying to figure out who I am and where I want to be in
life, but it's hard when you are trying to dictate the answers to me – "ugly,"
"hideous," "probably going to die alone."

MIMI: The truth is there is no universal truth when it comes to attractiveness.
This is what I know attractiveness to be: uniqueness, you-ness, me-ness, a
quintessential quirkiness that says not every human is the same and that's
what makes us gorgeous.

EVINEE: I am still trying to figure out how to truly be happy and confident
with myself.

ALL: We're all still figuring it out.

MONICA: So, fellow teenagers, my partners in the confusing, emotional and
plain weird journey that is adolescence: can we please stop judging one
another on something as weak and twisted as society's idea of what *perfect*
is? Because I am sick and tired of trying to follow a yellow-brick road to
perfection when I don't need to: perfect is whatever we want it to be, perfect is whoever we are and however we feel, and right now,

ALL: I just want to be me.

KAIA: So, dear audience member, please look under your seats. You all have a
piece of paper and a pen under there. We invite you to write a letter about
how YOU feel about anything we've been talking about in this show. What
did you learn tonight? Who else in your life needs to hear it? Maybe a
friend? A little sister? A niece? A teacher? The editor of *Seventeen Magazine*?
Write what you want to express to them and put it in an envelope, write
their name on the envelope and give it to them! Or hand it to us. We'll post
it on our website SPARKmovement.org or we'll mail it for you!

The lights over the audience brightened and washed the room in light as audience members adjusted their eyes and awkwardly looked around as if to say,
"We're really supposed to *do* something?" A few bent forward and rummaged
under their chairs to find the paper. Others looked on, and then followed. Music
flowed through the space and harmonized with the scratching of pens across
paper, beginning slowly then building with intensity as the energy coursed
through the room. The performers dispersed to give any guidance or assistance
to the room of letter writers. After ten minutes, we faded the music out and
Kaia asked if any audience members wanted to share what they wrote.

One woman raised her hand and told a story about how she worries about
her niece and a man spoke up about the challenges he was facing raising his
daughter who would leave the house in "inappropriate clothing." Other audience members piped in and offered advice or guidance. A woman in the back
shouted, "You have to talk to her!" Another added, "Let her know she can trust

you. Stop punishing her for her clothes – let her express herself!" We were witnessing strangers connecting over the shared goal of helping parents and adults heal ruptured relationships with teenage girls and offer support to each other. Maybe the issues were not fully resolved, but people could start to see how opening up lines of intergenerational communication was necessary and that at least, they were not alone.

After several audience members shared their letters or their stories, the girls collected any envelopes that folks handed to them, the lights over the audience dimmed back to darkness again and the show went on. This is but one example of how performance can ignite individuals to consider how they can make changes in their own lives, or can take one small step toward demanding a corporation or a person in their life make a change.

I appear to be j[=ust like you

When considering girls' bodies and live performances as sites of activism, I must acknowledge the power, potential, ethics, and challenges of girls with disabilities[2] and the specific challenges and needs for their use of the theater as an activist space. Jen Slater (2012), a disabilities scholar, writes about the routine positioning of disabled young people as "passive youth." They then expose the hypocrisy and danger of this label within the Neoliberal context that demands that in order to survive in our capitalist world, individuals:

> deliberately using an ableist idiom, need to "stand on your own two feet," … Discourses surrounding those construed as passive therefore soon slip from the paternalistic (victims/charity cases), to the demonising (burdensome/a drain on society).
>
> (p. 183)

Their work highlights the need for young people with disabilities to flip this script and perform their own agency as a counter to the inaccurate and damaging perceptions of their "passivity." How might theater counter these false narratives and provide an opportunity for girls with disabilities to challenge the injustices they face?

Along with some clear opportunities for enacting positive change within the disability rights movement, theater as an activist tactic also comes with a hefty warning label of dangerous side effects. Disability scholars have long critiqued the dangers and exploitation of nondisabled activists or advocates using disabled bodies to cultivate empathy or draw pity in order to make the case for resources for their community and the need for disabled people to speak for themselves (Charlton, 2000). Feminist theater scholar Stacy Wolf (2005) warns:

> valorizing "positive," "accurate" images necessarily calls up the conundrum of visibility: What exactly is a positive representation? To whom? And who can decide? What is an authentic representation? These questions echo those of other identity-oriented movements that have been preoccupied with the politics of visibility, and that continue to raise similar concerns about representations of women, people of color, lesbians, gays, bisexuals,

and transgendered persons, and so on. Proliferating representations can increase understanding, empathy, and tolerance, but they can just as easily delimit identities as expand them. Visibility does not necessarily promote social change.

(p. 317)

As complicated as issues of representation and visibility can be, theater has been a positive and useful space for disabilities activists with a rich history (Kuppers, 2013; Sandahl & Auslander, 2005). Colette Conroy, a disabilities activist, scholar and theater artist writes (in ironic pairing next to Slater's analysis of "passivity" whereby the audience's passivity is useful):

The enforced passivity of theatre offers a reversal of the usual habits of looking at disabled people. The individual performer is empowered and is accorded status because of his presence on stage as performer, as speaker and actor, as object of the audience's attention.

(2009, p. 7)

Though all girls are impacted by unrealistic images of "beauty" that the main-stream media perpetuates, girls with physical disabilities can often have add-itional layers of insecurity, shame, and tension as they compare their own bodies to the airbrushed supermodels or Hollywood celebrities alongside their able-bodied peers. Within an activist devised theater process that encourages girls to share their own stories of injustice or struggles at various points in the play building process, girls with disabilities often write and perform stories related to their experience of living with a disability.

It was rare for girls with disabilities to sign up for viBe Theater. This was likely due to our lack of specific recruitment of them and the dearth of images on our website and marketing materials that showed images of girls with obvious physical disabilities. Though, despite this failure on our part, in one program, we did attract brave and outgoing Angelique, a 16-year-old Black girl with a self-identified "hearing and vision impairment and speech impediment" (personal communication). The ensemble of girls in this par-ticular program rallied around her and offered her much support and encour-agement throughout the program. Additionally, there was one rehearsal where Angelique taught the other girls one line of sign language that they all performed together in the show. This was an important moment when Angelique stepped into a leadership role and became the expert who needed to teach the others a valuable new skill.

Though her speech impediment made it difficult to always understand her, everyone was patient with her and ensured that she had what she needed to best communicate with us. For example, she was an excellent lip reader and relied on this skill to understand what others were saying, so we would always make sure to face her when speaking to her and to stage each piece of the perform-ance ensuring she could see the lips of her fellow performers. In the final show, she wrote and performed:

ANGELIQUE: I appear to be
just like you
"normal"
good body
good height
perfect teeth
pretty face
good dresser
great personality
but wait …
as they say,
no two persons are the same
no two people are alike
each person is different
because that's how God made us
I have a hearing loss
'cause that's the way God made me
I have a small vision problem
'cause that's the way God made me
I have the voice that I have
'cause this is the voice God gave me
I have a speech problem I live with everyday
'cause God loves me so much
he made me this way
unique
ALL: Unique
ANGELIQUE: you don't have to like me
you don't have to accept me
I'm not asking so
please don't feel sorry for me
Just know that
I'm me for a reason
'cause that's the way God made me.
That's why I am the way I am.

When Angelique performed this piece, the entire audience leaned in to the stage, struggling to hear and understand her. The specific text of her monologue was likely not fully transmitted, but the emotional core was crystal clear and the audience responded to her proud smile at the end of it and rewarded her with a round of cheers, hoots, and ecstatic arms-in-the-air "jazz hands" waving from her friends and family more familiar with performance norms within the Hard of Hearing community. She beamed with confidence and joy throughout the entire performance and in her postshow assessment told us that she now wanted to pursue an acting career which is definitely not the goal of viBe's programming, but shows that she had such a positive experience on stage that she wants to continue in the field.

This example is one of many that illuminates how youth theater companies adopt inclusionary practices where young people with disabilities are welcome, and encouraged, to participate alongside and in collaboration with their able-bodied peers. By implementing a range of legally mandated accommodations such as accessible ramps or elevators and sign language interpreters, artists with disabilities should have the same opportunities to express themselves that all young people deserve. For solid guidance on what these accommodations might look like in youth theater spaces, see Kathleen Juhl and Lindsey Smith's "Adapt the Space! Working with People of Diverse Abilities," from the *Staging Social Justice: Collaborating to Create Activist Theatre* (2013). In this chapter, as two nondisabled theater directors, they recognize that they need to deliberately engage with and ask performers with disabilities what they need and to supply necessary items such as hearing aid batteries and electronic communications that could be adapted into a Braille computer device.

Another positive impact of this intentional inclusion is that the nondisabled participants learn more about the challenges in the environment that favor nondisabled folks and that people with disabilities are forced to navigate through authentic relationships and friendships and can better advocate on behalf of their friends and collaborators throughout their lives. Access To Theater, a program of Partners for Youth with Disabilities, is "an award-winning inclusive theater program for teens and young adults. Its purpose is to develop communication, artistic, and leadership skills, and lasting professional and personal friendships" (Partners for Youth with Disabilities, 2018). One of the participants quoted on their website expressed the impact of the program on them:

> [Access To Theater] has taught me innumerable lessons in patience, cooperation, teamwork, leadership, and compassion. It's just one of those moments that make you realize that you do have an effect on your surroundings, and you can make a difference.
>
> (Partners for Youth with Disabilities, 2018)

In addition to including young people with disabilities into theater projects, there are many youth theater organizations specifically created for young people with disabilities, though at this point I do not know of any that works primarily with girls or nonbinary youth. They include The Miracle Project, "a fully inclusive theater, film, social skills, and expressive arts program for individuals with autism, other disabilities and all abilities" (The Miracle Project, 2019); Solar Bear's Deaf Youth Theatre in the UK for "young deaf people to meet, play, learn skills and create new work" (Solar Bear Deaf Youth Theatre, 2020); the DisAbility Project in St. Louis, "comprised of people with and without disabilities to model inclusion, the project creates and tours original material about the culture of disability" (The DisAbility Project, 2020); and Action Play, "an inclusive improvisational music and theatre residency for teens and adults on the autism spectrum and with related conditions … the goal of this program is to encourage greater confidence and increase communication and social skills" (Action Play, 2019).

The literal etymological definition of theater comes from the Ancient Greek word, theatron – "a place of seeing." For marginalized girls who are often perceived to be invisible, the theater is a powerful site to claim their place and assert their significance. Aaron Philip, the internationally renowned and first Black, transgender, disabled model, spoke out at the WE Day UN conference in 2019, an event with 18,000 young changemakers and their teachers held in Brooklyn's Barclays Stadium. She claimed that the visibility of marginalized groups is the foremost important aspect of activism. "Visibility is a statement within itself. I think that the more statements that are made, the farther it will push change and inclusivity" (Kim, 2019).

Providing specific opportunities for young people with disabilities to create and perform theater is one step towards breaking the physical, societal, and institutional barriers that prevent them from pursuing the greatest possible quality of life. I know that I can do better in ensuring that girls with disabilities know about, have access to, and are encouraged to join activist theater creation projects. Their voices are necessary within any movement for social justice and I regret that my work has not been more inclusive. Being more intentional about where I post notices about new projects, specifically partnering with young activists and artists with disabilities at all stages of the process and committing to representing bodies with different abilities in our promotional materials are a few steps towards necessary inclusion.

(Miss)empowered

"Miss Empowered" evokes the image of the strong, bold supergirl. I imagine her feet grounded and steady, hands on her hips, chin tipped up to the sky, her superhero cape rippling behind her. She speaks her mind with a confident, clear voice and articulates majestically how her actions will change the world. She is that girl quoted on countless nonprofit organizations' glossy brochures shouting "theater changed my life!" and "After participating in _____'s program, I am a smarter, braver, more confident, less shy, happier, louder, better person!"

Though, if read as "misempowered," I envision the evil twin of this girl, confused and conflicted, faking a confidence she does not actually possess. I see a girl who still hears the echoes of applause and cheers from her performance, but then once the lights dim and she washes off her stage make-up, she hates the familiar face she sees reflected back at her in the mirror.

Despite, and in many ways a response to, the infinite messages girls receive that they are not pretty, smart, strong, [fill in the blank] enough, I have seen girls perform a heightened and often exaggerated confidence on stage. Trained by society to be polite, pleasing and modest, girls learn that to brag or boast in their real lives is a sign of crassness, a masculine arrogance.

Lyn Mikel Brown (2003) writes about the ways these social expectations cause girls to silence themselves:

> They are judging other girls against dominant cultural ideals of femininity: on how well they contain their sexuality and negotiate heterosexual romance, conform to white middle-class ideals of beauty, and collude in passive, nondisruptive, "nice girlness."
>
> (p. 116)

In the theater space, girls can more easily leap over these social hurdles through the loose mask of a character or a heightened version of themselves, or speaking whatever they want, uninterrupted on stage. When defining self-esteem as a core issue they want to address, many teenagers then write superlative, saturated odes to their own greatness. At its best, these boastful pieces seem to shatter the stereotype of the timid, insecure, passive, body-hating girl by asserting her confidence. Watching a large-framed girl with abundant curves whom society often would label and shame as "fat," proclaim that she loves her big body, can be an empowering moment for both the girl and for others in the audience who have felt insecure about their size. Her words might offer a new narrative about what it means to accept yourself the way you are. Challenging these cultural ideals of "beauty" can be liberating. And yet, as activism as well as self-empowerment, it can backfire.

The evidence within our playmaking process where I would see most distinctly the disconnect between how girls perform an exaggerated confidence versus how they represent insecurity is most apparent through an analysis of, what we called in viBe Theater, the "Cheers." As African American Studies scholar and Ethnomusicologist Kyra Gaunt, who studied the history of cheering, writes in *The Games Black Girl Play: Learning the Ropes from Double-Dutch to Hip-Hop* (2006):

> [Historically cheering] involves creating in-body formulas that represent the unique identity of each group, by sampling and re- composing aspects of black vernacular style and expression as well as moment of popular recorded song from gospel to hip-hop, from preaching to playing Dozens. Competing groups try outdo one another by choreographing a funky routine of embodied percussive beats and chants, collectively enacted by the group that names the individual members, while also signifying their unique group identity.
>
> (p. 76)

The Cheers, as created for our show, are usually performed at the end of the performance as a curtain call or encore where the audience has the chance to "meet" the girls as themselves as opposed to as the characters they have created and performed throughout the rest of the play. Occasionally they would open the show with the Cheers as a "curtain warmer" introduction to get the audience hyped for the show they were about to see. The irony is that often, it is in these cheers that the girls have constructed "fictional" characters and the "characters" they play in the play are often closer to who they are offstage, than this heightened persona represented in the cheers. In reading through the "cheers" of every one of the nearly 400 viBe girls in the ten years I was co-directing the shows, I can proclaim that each one introduces herself in inflated, exaggerated positive language.

Allow me to set the scene: The play has ended, the lights black out, but then pop on again as the audience applauds and the girls perform their individual Cheers, one after another. They choreograph intricate movement and dance sequences as well as rhythmic beats, clapping, thigh-slapping, and stomping. The Cheers, in performance, are a celebration of the work and effort from the rehearsal and performance process. They highlight the girls' pride, strength, joy, and humor. Often the shyest or quietest girls burst out with big and bold expressions of confidence. The structure of the Cheer with its frequent rhyming, in some ways, mimics a hip-hop verse enough that the girls assume the energy and confidence of hip-hop stars. But by imitating some of the drive and structure of their favorite artists, they also assume their arrogance and ego. For adolescent girls who have been presenting evidence that they feel they don't measure up to the standards set by their family, by the media, by their schools or their communities, these Cheers become a space for them to taste what it might feel like to express total confidence. As dozens of research studies have shown over the past several decades, the physical act of smiling can boost your mood toward happiness, even when you are feeling sad (Coles et al., 2019). Can the same be said for embodied, choreographed joy and confidence? Listen to Brea:

> BREA: My name is B to the R to the E to da A
> I'm known for my originali-tay
> I'm fresh and fly and that's no lie
> Every day's a happy day cause I'm givin out smiles
> See I'm known to be cocky and I'm known to crack jokes
> Wait I thought you had something to say – oops. Ya just choked.
> Cause my fate is to be fabulous and to do great
> That is why all dem otha chicks hate
> NYC Brooklyn Hay

In performance, the ensemble of nine girls creates a cypher around Brea. Izzy starts by stomping her turquoise Nikes, sliding her hands across her thighs in a shwooshing rhythmic beat and releasing her hips to accent the movements. The other seven girls pick up the beat. The circle closes in and gets tighter around Brea as she belts out her first line, in a voice louder than the audience has heard her use all night. She swings her long, lean arms out at her sides, taking up as much space as her body can allow. Her legs, in tight black jeans with black and white polka-dot leg warmers scrunching around her ankles, match Izzy's stomping. Her face beams, smiling with pride and excitement. "I'm fresh and fly and that's no lie," she belts out as the other girls back her up with "uh huh!," "Yeah, Brea!" "Say it, girl!" and the audience erupts in claps and hollers.

Brea, a 14-year-old ninth-grader is one of the youngest in the project. Compare Brea's cheer with a monologue she tells about pain and insecurity earlier in the play, including a direct contradiction with the power and positivity of her Cheer. Approximately 20 minutes earlier in the play, she performs the following poetic monologue:

> I'm sick and tired of people sayin I think I'm so fly
> but I'm not simple I try
> and at one point I wanted to die
> cause I was sick and tired of judgment with only my sister on my side.
> and just some foster parents who said they loved me
> but I never knew why
> Most of my life has been a roller coaster of pain
> going from sad to happy to depressed
> and at one point I thought I was insane

It is a jarring contradiction to watch the same girl expressing so much pain, insecurity about whether she was loved, and suicidal thoughts with the explosive joy and presumed confidence in her Cheer. She literally goes from saying, "I'm sick and tired of people sayin I think I'm so fly" to later shouting the opposite, "I'm fresh and I'm fly!" Brea is in no way unique in this respect and I could offer dozens more examples of almost the exact same occurrence of a girl going from speaking out about her insecurities at one point in the play to then, at the end of the show, singing her own praises.

I question: Just because girls are performing very confident versions of themselves, are they actually building self-esteem and benefiting from this experience? Obviously, people can hold contrasting truths about themselves and feel good about themselves in one moment and melt into tears at another. But to present both within the same performance hour can be whiplash-inducing, confusing, and complicated, for both the girl and the audience.

When considering where this performative ego and cockiness comes from, I look to hip-hop culture. Particularly for Black and/or Latinx girls, hip-hop reinforces the concept that an exaggerated ego is the norm, or at least that the performance of extreme confidence is expected and celebrated. As a vocal assertion that challenges and contradicts the racist notions and stereotypes about people of color, bold and narcissistic declarations are celebrated.

Feelings of powerlessness, expressed by marginalized teenage girls, can be easily masked by outrageously confident lyrics proclaiming their prowess and strength. The music then becomes an anthem to young people, an anecdote to their experiences of oppression. The mass popularity of hip-hop music and the celebrated arrogance of its frontrunners and pop idols such as female megastars from Lil' Kim "I am a diamond cluster hustler, queen bitch, supreme bitch" (1996), to Nicki Minaj "I am a rap legend" (2014), Cardi B's "I think us bad bitches is a gift from God" (2018), and Beyonce's epically simple declaration, "I slay" (2014) reinforce this assertion that boasting breeds respect.

How might ending the show with the powerful, heightened confidence of the cheers release the audience from worrying about the girls' lives and futures both specifically and generally? As the finale encore moment of the show, the girls burst back onto stage often with more energy and enthusiasm than they've shared in the performance yet. The cheers are a cacophony of exclamations, shout-outs, and explosive joy that usually erupt in raucous applause and cheering from the audience. This final moment allows the girls to end on a note of enthusiastic celebration that flows into their post-performance glow and pride. But ending performances with this lingering energy colors people's memories of the earlier parts of the show when the girls revealed more subtle narratives and shared personal challenges and struggles. Audience members often comment about how confident and strong the girls seem in their performance. Dramaturgically, the cheers provide the relief of a "happy ending" despite any unresolved narratives or stories of heartache and violence presented earlier in the production and let the audience off the hook for worrying about girls' self-esteem and feeling impelled to take action to support them.

Another repercussion of confidence performed, but not necessarily embodied, is the pain that can accompany an unsupportive audience. As a way to ensure their messages were impacting other teenagers who could identify with seeing girls who looked and talked like them onstage, we would often perform in public high school auditoriums during all-school assemblies when the audience was filled with hundreds of teenagers who were required to attend. I remember many instances when, after crafting an original show that often included personal testimonials about their own strengths and confidence, the girls would bravely speak their truth only to be heckled by teenagers, often just wanting to impress their friends or get attention. And sometimes even worse than the snide laughter would be the chattering across to the aisles or the blank faces or the heads nodding to music through headphones or the scrolling through phones, ignoring the stage entirely. These disruptive young audience members could sabotage many of the gains of the theater process on the performers and chip away at much of the confidence that had been fostered.

And yet. It was often these high school performances where girls in the audience would linger after the show and ask how they could join us, create and perform in the next show. As with so many aspects of this work, there was rarely a clear or obvious choice to make. Yes, cruel audience members could sabotage many of the gains of the process and production. And yes, the girl performers also knew to anticipate and expect this pushback. And yes, it still hurt. And yes, these performances still reach some audience members in powerful ways. In the end, after learning from these experiences, we would try to best prepare the performers by inviting friends and alumnae to attend a final rehearsal and act like a disruptive audience to give the girls practice in how to navigate these potential situations, discuss the presumed intent of the unruly students, identify the kind of audience members they most wanted to impact and ensure they were prepared – and energized – to perform.

Gendered bodies in performance

During the summer of 1998, I worked as an intern at the Institute of the Arts and Civic Dialogue, a project created and launched by renowned theater activist Anna Deavere Smith at Harvard University. One of my assignments was to serve as the stage manager for an innovative new live/digital performance piece that explored two sites that were strikingly new to me, and much of the world. Co-created by artist Shu Lea Cheang and theater director Liz Diamond and co-produced by the Guggenheim Museum, "The Brandon Project" investigated this new site called "the world wide web," that was emerging rapidly and some were saying it was going to be quite popular in the real world. The content of the piece was inspired by the story of transgender man Brandon Teena's hate crime murder in Nebraska in 1993, a case brought to film later as *Boys Don't Cry*.

Travel back with me to 1998 for a few breaths. A world wide web sounded like a cartoon spy thriller. The word "google" was maybe your baby's first garbling or evoked plastic arts and craft eyeballs. A phone, a camera, a map were all different material items that you held in your hand and were your only options for communication, documentation, and navigation. I remember sitting in our rehearsals with my mind shaking to expand to understand this space where they told us you could create a new identity and interact with other people through your computer screen (your computer screen! Not just for word processing and writing college essays!) who were also testing and tasting new identities with new names, new histories and new genders. At that point in my life, as a cisgender woman born in 1975, I had never met (that I knew of) anyone who did not identify with the gender they were assigned at birth. My understanding of transgender issues was almost entirely academic, through my women's studies college courses. Though through working on "The Brandon Project," I learned about his story and the stories of other people like him who had suffered tremendously because of the transphobic world's response to their truth. Theater was my portal into understanding trans issues.

And not coincidentally, as the world wide web expanded and grew, so did the visibility of people of diverse gender identities. They were always there, of course, but the (newly branded) internet finally provided a protective glass screen between their bodies and their genders. Particularly for young trans people, online research, blogs, forums, and social media became lifelines for them to foster connections, realize they were not alone and begin to shape and co-construct the language that would represent them. Trans scholar and activist Eli Erlick writes:

> Trans youth online continue to develop transformative justice-based meth-
> odological approaches and bring these practices to the forefront of our
> community. Whether crowdfunding, creating new language, or organizing a
> protest, trans youth are centering the Internet in our work as young activists.
>
> (2018, p. 86)

As the forums filled, the blogs became public, the shared rage at the injustices
they faced built a movement and their numbers en mass began to tip the culture
to see and hear them. This emerging cultural shift allowed for select and excep-
tional trans folks to gain mainstream media visibility such as actress Laverne
Cox appearing on a 2014 *Time Magazine* cover and Olympian gold medalist
and reality television celebrity Caitlin Jenner gracing *Vanity Fair*.

Erlick shares, "Visibility itself must embody a strategic methodology in order
not to be co-opted by transnormativity. This most often entails critical practices
led by transgender people ourselves when sharing narratives, statistics, or epis-
temologies," (2018, p. 75) As we have also tragically seen in our political spaces,
this increased visibility has led to increased physical and legislative violence as
trans bodies are sacrificed in our streets and our laws.

Fortunately, now there are many more sites and resources to explore, understand, and celebrate diverse gender identities that don't sensationalize stories of
violence. What role can theater play here?

As with many marginalized groups, sharing their self-crafted stories with live
audiences can work to foster empathy in the hearts of audience members as
they hear firsthand about the true lives, struggles, hopes, and joys of trans folks.
Erlick writes:

> Although visibility is a neoliberal practice that functions to assimilate
> transgender people instead of working against institutional violences, these
> public education campaigns on the intersections of transgender identity
> remain effective at representing critical issues the community faces.
>
> (p. 75)

Recent research about the ways that theater addressing queer and trans issues
can impact audience members and inspire them to change their feelings and
behavior has shown promising results. An intensive 2013 study examined the
impact of a production from Gayrilla Theater Project: Riot Youth in Ann Arbor,
Michigan. Through pre- and post-performance surveys, researchers tracked
more than 800 audience members' feelings and intended behaviors in response
to Gayrilla's devised performance piece. The production included personal
stories about the LGBTQIA+ ensemble who spoke passionately about their
lived experiences and struggles with homophobia and transphobia. Following
the performance the youth performers led the audience in an interactive
activity and a guided discussion about why and how to safely intervene when
witnessing violent language or actions towards queer and trans folks in their
community. According to the researchers:

After viewing the Gayrilla performance and participating in the dialogue, across all responses, more participants indicated that they intended to intervene in all cases, including cases in which participants were not absolutely sure whether an offense has occurred and whether or not an LGBTQQ student is present.

(Wernick et al., 2013, p. 1582)

The Pride Youth Theater Alliance includes more than 30 member companies that all offer theater programs specifically to lesbian, gay, bisexual, transgender, and queer youth (Pride Youth Theater Alliance, 2020) serving as beacons for young people marginalized by their sexuality and gender identity and local opportunities for community audiences to be impacted by the performances, shift their perceptions of LGBTQIA+ youth and hopefully also tilt the culture towards enforcing LGBTQIA+ legal rights.

As I wrote earlier in this book, through my decades of creating theater with teenagers in Inside/Out, viBe Theater, and SPARK, I have likely collaborated with more than 1,000 young people who identified as (cis)girls, and two who (at the time I was making theater with them) identified as nonbinary so my personal experience with transgender, gender nonconforming and gender expansive youth is limited. Sexuality though has been much more visible through our projects and I estimate that approximately one quarter of the girls in our shows identified as lesbian, gay, bisexual or queer. And as the lavender tide roared in and shifted US culture and policy closer to equal rights for all people regardless of gender identity and sexuality, performing artists were at the crest.

In terms of political change, the decades from the 1970s through 2020 have marked one of the fastest paced social and political movements in our nation's history. Launched by trans women of color in the 1966 Compton Cafeteria Riot and in 1969 in response to a homophobic and violent police raid of the Stonewall Inn, a gay bar in New York City, queer and trans activists and their allies forged through the next 50 years, securing legislative victories and shifting popular culture. As American culture began to catch up with the young people demanding the same rights as their cisgender and heterosexual peers, performing in arts spaces were at the forefront of the movement.

As many have argued, we must first change people's hearts and minds before we are ready for policy change and our media narratives are a vital part of shifting people's perceptions about social justice issues. By providing opportunities for audiences to see the full humanity of marginalized people and to empathize with their struggle, they are more likely to fight for (or at least not protest against) their rights. Popular television shows such as "Will and Grace" (Mutchnick & Kohan, 1998–2006), and "Modern Family" (Lloyd & Levitan, 2009–2020), which featured gay characters in lead roles along with successful and award-winning theater productions of plays that "humanized" gay characters and directly addressed the impact of homophobia such as "The Normal Heart"

(Kramer, 1985), "Angels in America" (Kushner, 1992), and "The Laramie Project" (Kaufman & Tectonic, 2001) all helped pave the way for an American majority that supported LGBTQIA+ rights and led to elected officials enacting legislative change. Same-sex marriage was declared legal in the US in 2015, and then five years later the US Supreme Court extended the Equal Rights Act to protect Lesbian, Gay, Bisexual, and Transgender people in the workforce.

Young people have consistently been part of this growing movement; though have faced some of the harshest barriers to participation. According to a 2012 study, 81.9 percent of LGBTQIA+ middle and high school students reported feeling unsafe at school and bullied because of their sexual orientation or gender identity (Kosciw et al., 2012). As too many LGBTQIA+ youth live with unsupportive and/or violent parents, being part of the gay rights revolution was often a matter of their survival. And though just 10 percent of American youth identify as LGBTQIA+, 40 percent of the homeless youth population is LGBTQIA+ mostly due to young people running away from abusive homes (National Coalition for the Homeless, 2020). According to the 2019 National Survey on LGBTQ Mental Health by The Trevor Project, 71 percent of LGBTQ youth reported feeling sad or hopeless for at least two weeks in the past year (Paley, 2019).

Lily's story – "thirsty"

As activist theater can be transformative both for the audience, and for the artists creating it, I wanted to share Lily's story and follow this one teenage girl over three years of high school, grappling with and finally embracing her sexual and romantic desire for other girls and the impact her journey can have on her family, audiences, and community. She challenges the narrative that girls are passive sexual objects by writing and then performing a diverse variety of female adolescent characters who express their sexual desires directly and vocally. She uses the theater *rehearsal* process to explore these emotions. She uses the *performance* process to test her audience's response, build confidence to come out on stage and then off stage, and finally to develop her own bold, erotic voice, a rarity for a young Black woman to share so publicly.

> She never knows that I watch her and she doesn't feel my eyes burning a hole of desire into her body. God, if she knew, things wouldn't be the same. Never again. She'd tell everyone I was a freak who liked to look at girls and I'd have to deny it, but in my mind I'd be thinking: "Who *doesn't* like to look at girls?"

Lily spoke these lines on stage during a solo show she wrote and performed in 2005. Though this production was 15 years ago, her story still resonates and captures a homophobic reality that queer girls still deal with today. I worked with Lily – a tall Black teenager with long burgundy locs – from the time she was 16 until she reached 18 as she journeyed through various sexual identities. She was a fiercely independent young woman from the day we met her and seemed to prefer solo work to group work. Strong-willed, highly motivated, and a perfectionist, Lily was always an intense and powerful presence. I was thrilled and somewhat surprised when she eagerly agreed to participate in my dissertation research study. I had told her that I would be asking her to reflect upon personal experiences and stories and I had always pegged her as a somewhat introverted and private person. But her openness during the interviews was surprising in its unfiltered honesty, and very powerful.

Describing her teenage exploration in her slow-motion interview[3] on her personal tape recorder at 18 years old, Lily says:

> I'm still kinda confused. I don't know too much about sexuality, to be completely honest. I mean, I went from being straight to being bi to being asexual to being ... um ... I guess gay or whatever.
>
> (interview)

The ambiguity she expresses about her sexuality ("I don't know ... I mean ... I guess ...") is directly explored through her experience of embodying various sexualities during three different viBe Theater projects in which she participates.

During that first program, when Lily was identifying herself as "straight," she created, wrote, and performed the character "Cupid," a teenage boy who has a crush on another girl in his high school. Within the context of that collaborative production, she dressed like a boy, and was proud that at first, audiences thought she, the performer, actually was male.

She describes the audience's reaction to her gender-bending perform-ance: "At first no one really realizes, 'oh is that a female? Oh! That's a female!' Um, yeah. So that was exciting" (interview). Listening to her voice on the cassette, I can "hear" her smile. Her "excitement," at being mistaken for a boy rang as pleasure, as she used the security of playing the character of Cupid and enacting "his" desires, while still remaining free from homophobic outbursts either in our rehearsal process or from the audiences, which included her friends, parents, teachers, and community.

"Deviations from traditional gender roles – feminine boys and masculine girls – are most frequently and severely punished" (Raymond, 1994, p. 125), though Lily didn't deviate in "real life." She was using the stage to test and taste what it might feel like to express desire for a girl, protected by the baggy jeans and baseball cap of Cupid's costume. She was able to use this theater experience as a testing ground to seduce another teenage girl, but through writing, acting, and speaking. Pointing to another girl on stage, Lily, as Cupid, describes her, then speaks to her:

> This is Dwendolyn. Damn, she looks fine! But she doesn't think so. She has really shady friends and her enemies are FIERCE! I plan to be the one who steals her heart.

It must be pretty boring with you all the way over there. Come a little closer. What happened? Are you scared? Don't be scared. Don't worry, I won't bite. Come a little closer, shoulder to shoulder. Come a little closer. It's really boring with you over there and me over here. Come a little closer. Let's have some fun.

Staged, this second moment appears to the viewer like a heterosexual courtship between two teenagers. Lily, sitting in a school chair with her long legs spread wide like a baseball catcher over home base, leans in towards "Dwendolyn" and attempts to lure her closer. Dwendolyn resists coyly by smiling back at Cupid/Lily and gives Lily the chance to rehearse persistence. S/he says, "Don't worry, I won't bite," which can be read as Lily's defense of her sexuality and attempts to convince her peers that she's not dangerous, that her desire will not hurt anyone.

For Lily, living in the clothing and voice and desires of Cupid allows her to think, write, fantasize, and perform desire for a girl in a more socially acceptable way for the time period, onstage in front of her community. During the playwriting process, it made sense to Lily to create a character who spoke love poetry to another girl, though her own insecurity or reluctance to reveal her attraction to other girls that year prevented her from creating a female character who desired a girl. Instead, by writing and performing as Cupid, she was able to act and speak according to her own heart and loins, yet also remain safe from potential ridicule, misunderstanding, or violence. Though it is clearly a baby first step towards an acceptance of her own attraction to girls, it is significant in her development as part of a process that continues for the next two years.

I interject here my 2021 sensibility into this analysis of events from 2006. In the past decade and a half, the culture shift around transgender issues has evolved at racecar speed. If I had been collaborating with Lily today, I would have found gentle ways to offer support for her exploration of masculinity. I would have assumed more immediately that she might be testing the boundaries of her gender identity, not her sexual orientation. Also, in 2021 New York City, it might have been less likely that her performance of Cupid would have even been a necessary step in her own coming out journey as young people exploring their sexuality, especially in progressive metropolises such as New York City, is somewhat less risky today. I have stayed in contact with Lily through the years and confirm she has consistently presented her adult self as a femme cisgender gay woman. I include this seemingly dated story and my interjection to remind us adults how quickly young people's acceptance of new norms can be and how it is often adults' inflexible assumptions about the stasis in the culture that prevents more urgent cultural evolution.

Fast-forward about six months from her performance as Cupid. Lily returns to viBe as a participant in the viBeSolos program. She tells me about her writing process for her one-girl-show:

My first solo show, *Sessions,* um I kinda dipped into homosexuality. Not too much but enough where I guess the audience understood that Naomi … not that she was *gay*, but that she had feelings for her roommate.

(interview)

During this process, Lily wasn't ready to identify this character (or herself) as "gay," but she pushes further than she did as Cupid by playing a female character who "has feelings for her roommate." As Naomi, Lily speaks to her audience, admitting aloud that she is not just attracted to a girl, but that she watches her in her bed sleeping[3] and has explicit sexual fantasies about her:

How her eyes flutter slightly in response to a dream she can't control. I count how many times she sighs and moans and her mouth, with those lips. What I really want to hear is my name ripping from her lips while the waves of an orgasm crash over her body.

It is significant that Lily's play presents four different characters that she, quite effectively, transitions between. She plays Naomi; Felicia – Naomi's object of affection; Felicia's abusive boyfriend; and she plays an adult therapist, a Muslim woman who is treating the three teenage characters. By constructing a play with these multiple characters, Lily alleviates the fear and weight that the audience will assume she is speaking autobiographically or simply telling stories from her own life. She uses the mask of the character not only to hide behind, but also to speak through. In performance, the character of Naomi was definitely the closest to Lily's own personality and physicality. As Felicia, Lily jutted out her hip, assumed a fast-talking accent; replete with teeth sucking, neck rolling, and wrist-heavy hand gestures. The counselor was portrayed as a middle-aged woman wearing a hijab, speaking slowly in a lower register with a calm demeanor.

Also, significantly, the character of Naomi never actually "acts" on her attraction to girls. She fantasizes about Felicia and gazes at her but only while Felicia is sleeping, eyes closed, unaware. Naomi is not risking anything. But as a performance, it allows Lily a further opportunity to test out the language of female desire and listen to the audience's responses and reactions in the moment and following the performance. She can have a conversation about the character, "Naomi," and gauge her audience's responses, while still protecting her own sexual identity. Lily describes this:

I remember the character of Naomi kind of being a steppingstone for like a gay character that I would write, but me not really wanting her to be gay, but me wanting her to be – it was – it was – it was a lot going on.

(interview)

"Naomi" as a steppingstone is a powerful metaphor when examining how queer youth make the leap from a heterosexual identity towards a queer identity, and how theater performances can add an extra stone in this constant flowing current, both for performers and audiences. This proverbial steppingstone can be a safe transitional space in the journey towards coming out. The girls' community – family, friends, peers, teachers – start to recognize and hopefully accept the humanity of the queer characters, and in turn, the queer girls themselves.

Lily stutters during her interview in her attempts to explain her playwriting decisions at that time. "It was – it was – it was a lot going on." I remember working with her in rehearsal for this production and she did not discuss her own sexuality at all. She would talk about the "person" she was dating using only they/them pronouns.[4] Wanting to protect her desire for privacy, I never pried though I distinctly remember one particular rehearsal when Lily and I were working on Naomi's monologue.

In the fifth-floor public high school classroom, we slid and scratched the desks and chairs across the checker-tiled, linoleum floor, taped paper from the recycling bin to the rectangular window on the door to block out the boys' craned-neck peeking into the room. We don't often rehearse in schools, though that particular day, our usual rehearsal studio was booked, and we were on a tighter-than-usual budget and accepted the free classroom space, despite its inherent restrictions. I started asking Lily questions about the character, Naomi, pushing her towards an understanding of Naomi's objectives both within the text of the monologue and in Naomi's life. At first, Lily spoke in the third person. She said statements like, "Naomi is afraid that Felicia will want to move out if she finds out that she's attracted to her. She can't tell her … She wants … She is …" Then I asked her to run through the monologue, so Lily embodied Naomi and spoke as her. My coaching style involves talking at the girls while they are performing, asking questions that demand they clarify their intentions. Or I might offer staging suggestions or technical suggestions such as, "louder … faster … make her look at you … walk away …" As is often the case during these types of rehearsal sessions, Lily starts to respond *as* Felicia.

Lily's pronoun shift in her talking about Felicia and rehearsing as Felicia, allowed her to respond in the moment to my questions about sexual desire, the challenges of coming out to a close female friend, and the potential social punishments she might face. The theater rehearsal space becomes a site of exploration where Lily can explore and perform – not only the text she has written – but can improvise responses in the first person to my questions, such as,

> What if Felicia wakes up while you're standing over her bed, staring at her? What do you like most about her? Is there anyone in your life you would feel comfortable talking to about this? Why haven't you told anyone about your feelings for Felicia?

The rapidity of the questioning and the vague physical characterization of Naomi blurs the distinctions between the character and Lily herself.

Drama teacher and scholar Kathleen Gallagher (2000) describes a similar process in her theater classroom and theorizes about what girls learn during this improvisational rehearsal process:

> What I have called "expressive learning" here emerged from what might be best understood as the articulation and resolution of emotional conflicts and tensions in our improvised story. It is this quality of interaction among students often witnessed by drama teachers that suggests the important role drama will play in the development and exercising of communication skills. Negotiating in role enhances the students' opportunities for understanding the qualities of successful relationships.
>
> (p. 51)

Skip ahead almost a year and Lily returns to the viBeSolos program for her final production with viBe. She now speaks candidly about her girlfriend and writes explicitly and erotically about her thirst for sex with women. Her solo show also challenges the silence and shame surrounding girls' desire. In *Sister/ Outsider* (1984), Black feminist scholar and poet Audre Lorde writes:

> We have been raised to fear the *yes* within ourselves, our deepest cravings. But, once recognized, those which do not enhance our future lose their power and can be altered. The fear of our desires keeps them suspect and indiscriminately powerful, for to suppress any truth is to give it strength beyond endurance.
>
> (pp. 157–158)

As Lorde warns, when girls repress and suppress their desires, they build shame and fear around them, preventing them from actually following their desires and getting what they want. Though written 35 years ago, Lorde's warning still rings true today. Lily's *Thirsty* counters these fears and quite explicitly expresses the "yes" that Lorde refers to. The full text of the play includes a dozen characters, girls and women who speak honestly, boldly, and shamelessly about their sex lives:

> I wanna smile like those people on TV
> Who demonstrate what the outcome could be
> If one perfectly were to seduce, have foreplay, then sex
> In a maximum of five minutes or less
> In real life that's nothing to brag about
> But if you could make me climax within that time span
> Do more than most could do if they had all night

Lily's text pulses with the energy of desire. She satirizes the ridiculous ways the media portrays sex and demands pleasure for herself, challenging the "you" she is speaking to. She uses humor and metaphor, writes boldly about her queer identity (in other parts of the show), and mocks anyone who stands in her way of fulfilling her desires. Her poetic play: written in private, workshopped, and edited in collaboration, was performed live for hundreds of audience members.

> That just made my throat dry
> My palms sweat
> I don't know it's been a while
> But I think I might be wet
> And you all might be wondering
> What my point may be
> I honestly, just want to know
> If anyone has a glass of water
> 'Cuz I'm really … thirsty

Lily's words embody her hunger and provide a visceral context for where her desire lives in her body. The parameters of poetry and performance beg Lily to invent language and images that allow her to express her story in her unique voice. She represents a refreshing future where girls are forging their own paths, lined with stories, poetry, and drama that challenge the assumptions of silence and passivity by speaking about their desire and taking the risk of letting someone hear them. Demanding to be heard.

Lily's journey is not only transformative for her, but it is transformative for the community audience members who come again and again to performances over the years. These young people, girls mostly, see Lily's shift from "Naomi" to the rainbow of girls and women who boldly speak about lust and desire for other girls. Though the political impact on her audience wasn't Lily's specific agenda, its power cannot be denied as her successful, applause-heavy performances give permission to other girls to explore similar themes.

> When I was writing my – my second solo show I kinda – I had the premise of female sexuality and believe it or not I was gonna leave homosexuality out because I didn't feel like – I felt like it was necessary, but I didn't wanta – um – I didn't wanta write about it and then, I don't know – I just had an epiphany and I realized it's – it's important that it's there. Whether or not it relates to me, it needs to be put into the play.

In viBe's history, *Sessions*, produced in 2005,[5] was viBe's first play to introduce a female character who was exploring her sexuality. Lily was the first girl to really challenge heterosexist narratives.

Anecdotally over the years, Lily held a highly respected position among the younger girls at viBe. Her show, *THIRSTY*, was often mentioned in awed tones and it was clear that her work had an impact on other viBeGirls. In the next five years, there were more than a dozen other characters who openly identified as gay or bisexual. Her bold, unapologetic performances and the enthusiastic and loving response she got from the audience, gave permission to other girls to explore their own sexuality – both onstage and off.

Confidence as agency

While scholars (American Association for University Women, 1992) and journalists (Kay & Shipman, 2018; Orenstein, 1995) have been writing about girls and confidence for decades, they have often focused primarily on the Neo-Liberal theory that challenges and successes begin and end with the individual. Yes, they all found extensive evidence that girls are reporting low levels of confidence and self-esteem and that these feelings and inner psychological churning is holding girls back from achieving their greatest potential, making them depressed and causing rupture in their relationships. It has been, undeniably, an issue. As an activist who wants to ignite revolution alongside girls to challenge all systems and structures that harm them, I read the research with a festering rage and a raised eyebrow.

When we identify the problem as a crisis within girls, then the effective framework for a solution must also be found within girls. What is necessary is an awakening to a critical consciousness that allows them to see the ways they have been duped into believing that if they only try harder, love themselves more, and stop talking about their flaws, they will soar. As Lily and the other girls through this chapter showed me, their process of rehearsing and then speaking their truths, watching their words float into the air without being shot down, gradually allowed them to trust their voices. This though, as potentially transformative as it might look for the girls, is not officially changing the world that was trying to silence them. Lily bravely sharing her stories about her attraction and desire for girls did not end homophobia, but it might have granted her healthy doses of self-efficacy, the necessary feeling and faith that you are up to a challenge.

Renown psychologist Arthur Bandura described this difference between confidence and self-efficacy:

> Confidence is a nondescript term that refers to strength of belief but does not necessarily specify what the certainty is about … Perceived self-efficacy refers to belief in one's agentive capabilities, that one can produce given levels of attainment.
>
> (1997, p. 382)

The theater space allows young people to believe that they can accomplish feats they might previously have never attempted. Though these are first steps towards building the self-efficacy young people need to develop in order to trust their voices and take action, it is only a first step. Once they feel "confident" that their voice can have an impact, they need to point it at the people in their lives and communities who hold the power over them that holds them back. Recognizing who needs to hear them, and then making sure that person is in the theater listening, is the next step.

Notes

1 www.nyc.gov/html/girls/html/home/home.shtml
2 As I write, in 2020, the phrases "people with disabilities" or "disabled people" have emerged as the respected norm from disability scholars, activists and disabled people themselves. There are certainly other folks who prefer "differently abled" or desire to reclaim the word "crippled." At this moment in time, I use the phrase "girls with disabilities." https://adata.org/factsheet/ADANN-writing
3 Though Lily was in high school at the time she wrote this and living at home with her parents, it is significant that in her fantasy/fictional monologue, she was not yet able to imagine a scenario closely related to her own life but instead created a character who was a college student.
4 This experience, in 2006, was more than a decade before the mainstream usage of "they/them" pronouns and the quickly growing acceptance for gender nonconforming youth. I later learned from Lily that her romantic partner had in fact been another girl who used she/her pronouns.
5 This work is not publicly available.

4 "Held momentarily"

For an audience of one … plus[1]

For many girls, the fistpumping chant, "I want to change the world," is often replaced with, "I want to change my mom," or "I want to change my ex." Sometimes, the more specific the audience is, the more powerful, and potentially universal the impact. As theater artists, knowing your audience and directing your message toward specific people (or composites of specific people) is vital in helping to find a clarity of messaging. Theater director Anne Bogart writes, "The paradox in an artist's relationship to an audience is that, in order to talk to many people, you must speak only to one" (2001, p. 110).

In this chapter, you will meet girls who began their process with a focus on one person in their lives who they felt needed to hear their story, but ended up creating theater that rippled through the audience.

Isabella: "If mom only knew"

According to the Guttmacher Institute, in 2016 approximately 19 out of every 1,000 teenage girls in the United States had an abortion (Maddow-Zimet et al., 2020). Reproductive justice is an issue with millions of crusaders fighting from every side, some working to limit or deny access to abortions and others determined to ensure full reproductive health resources, including the right to terminate pregnancies. In my decades of work with teenage girls, I have heard dozens of personal stories about pregnancies, miscarriages, and abortions. I have become familiar with the stained maroon chairs in the Planned Parenthood waiting room where I have sat while accompanying girls for abortions that they couldn't tell their mothers about. Despite what we know about sexual activity and teenagers, the cultural narratives dating back centuries still swirl around that having heterosexual sex can make a boy's reputation, and destroy a girl's. Fear of being labeled a "slut," prevents many girls from sharing their stories with their peers (Tolman, 2018). Generational, religious, and cultural differences between teenagers of color and their parents along with the general squirmy embarrassment of talking with their parents about sex often leads to girls zipping their lips about their most intimate experiences (Ogle et al., 2008). Though the following example shows that the stage can be a space for girls to share a real story that cuts holes through the narrative and defies the cultural norm that girls should never talk about sex, and its impact.

Isabella is a tall, 18-year-old Dominican girl with braces, dimples, and a boldly bleached bronze streak in her long dark curly hair. On the first day of our rehearsal, she declares that she wants her show to deal with her experience of getting an abortion three months earlier. She never identified herself as an "activist" and would likely balk at that label. Choosing to write about abortion, for her, is not an overtly political act, but a choice to find poetry and metaphor to make sense of an intense and transformative life experience. That afternoon, she curls into a chair in the front row of the theater with her spiral, pink notebook in her lap and begins to scribe her story. She reconstructs it in raw, detailed, unfiltered, poetic text, as a day in the life of a teenage girl getting an abortion. Without the politically charged and divisive rhetoric about why abortion should remain a choice for women or about specific hurdles or gratitude for the relative ease of access she had to a safe, affordable procedure, her show has an impact.

As I do with every girl as part of our theater process, I question Isabella: "Who needs to hear this story?" She responds, "my mother," and states that she wants her mother to, "Stop scolding at me like I'm a little girl. I'm old enough to know things, like, you know, right from wrong. I don't need to hear it from an adult" (interview). Though in her "real life," Isabella does not tell her mother about her pregnancy or abortion, she invites her to the performance.

Bright lights come up and reveal Isabella sitting alone on two black blocks, pushed together to signify a subway bench. Her solo show begins:

> Here I am on the subway. 8:50 am. Going downtown knowing damn well that school is uptown. I don't want to do this. I don't want to lie to my mom. I know when she finds out, she's gonna kick my ass.

In the intimate 60-seat theater space, Isabella's mother sits in the second row. Isabella continues with her story detailing stories about the judgmental eyes of the security guard at the clinic, her post-procedure call with her sister, getting food at Burger King, and then coming home to her mother nagging her about the dishes:

> Mommy, please don't make me clean. I don't feel well. Please listen to me. You never understand.

During this scene when Isabella's "character" is speaking directly to her mother, she walks downstage even though she is out of the spotlight and ignores the staging we had rehearsed in order to look out into the audience, lock her gaze and direct the poem to her actual mother, sitting before her in a burgundy velvet theater seat. She performed with tears running down her cheeks:

> You know I can't imagine living without you
> Yet sometimes I feel I'll be better off without you

The love you translate traps me into confusion
One day you're weak, another you're superwoman
Every wrong door I opened you came to the rescue
Although you're never on time you put your best effort through
But sometimes you don't understand who I am
It's hard watching you become my number one fan

Though considering her audience of one, I push Isabella a little further and ask who else might need to hear her story. She thinks about it for a few seconds and then her voice erupts with growing passion:

> Probably people who are against abortion, because the people – yeah definitely – the people who are against abortion, because they say, "Oh my god. You can't kill a baby. What's wrong with you?" this and that. But they don't know the pain and hurt behind it. It's like – I guess they think that they went to the clinic – "Oh I'm done! that's it. I could move on with my life." It's not like that. I mean for some people it is. But for me, it's not. That's gonna stay with me forever, like in the future when I'm like 35, I'm gonna have, I don't know four kids and I could be like, "Oh I could have five kids" you know. Like sometimes I picture, "Oh my god, what if I had a boy? What if I had a girl?" It stays with me. It's never gonna leave me.

Months later, I speak with Isabella about her experience that night in the theater. She tells me that one recent evening she was doing dishes with her mother and without looking her in the eye, her mother told her a story from her own adolescence. She said that she had accidently gotten pregnant and had had an abortion when she was a teenager and that she had never told her own mother. She wanted Isabella to know that she could always come to her. That she would understand.

For Isabella and her mother, the theater space became a safe site for seeds to be planted for a conversation, through the lens of a "fictional" character telling a "fictional" story. As a space that is both "real" and "not real" (McAuley, 2000), the theater allows young people to share detailed experiences that they might be unable to express in other spaces in their lives. Isabella had the rehearsal space to write the exact words she wanted to speak, practice her delivery and have full control over sharing the experience of getting an abortion – without being interrupted, yelled at or dismissed. The stage was real enough to communicate a story about an issue teenage girls deal with, but also was "imaginary" enough for girls like Isabella to create the façade of a character and not risk getting in trouble or revealing too much. Additionally, beyond the personal impact this event had on Isabella and her mother, other girls and parents in the audience could also have heard her story and related it to their own lives, relationships, and experiences. Because girls, particularly girls of color who are disproportionately sexualized (American Psychological Association, 2007), often are treated negatively, "slut-shamed," or ostracized for revealing too much about their sexual activities, the performance space can be a safer space to share the nuances and unique details of these stories and move beyond statistics and stereotypes.

Diamond: "I need to perform him out of me"

Using the fourth wall of the stage as an invisible, protective barrier to communicate rehearsed lines to a loved one happened again and again in my theater work with girls. Another powerful example of this is Diamond, an ebullient Black teenager with the husky voice of a Jazz singer, who was involved with viBe every year of high school. She had created and performed in at least six productions and had clocked hours and hours of live performance time. During the summer after her sophomore year, at the age of 16, Sean, her first boyfriend, of nearly two years, broke her heart. Awash in tears, grief, anger, and confusion, she stumbled into rehearsal for her record release performance in our song makers program. Face glittery with fresh tears, shoulders curled inward with sadness, her voice cracked to me: "Dana, I have to make a solo show. NOW. I need to perform him out of me."

One quick week later, Diamond was on stage performing a glorious, uplifting, emotional, brutal solo show. As part of the performance, she had written Sean into the show and she seized the opportunity to speak "in his voice" and to create and share the words that she thought he might be feeling. She stood before a packed theater, with Sean himself in the fourth row and her voice resonated, piercing several hearts in the crowd:

> You said, "I love you more than you love me"
> But when I think about that shit now I chuckle because
> If you loved me more than I loved you
> Then it would be *you* who cried night after night,
> It would be *you* who pleaded for one more chance,
> It would be *you* with the heavy eyes, broken heart, and spiritless Soul
> And if it was *you* …
> Then your ass would be up here saying this poem.

Beyond the catharsis of sitting alone in her bedroom and scribbling this poem, Diamond understood the impact of performing the words aloud, before an audience. She needed her community to understand – as well as her own heart. Performing this piece seemed to contribute to her holding onto a sense of her own worth. Sometimes, a romantic rejection can erode self-confidence and fill one with insecurity, self-doubt, and fear that no one will ever love them again. Yet Diamond used her flowing poetic voice to make positive meaning from her experience of pain, her exuberant and well-received performance cushioning the prickles of the narrative as it glided out of her voice. The raucous cheers and applause that followed her tear-soaked performance lifted her spirits out of the gloom of her break-up. The laughter, finger snaps and recognition and "uh uh"s, "ummm hmmm"s and "you go, girl!" that leapt from the lips of audience members formed a vocal duet of women's voices of all ages sharing and supporting her experience of that lost first love.

To an extent, Diamond's past experiences and comfort on stage performing provided her with the confirmed confidence to express such a personal story so publicly. Over the prior years, she had built a repertoire of self-written performances and therefore she could anticipate an audience's response. Her goal was to not only communicate to Sean how she felt, but also to use the stage to work through her own feelings and responses to his betrayal and to implicate him as a cheater who broke her heart and warn other boys about the consequences of betraying their girlfriends' trust. Performing as Sean, slouched in a chair, wearing a Yankees cap, she spoke:

> I love her. I really do. I don't mean to hurt her, but I guess I find a way to do that. It's not that I don't want her ... it's just that I'm not happy right now.

She clutches the main tenet of the cultural narrative of romantic love that states that the boy does love the girl, even if his actions seem to express otherwise. She also assures herself, and her peers in the audience that she is still desirable. "It's not that I don't want her ..." The form of solo theater makes it particularly challenging for an amateur performer to write and perform a realistic dialogue between Sean and herself. Its structure invites her to construct Sean in isolation where his discoveries are internal and self-motivated. She uses this structure intentionally to reinforce her mission of convincing Sean – and in turn, the audience – that he was wrong and made a mistake in breaking up with her.

She releases herself from any blame for the break-up by laying the weight of it on Sean and his cheating. She absolves herself of guilt or responsibility and reminds herself, and her audience and Sean himself, that there was nothing she could have done to prevent it. She protects herself from the horror of total rejection by writing his voice as confused and wistful and still in love with her.

> But Imma step up and admit: yea I was wrong for doing that, cuz if she woulda did it I prolly would have broke up with her. Yea, I said it. We would have broke up becuz for some reason that's my solution to everything.

Here Diamond is able to use the theater space to express exactly what she desires Sean had said to her. And she is able to express it loud and clear to her community. "Yea, I was wrong for doing that ..." She doesn't try to imagine a solution or defend his actions according to any logic she might devise. This speech is a cry out for her to express her desire for Sean to just admit that he was wrong. Her performance of this request is twofold: she knows that Sean, sitting in the audience will actually hear her and also she knows that there will be hundreds of witnesses. Even if Sean is tuning her out or not actually listening, there is a cheering crowd that provides the response Diamond seeks. Other boys in the audience, besides Sean, also are listening and hearing a teenage girl express how she feels. They bear witness to the support she receives from her community.

> Madison's[2] always telling me that I need to talk to her instead of breaking up, but shit Imma [young Black man]. I ain't with all that talking … so we break up. As I said before, I don't like to hurt her and the last thing I wanna do is make her cry. But I guess I haven't been showing that? Have I?

This final section of Sean's monologue, as imagined through Diamond's pen, reinforces a stereotype about teenage boys' accommodations to constructions of masculinity that tell them to avoid talking about their feelings (Way, 2011). It is significant, here, to examine how girls perpetuate this stereotype. Though the very action of expressing through his speech Sean's adamant refusal to talk is ironic, poignant, and revealing about what girls know about boys, and what they want them to be. His final lines in this monologue, also his final lines in Diamond's play, invite the audience to respond and react to him. In perform- ance, there was a smattering of "No," and "uh uh!" and "you gotta tell her!" from the crowd, which the real Sean, sitting in the audience, undoubtedly heard.

   Diamond's performance of Sean offers meaning on two levels, as we are aware that we are watching Diamond portraying what she imagines a teenage boy might be feeling, yet this duality allows us to recognize how differently, and similarly boys and girls speak and act. Performance anthropologist Diana Taylor theorizes:

> Whether it's a question of mimetic representation (an actor assuming a role) or of performativity, of social actors assuming socially regulated patterns of appropriate behavior, the scenario more fully allows us to keep both the social actor and the role in view simultaneously, and thus recognize the areas of resistance and tension.
>
> (Taylor, 2003, p. 30)

Because we listen to Sean's voice through Diamond's body, we don't know much about the actual Sean, but we do have the opportunity to witness one girl's hopeful desire for how a boy might be feeling. For Sean, slouching in the third row of the audience with his fitted baseball cap tipped low over his brow, the experience of watching Diamond perform the intimate details of their relationship obviously would have been quite different. I did not speak with Sean, but based on conversations with Diamond afterwards, she revealed that after the performance, she didn't really have much to say to him. "I said every- thing I needed to in the show. I was done" (interview). Performing out the story gave Diamond the closure she needed on their relationship, despite the fact that it was a one-sided "conversation." She spoke to Sean, at Sean, for Sean, but he had no space to respond in those moments. I'll never know if watching Diamond perform as him had any effect on Sean's feelings about his actions, their break-up or his later relationships, but it clearly impacted Diamond and her girlfriends. The experience and flow of support gave Diamond the confidence to move on after the break-up, put the pain behind her, and start dating other boys. Another signal of her feeling of success through this process is the fact that three years later, at the age of 19, Diamond breaks up with another boyfriend, and writes a second solo show exploring the details of the relationship and its demise.

By examining how a teenage girl writes and performs the teenage boy she is in a relationship with, we can see her unconcealed desires leak out and notice what she wants from him. She challenges boys who reject showing evidence of intimacy and vulnerability, by showing her audience what a boy might gain, not lose, by expressing his emotions. Diamond's performance could also serve as an educational model for boys to learn different aspirations and help them redefine what masculinity means to them. She perceives boys as possessing and experiencing feelings of love, intimacy, loss, doubt, and insecurity and sees through their attempts to mask these feelings behind a carefree nonchalance.

But is it activism? In the need to shift cultural norms whereby women feel confident and supported to express agency in their personal and professional relationships, and advocate for what they deserve, Diamond's personal journey can inspire other girls to interrogate their own passivity in their relationships. For girls who sit in the audience and actually witness, in real time, a peer speaking her mind and calling out a boy for his mistreatment of her, this performance could be transformative.

Zahriya: "Sorry. I'm sorry."

Another, more joyful example of a fourth wall tennis match of bouncing words, came two years later. Zahriya was Diamond's estranged best friend, at least until this theater production. Zahyria, an introspective, 16-year-old Black poet who had been making theater with viBe for three years, often came to rehearsal and spoke about tensions in her relationship with Diamond, who was not in this show with her. She would describe how she felt that they had grown apart since Zahyria came out as queer, fell in love with, and started dating a girl at her school. As she began to write text for the play that presented this complicated issue, she decided she wanted to focus on this for her "Two Minutes in the Spotlight."

Two Minutes in the Spotlight was a specific part of the structure of the viBe Theater plays during the years I was there. The entire show is written collectively and collaboratively with a consensus structure whereby every girl has to agree to every plot point, structure, content or action, except for the "Two Minutes." This is the chance for each girl to "own" two minutes of the show where she has 100 percent control. She can write whatever she wants, about whatever she wants, in whatever form or style she wants, addressing any issue she wants. If the play has a fictional structure and she is portraying a character, this is an opportunity for her to break the character and play herself. She is the director of those two minutes and does not have to collaborate, compromise or cut anything within that block of time. She can invite other girls to perform with her and join her in any way she asks to support her vision. Past Two Minutes have often been original songs, choreographed dances, poems, or rants. As part of the activist training and mission for the project, this is a chance for each girl to learn and practice leadership. Audiences likely would not realize what is happening during these moments and they often contribute to creating a collage-like style to the production where it's expected that at random moments, the action of the play might break and one girl might start singing or dancing about a totally different topic. viBe Alumnae, though, often know exactly what these moments are, and the specific care and pride each performer takes in crafting them. The Two Minutes, similar to the Cheers I write about in Chapter 3, become a form of currency whereby girls trade stories about what they did for theirs and the most memorable ones live on for years through the retellings.

Organically, as Zahriya started to work on her piece, the other girls chimed in with their own experiences and strategies for dealing with ruptures in their close friendships. With suggestions from the other girls and many discussions about friendships and their sometimes tragic demises, Zahyria worked on her own to create, direct and then perform a poetic monologue in the play as if she were directly speaking to Diamond. On stage, other girls surrounded her supportively as she spoke her truth about missing her best friend and apologizing for allowing her new relationship to interfere. The other girls in the show gave her feedback on her poem and offered staging ideas for the performance. Through this collective, creative problem-solving, girls learned new ways to address their challenges and they began to trust that their peers may offer powerful solutions to their personal dilemmas. Leading does not have to look like working alone. On opening night, Zahyria stood in her spotlight and spoke out into the darkness about missing her best friend:

> Subliminal messages have been sent through our silence
> Trying to fight against the odds
> Wanting more than air to be with her and only her
> Wanting to feel like I'm hers and she's mine
> That's all that matters, nothing else is relevant
> Trying to find the solace in our peace of mind
> Is a needle in a haystack
> Yet she's got the golden ticket
> And I love her. I love her and what more is there to say
> I don't see regret in my future, I don't even see tomorrow
> I see right here, and right now with her faint smile and dark hair
> On her Batman sheets I see the first girl I've ever loved
> And I see the person who gets me the most
> Our silence is conversation all the time
> Never have I felt so connected
> But my situation has caused a complication

And I'm wanting a relationship
But time has got me facing shit
Wanting to be patient
But I need her
Never would that word come through my vocals if it wasn't true
But her and me and this friendship must be
Us coexisting with each other is what I need. Don't you see I said it again
The reality is crystal clear …
For me to be happy, slightly selfish and a lil indulgent
Inside I have emotions untold, unheard,
Can't seem to comprehend my actions, wondering how I got here
My intentions were not to hurt her …
I can't seem to grasp this hurt
My chest, my mind my heart my conscience aches
Realizing my apologies are of no use
My actions could do no good
'Sorry' does not change it or make it any better …
But that's all I am
Sorry. I'm sorry. I don't deserve.

And from that darkness, a deep, husky voice trembling through tears, shouted back at her using her childhood nickname, "I love you, Pookie!" Two best friends needed the structure of the theater to communicate their thick love for each other. And the 100 people in the audience were there to witness this emotionally charged reunion and perhaps consider the broken friendships in their own lives and see the hope for reconciliation. A communal celebration of girls' friendship is not to be taken lightly in a world that always seems to privilege romantic relationships and assumes girls are more often petty, gossipy and cliquey. Researchers have recognized the positive impact of close friendships and moments such as this one confirms such findings (Graber, Turner, & Madill, 2016).

In this story, the performance space is a site to express, as Zahriya describes, her inside "emotions untold, unheard." She had shared stories with us during the rehearsal process about how she and Diamond had been at the same party recently, and they texted back and forth *while in the same room* but neither walked across the floor to engage face to face. Diamond would have immediately recognized this moment as Zahriya's Two Minutes, and would know what it meant that she chose to use this precious time to write a piece for *her*. Perhaps because she herself had also used the stage to express something to a loved one that she could not share offstage, Diamond was ready to listen.

I am not implying that every time a teenager needs to communicate something they can't express in real life, they should make a play about it or use the stage to say it. Yet, witnessing dozens of moments such as these, I see how the stage can be a training ground for teenagers to practice what they need to say and how they want to say it. Once they experience the release and relief of expressing their truth in a way their audience can hear it, possibly next time, they won't need the rehearsal, lighting, costumes or characters and their heart muscle memory can guide them.

Kuenique: "Mom. I need a listener. I need you"

For adult activists, campaign targets are often leaders or people with vast amounts of power such as elected officials who can impact government policy or corporations whose footprints devastate specific communities. Not that these targets do not also impact the lives of teenagers, but as adolescence is a time of identity formation and self-awareness (Erikson, 1968) teenage activists often focus on the systems of power closest to their lived experience. Few people have more power over a legal minor than their parents.

For almost every child, the first person to have authority over them is their parent or guardian. From deciding what food they will eat, which activities they will engage in, where they will go to school, and who they will – or won't – play with, parents have near total control in the early years. As children grow and spend more time away from their parent or parents, they experience new gasps of freedom. They might taste the surprising sweetness of their first birthday cupcake at a preschool party or discover that at Grandma's house, they can watch endless videos. Then as teenagers, comparing the rules and freedoms of their friends and peers to their own unique homes can ignite rageful bursts of, "But [fill in friend's name] is allowed to [eat sugary cereal, wear make-up to school, stay out past 9 PM, etc. …]." And often followed with the whine of, "It's not fair!"

From the standpoint of many parents, authoritarian rules and decisions are most often made in the perceived "best interest and safety" of their child, but for girls growing up, these rules can often feel overbearing and unfair. And to girls' credit, sometimes the rules truly are arbitrary and often sexist such as, as many girls reported to me, realizing that they have to help their mother with the cooking and the dishes while their brother lounges on the sofa watching television. Or their younger brother is allowed to ride the subway by himself before they are. As they attempt to make their case and reason with their parents, or defy the rules and rebel, girls see the limits of their power and the harsh impact of their resistance. In example after example, I saw girls using the stage as a space to express their feelings to their parents.

Kuenique, a bright 16-year-old whose frequent smiles include deep dimples, was born in Guyana and raised in Brooklyn. She had been involved in several viBe programs throughout high school. During our rehearsal check-ins, she would often vent about how overprotective her parents were and how they did not understand her, an issue far too common for teenage girls, particularly for children of immigrants (Salami et al., 2017). In the summer of 2019, she wrote a monologue telling them how she feels. Her mother attended the show and after performing her monologue, Kuenique shared with me why she wanted to use this performance as a space to communicate with her mother. She said:

KUENIQUE: When you're on stage, they're not right in front of you, judging you. You can say what you want to say.

DANA: Can you give an example of that?

KUENIQUE: Mm-hmm. I recently wrote a piece to my mother and father. Because I feel like every time I complained about anything they did, they were like, "Well, we feed you, so you shouldn't complain." And it felt like to me, it was not … I was trapped in my own home because I couldn't say what I wanted to say without it being a judgmental thing. I'm not judging you, just asking for one thing to be fixed.

DANA: And so, what did you do in the performance?

KUENIQUE: My piece was about me telling them that I wanted more than just to be fed and to be clothed. I wanted an actual person to talk to, to go to.

Flash to Kueniqie, crossing from the back of the theater behind the audience, down the center aisle until she reaches the stage. She speaks this monologue as she walks, starting with a rushed, nervous delivery but then slowing into a more natural and dynamic rhythm as she seems to trust her voice and gain confidence. With her back to most of the audience for much of her speech, she bypasses the potential awkwardness of seeing her mother's face as she speaks:

> Dear Parents,
> I hear … 'no matter how old you get, you'll always be my baby.'
> But how come, I'm not your baby when I need space?
> When I need protection? I am lost and confused and angry
> Mom. I need a listener. I need you.
> Dad. You once told me the world doesn't expect Black dads to care for
> their Black daughters.

By the time she reaches the spotlight onstage and turns to face the crowd, she's loud and clear and her voice is filled with passionate pleading and strength:

> But care isn't judging me.
> Care isn't feeding me and clothing me.
> Because those are things you're supposed to do.
> I cry because you abandon me when I need you the most.
> I pretend to be someone I'm not because you can't see the real me.
> I'm too raw, I'm too sensitive.
> I am a fire in your icy world.
> Igniting a path of awareness, of hope that one day you'll understand
> who I am.

In our interview, months later, I ask her, "And what happened after you performed it?"

KUENIQUE: I feel like my mother – my father wasn't there, but my mother was there – and when we were going home, she was like, "Oh. I didn't know you felt that way." And so, I feel like now we've come to an agreement where she's like – before we used to argue, and I feel like arguing doesn't get you anywhere. So now it's more like, as long as we're not arguing, it's more of a conversation.

DANA: And what role did the performance have in getting you to that place? Why couldn't that have happened without the performance?

KUENIQUE: I feel like without the performance, if I said something to my parents directly, I'd feel small compared to them. I feel like if I said something to them, I would stop myself. I'd be like, no, I can't say that to them. You know when you're just like, maybe not say this to my mother before I get slapped. That's obviously what I'm thinking in my head. It was like, let me not say this.

DANA: But theater space made it so that you could say it.

KUENIQUE: Yeah, I couldn't look her in the eye. It was me looking at an entire audience and it was just … I don't know you people, but it's okay, I'm going to say it to you. But she heard it, too. Yeah. I definitely reached her. Yeah.

Kuenique was bathed in the brightness of a spotlight glowing onstage while 100 people sat in the darkness. There was nowhere else for them to look, nothing else for them to listen to except the quivering and emotional honesty of her voice. There was no vacuum roaring or pot of stew to stir; Kuenique's mother had no option but to hear her daughter. As Kuenique states, "Without the performance, if I said something to my parents directly, I'd feel small compared to them." The performance space ensured she was larger than life.

As further evidence for the impact of Kuenique's monologue on parents in the audience beyond her own mother, I offer the details of a powerful section of the show later in the evening. First, a little plot overview. *Through Different Lenses*, a show created by viBe girls in the summer of 2019, began in an empty community room where girls wandered in for a support group meeting. Throughout the show, through flashback scenes and in real-time, each character shared her story about why she was seeking support as they awaited the arrival of the support group facilitator. After each girl on stage shared stories, both fictional and true to life, about issues girls struggle with related to parent pressure, street harassment, mental health, and gun violence, they stopped the action of the play and announced to the audience, "Look, there are lots of other people who came here tonight also. Maybe they also have stories they want to share or support to offer about these struggles."

The girls each went to a different corner in the room and announced that anyone interested in working on one of the issues brought up so far, should meet in that corner. Then, each girl led her group through an arts-based activity and discussion about the issue at hand. Kuenique and another girl facilitated a group in the "parent pressure" corner. They welcomed many parents (though not Kuenique's mother who had gone to a different group) and other teenage audience members and led a letter-writing project where each person wrote a letter to their child or their parent, inspired by Kuenique's monologue, expressing things they wished they could say to that person. Kuenique told me about one parent who, after hearing the teenagers explaining how stressed out they are, said, "My child does a lot more than I thought they ever did, even if they're not really expressing it right in my face, they really are going through so much and doing so much." Kuenique commented, "I really loved that. We finally got that experience where it's like, 'Oh, this is what they go through everyday. This is the homework load.'" Kuenique's monologue earlier in the evening, ostensibly written ⋆just⋆ for her own mother, resonated deeply with the other mothers in the room who heard echoes of their own daughters in Kuenique's voice. Given the opportunity to talk with Kuenique and Leo, the other girl co-facilitating in the breakout session, parents had an opportunity to reflect upon the performance text as well as share their own feelings about their children *and* strategize together for a way to bridge the divide between parent and teen.

So far, these examples show girls who had people in their lives whom they wanted to tell something, but just couldn't muster the courage. Isabella, Diamond, Zahriya, and Kuenique might inspire girls to use the stage to perform their side of the story. Sounds great, right?! Well, let's pause. Not every example of performing for a specific, captive audience member ends with such a neatly tied up ribbon. As a warning example, I present another experience.

Marlena: "Daddy's girl"

In *Say It How It Is*, the very first viBe show ever, in the summer of 2002, Marlena, a 17-year-old, extroverted, supersmart Dominican girl wanted to tell her father how she really felt about him. As a novice director/facilitator, I was not prepared for the potential repercussions of this type of public reveal. She knew her father would come to the show, and she wrote and performed the following monologue:

> I was 12. As happy and innocent as any 12-year old is entitled to be. I was your typical "Daddy's girl," until he himself destroyed every good image I had of him. He took away the innocence I possessed. That sweet innocence that characterizes a child was gone from one day to another. He lied. He cheated. He betrayed me and everything our family stood for. I love my mother, because she is strong, and she is beautiful and she is selfless. I had never seen or heard my mother cry before age twelve. One night I heard her sobbing in the shower. And I mean sobbing. All out bawling, hysterical crying, in a way I had never heard in my life. And it was because of him. He brought the strongest, proudest woman I know to tears. How could I not hate him?

But wait.

He's the same man who taught me how to ride a bike. The same man who told me every day of my life that I got prettier and prettier every day. Well now what? At the age of 12, how do you pick up the phone and tell the 911 operator that the man who taught you self-confidence is hurting the woman who taught you self-worth? How do you put those words together? You can't. I couldn't. "Help me," were the only words that came out. Every night for the past five years, I have begged God to help me. To help me in any way possible. I've asked God to make them get divorced, so it would end. The life of hypocrisy that we were forced to live. The yelling, the tension, the pain. I just want it to end. I asked him once, why he and my mom were still together if they weren't happy together and he responded, because he was "comfortable" there in his home. He's comfortable. Cute, isn't it? He's comfortable! Not because he truly does love his wife. Not because he loves his children and wants to be with them. But because he's comfortable! Comfortable with going out and sleeping with a woman who is not his wife, and then coming home and kissing his children with that same mouth. Comfortable with knowing that he's ripped his wife's heart to shreds. Comfortable with being completely shameless!

If I were to put all the bad things he's done on one end of a scale and all the good things on the other, they would balance each other out. He has neither been a bad father nor has he been a good father. He's just been there. Since I was 12, he's simply been present.

I miss my daddy. Because the man who's been coming home for the past five years isn't my daddy. But I'm an optimist and I still wait for the day that my daddy might come back, and throw out the cold, selfish man who's been taking his place.

What Marlena did not know was that as she was standing on stage with her powerful voice ripping through this text, tears slipping down her cheeks, the man standing in the back of the audience slowly walked towards the exit. He gently and quietly opened the door and by the time Marlena had collapsed in sobs in the arms of another girl in the show and the audience had erupted in rapturous cheers of love and support for her, he was gone.

I had been watching him throughout the monologue and knew I had to tell Marlena after the show that yes he had been there, yes he heard much of her speech, and finally, yes he had walked out on her. In the celebration after the performance, she seemed okay. She expressed that she was grateful for the chance to tell her story and that she felt, "free" from the weight of keeping her feelings inside. But, when we gathered as an ensemble a week following the performance, she told us that her father had not spoken to her since the performance, that he had seemed angry, but quiet and distant at home. Then, when I checked in a month later, she again revealed that her relationship with her father seemed ruptured beyond repair. Eventually, her home life returned to "normal," and neither she nor her father ever mentioned the performance.

In retrospect, I see how potentially dangerous and irresponsible it had been to support Marlena's choice to perform that piece. On one hand, our work had always been about providing a space for girls to share any stories that they needed to express, uncensored. I wanted to trust the girls that they knew what was best for them and for their audiences. On the other hand, what if Marlena's father had reacted with violence toward her or her mother or brother? She had shared a story publicly about a man who had been abusive in the past. He might have felt shame, anger or humiliation for being called out so publicly and in turn, could have lashed out at Marlena. I felt we – possibly literally – dodged a bullet. I think about Marlena and her father often and use it as a lens to look at when and how girls use the stage to speak directly to people in their lives. We should have asked Marlena questions such as:

Why haven't you felt you could tell this to your father directly?

How is the stage "protecting you?"

If you speak this story, what is the worst thing that could happen?

Are we prepared for that?

Might you or anyone in your family be in danger?

What support networks do you have for after you share this story?

What resources can we offer to you?

Does your mother know you're sharing this publicly? What does she say?

How will she support you?

Ethics of the "hot seat"

Encouraging young people to focus their performance on reaching or changing one individual can be complicated (to say the least). We saw this again and again in our work. Lasering in on one specific person inspires the girls to craft a more detailed and impactful piece because they know exactly what they want to do, and they often know enough intimate details about that audience member to guide them as they find the right language and stories to share in order to best connect with and impact that one person. As other audience members, when we feel that the girl on stage is speaking directly to one person, we can more easily imagine walking in that person's shoes. Through identifying with the recipient of the message, we are more likely to connect with the girl and feel as swayed by her message as she is hoping her intended listener feels. Songwriters seem to know this best, as the songs on my playlist are always the ones that feel like the singer is speaking directly to me, massaging my wounded heart vicariously through someone else's breakup journey.

Though it is one thing for Anne Bogart to muse in *A Director Prepares* about the universal impact of creating a fictional work for her "friends … a love letter to the theatre community" (2001, p. 111), and for musicians to record songs about their exes in the protected solitude of the sound studio. It is quite another to invite a girl to use performance to publicly accuse her father of betraying her and her family. And join her as she confronts him, live from stage, while an audience of strangers watches. At its lowest, it might feel more like an episode of *The Real Housewives of Wherever* when the producers arrange for the betrayed housewife to unexpectedly show up at the baby shower of her cheating husband's lover. Unsurprisingly, drama ensues! Are we, as co-producers, manipulating the audience member by inviting them to a show where they might be called out? Avoid this. Within an activist framework, when the production's goal is often to raise awareness or change people's hearts and minds about an issue, sharing a personal story about a specific relationship can prove devastating and adults need to do everything in our power to take care of both the performer – and the unknown and often nonconsenting strangers sitting in the darkness. It is our responsibility to fully support the girls and guide them in the most effective methods of executing their mission, but we also have ethical standards to maintain to protect the girls from the potential of future emotional or physical harm. And yes, we also have a responsibility to the audience member who maybe bought their ticket to the Colosseum and halfway through the games realized they were the next gladiator.

If both the adults and the girls believe they have taken every precaution towards ensuring the performer's safety and eradicated the potential for the targeted audience member's public humiliation, defensiveness or anger, the theater space can be a site where girls can take back power from within situations where they had felt powerless before. The rehearsal process – or a theater workshop where the participants never perform for an audience – allows girls to practice their agency and taste the words they might have wished they could have spoken. We can help prepare them for every possible outcome by troubleshooting potential responses and reactions from their targeted audience member. Other ensemble members can help the performer by stepping into role as the audience member and improvise scenes about what might happen in the theater, on the subway on the way home, or at any future interaction. Another option is to avoid the "Gotcha" moment entirely and encourage the performer to share the text she wrote with the person first, engage in a discussion about it and then ask permission to perform it at the theater. We can let the performer weigh the potential outcomes of every option and assess for herself if the risk is worth the potential pay-off. Usually, it is. Then, we can all more confidently let the performance unfold. Once the performer releases the words into the theater, had taken power back for herself, she might more easily speak similar ones in her future, offstage.

Notes

1 Excerpts from this chapter first appeared in my chapter, "Theatre and Girls Resistance," in the book *Gender: Space*, edited by Aimee Meredith Cox (2018). I acknowledge with gratitude Cengage Learning Inc. Reproduced by permission. www.cengage. com

2 "Madison" is the name of the character that Diamond writes in order to provide some distance between the play and her own life, though the name, "Madison" is a name that Diamond often uses when she is talking about herself in the third person. It is the name she uses in her personal email address and as her name on Facebook, the online social networking site. Everyone in the audience who knows Diamond likely also knows that "Madison" is Diamond.

5 "Shut up and listen!"

Performance in public spaces

8:34 am. Rush hour on a crowded F subway car chugging along from Brooklyn into Manhattan. I dodge a sloshing cup of coffee attached to the hand hooked around the slippery silver pole in front of me. The smell of sweat tangos with a musky cologne and a fried egg and bacon whiff interrupts the dance. White iPhone earbud cords dangle muffled tunes, cell phone games beep, the conductor's gravelly voice announces each stop, and slicing through the routine of these every-morning rides, the distinct voices of two teenage girls slice through the subway silence. A striking, strong voice of poetic fury twinged with New York City slang, and curses erupt from the denim-clad, curvaceous body of a teenager leaning against the subway door. Her friend shakes her black cornrow-ed braids and gold hoop earrings swing back and forth. From full lips coated in gloss, her response ticks back. Back and forth. Back and forth. Words are tossed and pelted and slammed against each other. They rant about a boy at school, a girl from the neighborhood who "thinks she's all that." The girls' voices are shrill and loud, the only clear sound in the packed subway car. Except for the older white woman who makes a show of shaking her head, gathering her bags and walking to the end of car, no one looks at them.

Anthropologist Oneka LaBennett paints a picture of (primarily male) youth of color breakdancing on the subway and though they are explicitly demanding attention, she writes, "They are avoided, pitied, or exoticized … these urban, minority youth are negotiating the spheres of labor, leisure and consumption to turn a profit and to demand the attention of a public that rarely engages them" (2011, p. 8).

Like these subway entertainers, girls, particularly Black girls, occupy and perform in public space in contradictory ways. They are seen and not seen, heard and not heard (Koonce, 2012). In the hierarchies of power, they often linger at the far edges, marginalized by race, gender, class, and age. In public spaces, girls' bodies are highly visible, regulated, and critiqued, and yet also are often dismissed, and ignored. Wakumi Douglas, social worker and Executive Director of S.O.U.L. Sisters Leadership Collective described to me during an interview,

> Black girls are hyper visible around sexuality and around anger, but are very *in*visible around the caregiving they're doing, the trauma they're

experiencing. And so, what we've seen is they're using the arts to tell the stories of those experiences.

Assumptions and stereotypes swarm around girls' bodies when their voices are not heard. Intentional performance spaces can become contained, expansive, and temporal sites to potentially see beyond the stereotyping by encouraging audiences to listen to the stories and texts the girls choose to share about who they are and what they need. Alternatively, theater can also be a site for reinforcing stereotypes as certain tropes and narratives get perpetuated through unexamined storytelling (Edell, 2013). When considering who exactly needs to hear their stories and reconsider the stereotypes and assumptions about who girls are and what they are capable of, the space – and the specific audiences who occupy it – matters.

Here I offer an analysis of ways in which girls and nonbinary youth actively consider the public spaces where they perform and the audiences who inhabit them as they construct and present theater to raise awareness about issues, educate their communities and ignite audiences to change. The "where" of performance can provide girls with literal and metaphorical space (McAuley, 2000) to share their own truths and challenge the stereotypes and cultural narratives that have defined them for too long. In this chapter, I consider space through a three-sided pyramid, tilting for a different lens on each side. The first is the history of the space, its legacy as a site of violence, of hope, of liberty or of freedom. The second lens is the physical space and its natural and constructed elements. Buildings are never just bricks, glass, and particleboard, but they include the third lens: the energy and spirits of the people who have inhabited it and the decisions, actions and events that have happened there. A park is never just a park, especially when chosen as a site for protest or activism.

Foremost, as I am writing and thinking about space, I must name the bitter truth that the United States was built on occupied territory. European colonizers displaced, violated, murdered, and attempted to destroy the Indigenous people and culture that live here. I write this moment sitting on a wrought iron chair at an outdoor café, my laptop perched on a cold metal table, resting on ground that belongs to the Lenni Lenape tribe. As activists and theatermakers in the US in the twenty-first century, our first understanding of land and space needs to be anchored in respect and acknowledgment of the violence and genocide of the Indigenous people here and then the unpaid labor of enslaved people of African descent who built the foundational structures for this country to live and thrive within. Space has history and that history matters. Taking cues from leaders and artists in other colonized states such as Canada, Australia, and New Zealand, beginning your process and performances with a land acknowledgment to honor the local native people is a beginning step of the journey to be in a relationship of repair and accountability to harm we settlers have wrought on Indigenous communities (Territory Acknowledgement, 2020).

Taking it to the streets (and the sidewalks and the parks)

Visualizing sites of girls' activism, the image that most often reigns supreme is that of a street protest, young people holding picket signs in one arm and a raised fist in the other, faces flushed, mouths open, marching, chanting, and singing in front of epic crowds trailing like a multicolored bridal veil behind them. Throw the concept of performance into the mixer, and the next image that takes shape is often a poem at the mic, a song from the bullhorn or a synchronized dance to the drumbeat in the street. This classic performance-infused street protest site has a rich history and a tried-and-true usefulness, though its limitations are as necessary to outline as its impacts.

Marginalized by age and gender, teenage girls have been calling out injustice in public spaces through poetry since at least the time of the mythological prophetess Cassandra in Ancient Greece, 3,000+ years ago. Cassandra had the gift of prophecy and would wander through the roads and villages singing warnings about the future, yet was epically and tragically cursed in that no one would ever believe her, a prescient foreboding of the reality of girls in many cultures since then. Including poetry, dance, and personal story sharing is an age-old tactic to keep marchers, protesters, and passersby engaged so that they stay, listen, and learn about the issues the organizers are raising as well as build community and solidarity among the protesters (Davis, 2017; Lampert, 2013). During the Suffrage movement in the early twentieth century in the United States and the United Kingdom, teenage girls contributed music, public speaking, and performance to the cause of securing the right to vote for white women. For example, 16-year-old Dorothy Frooks, a young white activist speaking out about women's suffrage was condescendingly called by the press, "a baby Suffragette," and an "infant phenomenon" (Christensen, 2019) though her youth, energy, and attractiveness also worked in her favor. The *New York Tribune* reported about her in 1912, "She's not like those old maids that come down here … you see, they listened to her because she was interesting" (*New York Tribune*, 1912). The novelty of teenage girls speaking out during public protests has dimmed somewhat in the past century, but as Greta Thunberg, Malala Yousafzai, and Emma Gonzales showed us, it still makes ample headlines. As girls activism scholar Emily Bent writes:

> [high school] student-activists experience a similar state of precarious political (in)visibility in that they are at once hyper-visible as non-normative subjects laying claim to public voice and political rights, yet simultaneously trapped by their inevitable illegibility as not-yet subjects forever marked by the political boundaries of age.
>
> (2019, 59)

Oftentimes it is their very marginalization by age, gender, and often race that allows them to rise up and get attention as "media darlings," yet this same marginalization leads to the ease in dismissing them as not old enough to vote or not experienced enough to take seriously. Yet because of what they need to overcome in order to perform publicly as activists, girls often require an extra dose of courage, confidence, and real support before, during, and after the event in order to make their voices heard. A scripted and rehearsed performance can provide enough structure for young people to trust themselves and feel prepared. We also must consider the various implications of race, class, education, and able-bodied privilege that protesting in the streets requires.[1] Some people suffer from debilitating social anxieties that prevent them from marching through public spaces. Others have physical disabilities that make it hard to walk long distances or spend extended periods of time outdoors at certain times of the year due to cold weather or extreme seasonal allergies.

For many marginalized groups who have experienced overwhelming violence and generational trauma such as Black people in the US who are protesting and fighting for their very survival, naming their actions as "courageous" can imply that there is an equivalency between overcoming fear through public speaking and performance and fighting to protect your life and the lives of your loved ones. White people in activist movements are more likely to be branded as "brave" and "courageous," as they have the choice of whether or not to put their bodies on the line during a protest march with heavy and violent policing or they can choose to stay home and ignore the entire Black Lives Matter movement. Black people live Black lives and therefore they are always on the front lines, this is not something that is chosen (Cargle, 2020). Not engaging through sustained protest can mean accepting a status quo that will lead to violence and death.

There are significantly different roles and responsibilities for individuals who participate in organizing, protesting, and performing in public spaces. There are different levels of risk, need, and survival for protesters in the face of the obstacles and oppressions the movement seeks to address and to end. As a white organizer and theater director, I must be a useful accomplice to the work that Black girls do and perform through street protest. Within my own power and privilege, it is my responsibility to work with young people to ensure their physical and emotional safety. For example, as I guide and help craft outdoor street performances, I need to pay close attention to potentially dangerous areas because of their proximity to excessive police presence. For many white people, particularly white women, the presence of police officers can make us feel safe and protected, though for Black and Latinx folks, there is a legacy of trauma in relation to police brutality and racist violence (Report to the United Nations on Racial Disparities in the U.S. Criminal Justice System, 2018). In practice, this can mean literally using my own white, female body as a physical or metaphoric shield to serve as a barrier between police officers and Black teenagers. I can consult with Black people to map our routes through neighborhoods where they are less likely to encounter racist opposition. I can be transparent and honest about the possible backlash and verbal assault they might get barraged with when they raise their voices, share their stories, and name their demands.

Jamila Jones of the Montgomery Gospel Trio, a group of three teenage girls who sang at protests as part of the 1955–1956 Montgomery Bus Boycott reminisced about how within the civil rights movement, with Black people being murdered and Black leaders assassinated, participation was an absolute act of courage. She talks about what was at stake and the role of music during one frightening night at the Highlander Folk School when police raided their civil rights organizing space:

> I ain't gonna say that we wasn't afraid, but I'll say we used our music to strengthen us. What happened was the policeman came to me and put that gun down in my face and said, "Honey, if you got to sing do you have to sing so loud?" ... It was then when I recognized that the power of our music was so strong that it captured all that came from being in the dark and we didn't have any lights, it captured what they had as guns and billy clubs, that this man – shaking – put that gun in my face and I knew that night the power of our music.

> (Masters, 2020)

It was that night, while sitting in the darkness with the intergenerational and interracial group of activists singing the civil rights anthem, "We Shall Overcome," when 15-year-old Mary Ethel Dozier then added the line, "We are not afraid. We are not afraid. We are not afraid, today" (Davis, 2017). The trio harnessed that courage and went on to sing on the frontlines during the Montgomery Bus Boycott.

Arguably the three largest and most impactful activist movements of the twenty-first century were led and organized by women, primarily Black women. From the Black Lives Matter movement that was launched by Black women Alicia Garza, Opal Tometi, and Patrisse Cullors (Garza, 2020; Khan-Cullors & Bandele, 2020) to the tireless work of Tarana Burke, the Black woman who ignited the #MeToo Movement to the predominantly white organizing team that produced the Women's March, which led to the largest set of public demonstrations in the history of the world to the National Trans Visibility March, organized by trans women of color. The visibility of women as activist leaders in public spaces has shifted the image of what an activist looks like today, inspiring the younger generation of girls and gender- expansive young people to see themselves on the soapboxes, hanging the banners and holding the mics.

Teenager Makeda Zabot-Hall performed the following poem at a Juneteenth rally at a public park in Portland, Maine to commemorate the day that Texas, the last state in the union to do so, emancipated enslaved Black people within its borders. This Portland event was one example of hundreds around the United States in the summer of 2020, several led or organized by racially diverse teams of teenage girls or young women, as part of a global racial justice movement ignited by a series of murders of Black people by white police officers, and the spread of Covid-19 and its disproportionate impact on the health and economies of communities of color. These events erupted at the intersection between protest and performance where masses rally in the streets playing the simultaneous roles of both performers and audience members. Makeda spoke:

> I want to be peaceful, but where was the peace when my people hung from trees, naked and stripped of their lives?
> Where was the peace when Emmett Till was mutilated and murdered at the age of 14?
> Where was the peace when unarmed Breonna Taylor was shot eight times in the comfort of her own home?
> Where was the peace when two men in a pickup truck chased Ahmaud Arbery, an innocent man, and fired a shotgun into his stomach?
> We need more peaceful people like my father, but I won't wait for his blood to be spilled.
> So, let me ask you again,
> Where was the peace 400 years ago?
>
> (Zabot-Hall, 2020)

As organized by three other young women, the rally included dancers, poets, and spoken word artists who used a variety of performing arts tactics to engage and inspire a diverse crowd of hundreds of people to support their demands. Christina Donato, a recent graduate of a local high school, laid out their wishes to a *Bangor Daily News* reporter: "We are asking the city to defund the police and remove school resource officers from Portland and Deering high schools" (Schroeder, 2020). At one point, the young protesters lay on the ground for several minutes to mark and mourn the murder of George Floyd, an unarmed Black man killed by a white police officer. At another point, a young Black woman wearing a "HIP HOP IS BIGGER THAN THE GOVERNMENT" tee-shirt danced with her fist in the air in celebration as a multiracial circle of young people surrounded her and cheered her on.

The energy, passion, courage, and creativity that young organizers possess often includes weaving music and performance into the marching and using specific performative tactics as part of the larger protest. Though not explicitly "theater," as defined by a well-lit stage and an audience seated in darkness, young women in activist movements have used various tools of performance to make sure their message is heard. Poetic structures and techniques such as the use of repetition in Makeda's poem above reinforce the messages about the impact of violence on our community more than just news reports or statistics. Black girls leading the protests in the predominantly white city of Portland show their understanding of the urgent need to use their public visibility to express and get attention for their demands for local change.

We saw this in city after city in the US as Black organizers worked exhaustively to ensure the protests were peaceful events. According to research compiled and analyzed by scholars Erika Chenoweth and Jeremy Pressman for

The Washington Post based on 7,305 uprisings in support of Black Lives Matter in the summer of 2020 with millions of attendees in all 50 states:

> The overall levels of violence and property destruction were low, and most of the violence that did take place was, in fact, directed against the BLM protesters … our data suggest that 96.3 percent of events involved no property damage or police injuries, and in 97.7 percent of events, no injuries were reported among participants, bystanders or police.
>
> (Chenowith & Pressman, 2020)

The familiar structure of small-town as well as big-city protests across the country seemed to provide a cushion of protection for girls such as Makeda to appear and speak out. The multiracial and supportive crowds of mostly like-minded folks are there to cheer and connect with their comrades, and the mutual understanding is that the fellow demonstrators and attendees would prevent any blatant acts of violence or aggression.

For young people who are not out in the streets carrying banners and picket signs, the images of these colorful rallies splashed across television sets, newspaper frontpages, and Instagram posts, has an impact. Researchers in adolescent development are finding that the racial justice activist movements are influencing the identity development of Black and Brown children and adolescents. A 2021 study by Rogers, Rosario, Padilla, and Foo found that between 2014 and 2016 when Black Lives Matter protests and demonstrations were highly visible in the media and in the streets, the importance of racial identity among Black and Multicultural (not-white) young people increased. Whether the chants "Black Lives Matter!" come from their lips or are heard through their ear pods, the meaning resonates.

Taking over parks to reclaim public spaces

As the previous examples threaded girls' leadership through the traditional public street protest forms of marches and rallies, the following offers a different kind of interruption of public space with a project where girls "took over" a public park that "often endangers Black girls and their families." A Long Walk Home, a Chicago-based community organization that uses art to educate, inspire, and mobilize young people to end violence against girls and women, created the "Visibility Project: Black Girls Takeover Douglas Park," and filled the space with artwork and performance celebrating Black girls. Their Girl/Friends Leadership Institute "empowers black girls from Chicago to find their voices and advocate for justice in their schools, communities, and the larger city of Chicago" (A Long Walk Home, 2020). They use art to advocate for themselves and other girls, ultimately working toward the goal of changing the face of leadership in activist movements that work for gender and racial justice by supporting and empowering Black girls to enact change in their communities.

In July 2018, in North Lawndale's Douglas Park, as the sun arced from blazing yellow orb to gentle rosy glow, dozens of Black girls reclaimed the space and demanded to be heard. On a temporarily constructed stage, with microphones, "Got Consent?" tee-shirts and powerful, confident voices, Black teenage girls alternated performing poetry, dancing, and singing to a crowd of what looked to be a couple hundred people. The event also included double-dutch, a live music concert and the "Healing Tree," a special tribute created to pay homage to recently missing and murdered Black girls. In talking about her experience as part of this public performance, one girl proudly proclaims, "This [event] shows Black girls that we are allowed to take up space." Events such as this one, the Portland rally, and hundreds of others that have sprung up in the past few years where girls speak out in structured events in outdoor public spaces, seem to operate on a couple levels of impact.

The first ring of impact is on the girls themselves. The performance elements in these events include opportunities for young people to express themselves and share their own feelings, poetry, song, and dance so that they are personally invested in the project and motivated by the chance to be heard in their community, a privilege not often granted to girls, particularly Black girls. As Jesmyn Ward, a multiple award- winning novelist who writes stunning epic works based on her own lived experiences as a Black girl growing up poor, described in an interview, "Black girls are silenced, they are misunderstood, and they are underestimated" (Allardice, 2018).

The second ring of impact includes the public audience of both folks who came specifically to support the girls as well as random people who happen to be in the park that day, have the chance to hear firsthand about what it feels like to be a Black girl in Chicago and perhaps to find resonance, solidarity, and respect for the ways they have overcome struggles or have shared stories about how they survive. Assessing any long-term impact of these public performances on audience members is a heavy lift, beyond the scope of this research. We can notice that audiences stick around, that they cheer and applaud the girls onstage that they linger after performances to chat and remain close by. We won't know as much about the potential negative impact, such as people walking off annoyed that girls are taking up space and interrupting their quiet picnic. The performance could reinforce dangerous and racist stereotypes for certain audience members or passersby seeking affirmation for their worst assumptions. Additionally, teenage girls singing, dancing, and reciting poetry in public, could be a draw for sexual predators or adults to sexualize and objectify girls' bodies. As adult directors and program facilitators, we weigh the risks and the benefits. We fear and understand the potential for violence while also acknowledging that silence can be deadly, too.

Legal scholars and activists Kimberlè Crenshaw and Andrea Ritchie, in their African American Policy Forum report, "Say Her Name: Resisting Police Brutality Against Black Women" (2015) illuminate the lack of focus and attention Black women receive, and its dire impact on the lives of Black women and girls:

The failure to highlight and demand accountability for the countless Black women killed by police over the past two decades, including Eleanor Bumpurs, Tyisha Miller, LaTanya Haggerty, Margaret Mitchell, Kayla Moore, and Tarika Wilson, to name just a few among scores, leaves Black women unnamed and thus underprotected in the face of their continued vulnerability to racialized police violence.

Events such as the "Visibility Project: Black Girls Takeover Douglas Park," counter this narrative by demanding the stories and experiences of Black women and girls be heard. Recognizing their humanity through acknowledging their murders is a necessary first step toward achieving justice and changing the racist and sexist policies that lead to these brutalities.

Slutwalk and pussy hats: reclaiming violent language through public visibility

A more controversial example of specifically girl and young women-led, performance-infused activism is the "Slutwalk" in the early 2010s. In Toronto, February 2011, a police officer, speaking out about safety concerns on a college campus, told the young female students that in order to prevent rape and sexual assault, "women should avoid dressing like sluts" (Rush, 2011). His statement launched a massive global uproar, striking a nerve in young women, furious over the ongoing prevalence of victim-blaming after decades of legislation, education, and legal and policing practices that have underscored that a woman's appearance is never an invitation to sexual advances and assault. This event catalyzed young women and girls to protest and en-masse they took to the streets in what they called "SlutWalks," organized marches with over 100,000 people (mostly young women) in more than 70 cities worldwide wearing revealing clothing, bras and garter belts, sexualized attire or simply just marching in "regular" everyday or workout clothes calling attention to the problematics of marking women's clothing or behavior as an invitation to sexual assault. As a performance tactic, they used the idea of "costume" to make meaning from the ways a woman's clothing choice becomes a rapist's defense. By making what was quite private (the survivor's outfit during a sexual assault) into a highly visible performance, the activists demanded a legislative shift to disregard "what she was wearing" as permission to rape.

Feminist writer and activist Jaclyn Friedman (2011) spoke out about the controversial word echoed in too many legal courtrooms as too many rapists' defense at the Boston SlutWalk to a cheering crowd of thousands:

> The word "slut" is an act of violence. Not just metaphorically. It gives permission for people to rape us, and the person who wields it doesn't have to lift a finger. It sends a signal: this one is fair game. Have at her. No one will blame you.

Though successful in mobilizing hundreds of thousands of young women to march in protest, the SlutWalks were plagued with controversies related to issues of race, gender identity, and socioeconomic class. Mostly organized by white cisgender women who felt empowered and safe to "reclaim" the word "slut," and to openly march through the streets in their lingerie, the movement alienated many transgender women, nonbinary young people, and women of color whose long history of racialized sexualization contributed to their refusal to "reclaim" and "celebrate" this word for a few hours during a march (Black Women's Blueprint, 2011). There were, of course, exceptions, notably the viral video of model Samirah Raheem, a bold young woman of color who put conservative Reverend Jesse Peterson in his place at a 2017 SlutWalk. She said, "I own my body. My body is not a political playground. It's not a place for legislation. It's mine, and it's my future." When Peterson asked Raheem her age, seeming to imply she was too young to be taken seriously, she smirked and replied, "Grown" (Wang, 2018).

The emergence and rapid growth of the SlutWalks suggest that the sexualization of women and girls, and the violence and harassment it enables, is a significant mobilizing issue for a generation of predominantly white or otherwise privileged girls as their wake-up call to issues of gender injustice and violence. With their focus on reclaiming public and online spaces as sites for protest and focusing on individual storytellers sharing their experiences at the microphone at the rally at the end of the march, these activists, some committed for many years and others newly roused to action, count on and can ignite the power of hundreds of thousands of single voices and bodies joined together to reach the highest decibels.

Seventeen-year-old white girl, Molly Kirschner (2011) writes in *Ms. Magazine* about her experience at the New York City Slutwalk:

> I am at home here, despite the fact that it's unlikely I will locate my friends and acquaintances who are also participants. But everyone is a feminist here, and because of that I am empowered. Because of that I join the chanting: "When women's rights are under attack, what do we do? Stand up fight back!"

Kirschner writes about her experience of solidarity and mobilization through the shared experience of a collective performance to reclaim and reframe the word and concept of "slut." Though SlutWalk used the performative to successfully incite young women around the world to rally together, their focus and scope were limited. Their activism was organized to be primarily reactionary, drawing attention to the dangers of or support from those nearby *after* an instance of assault has occurred, as a tactic to prevent victim-blaming and as a movement-building strategy to ignite girls toward further activism. They provide valuable sites for venting personal stories and experiences of sexual violence as ways to log its prevalence and put pressure on law enforcement and policymakers to recognize that the blame and punishment for sexual violence is 100 percent the responsibility of the perpetrator.

Though the sheer size of the Slutwalk organizing efforts was admirable and impactful in terms of rallying the troops, this movement did little to offer strategies to actually prevent future occurrences of sexual violence. Missing from this model is a way or an effort to engage girls in the possibilities of participating in an intergenerational movement through creativity, collaboration, and being part of the solution to end sexual violence rather than reacting to the problem (Edell, Brown, & Tolman, 2013).

Troubled with some similar concerns about its racist and transphobic premise, the ubiquitous pink "pussy hat" from the Women's Marches of 2017 shares many of the strengths and limitations of the SlutWalks. Knitted and crocheted as a knee jerk reaction to presidential candidate Trump's shocking and offensive leaked recording where he boasted that, "I just start kissing [beautiful women]. It's like a magnet. Just kiss. I don't even wait. And when you're a star, they let you do it. You can do anything. Grab 'em by the pussy. You can do anything" (*Washington Post*, 2016). Almost immediately, these pink hat costume pieces were everywhere, seeming to signify the wearer's rejection of Trump and solidarity with an intergenerational "women's movement" to challenge him. Shared costume pieces can serve to connect and inspire many of the players of this global movement while also alienating other would-be members by insinuating that bearing a "pussy" means you are a woman while also assuming that all pussies are pink.

Additionally, raising awareness or offering one-shot opportunities to collectively protest does not constitute the sustained effort that is needed to breathe incitement into the SlutWalk's violence prevention movement building and the pussy-hatted generically watered down and pinkwashed "feminist movement" building. While these movements, and other similar street protests and demonstrations, signal the passion and motivation girls and young women have around the issues of gender justice and sexual violence, and offers them creative, activist outlets for their outrage, they do not offer girls the opportunity to hone their critical vocabulary to, as theater educator Maxine Greene writes, imagine the world "as if it could be otherwise" (Greene, 1988, p. 3), address the systemic racism at the rotten core of the crises and provide strategies to end the root causes of the violence and oppression they are marching against. To do *that* work, we need to build into our education systems: a sustainable long-term media literacy and criticism curriculum, critical race theory, and gender justice work alongside opportunities for young people to unpack their own experiences, understand their complicity in these systems of power and find inspiration and motivation in the lifelong work and effort to dismantle these systems. One march, one play, one class will not reverse the centuries of institutionalized racism, sexism, homophobia, transphobia, and other oppressions that impact our society's most vulnerable people. And yet, we must continue to work toward this. Everyday.

"This is not a safe space": performing in the streets

Physical theaters can be powerful spaces for girls to share their stories through traditional plays performed in front of audience members who enter the theater, knowing at least the general context of the show they will see. However, some girls or the organizations that support them don't have access to or interest in private theater spaces and want to reach people in more public spaces, spaces where they might engage the people who did not pay or choose to sit in the dark theater space and listen to their stories.

In an example of this, Laila, a 16-year-old Pakistani Muslim girl, stands on a milk crate in front of a large public high school. As the autumn wind ruffles the dark hijab that covers her hair, she raises her fist and shouts out to the crowd gathered on the sidewalk in front of her and to the passersby who turn toward her at the sound of her passionate and raspy voice. She tells everyone within earshot:

> America, a country built by white men for white men. America, a nation where the validity of one's natural rights is still, in 2015 for crying out loud, determined by the color of one's skin or a piece of cloth over one's head … Where the FBI has the right to delay immigration indefinitely for Muslims due to security reasons, where I am constantly told, and down-right harassed at times, to forgo my beliefs in favor of flashing more skin, because I'm making my fellow citizens uncomfortable. America, where Brooklyn High refused to take a yearbook photo of me in a hijab, because I "didn't fit its image of the school." We're legal citizens of this country, yet we're still considered outsiders to many. Why should our religion essentially make us less than everyone else?
>
> And it's not like we have it easy in our cultures either. Notice that I said culture, not religion. While over here, we're considered thugs hiding weapons in the folds of our scarves, our own people shame us for our hijabs as well. While over here, we're told that we need to put our bodies on display, our own people tell us that our coverage is never enough to protect the *male gaze*. It has gone to the point where we are made to feel ashamed of our bodies, where we are encouraged to forgo our individuality and take up as little space as we can, just so little Sammy over there doesn't jizz his pants …

Laila is a young writer/performer in *This Is Not a Safe Space*, a site-specific outdoor, public performance event addressing rape culture, sexual harassment, and gender injustice in high schools, produced by SPARK Movement in 2015. In this project, a trio of teenage girls intentionally create a performance that weaves throughout a neighborhood in Brooklyn with scenes and monologues in a public park, a trendy clothing store, in front of a mural of women's faces, on the stoop of a luxury Brownstone home, and along the streets and sidewalks. They created fictional high school students who were competing with each other to win a $1,000 school grant for a social justice project. The play included scenes where the girls get ready for that night's Nicki Minaj concert, plus scenes where the characters shared stories about being propositioned for sex by a man in a clothing store dressing room and a poetic scene about supporting a friend who had been sexually assaulted.

After Laila's speech which was staged like she was practicing for her application for the social justice prize, as part of her audience-engaged Call to Action, she distributes copies of a fictional petition she had printed demanding an end to the restrictive and sexist dress codes at her school; a page of a toolkit for future young organizers to challenge their own school's dress codes. Friends, family, and audience members who came to see her performance received this petition, but so did random passersby. Her soapbox rant attracted a collection of local residents, tourists, and shoppers. People who likely had not thought about restrictive, sexist, and racist dress codes in public high schools got an earful, along with a petition that outlined the details of the issue and an articulate, passionate strategy and roadmap for how to solve the problem. It advocated for creating a team of students to rewrite the dress code from their perspective to ensure that they could wear clothing that was comfortable and affordable, addressed their own fashion style, and was in line with their cultural values. We have no evidence whether they did or did not use them, but the distribution of the printed petitions offered the text and strategic plan for high school students anywhere to launch a campaign challenging sexist, racist, Islamophobic dress codes.

In an email interview, Laila described her passion for focusing on dress codes as the social justice issue she wished to challenge through her performance:

> When a girl gets sent home because of her clothing, she gets the message that how she presents her body and her male peers' education are more important than her own. She internalizes that men, because of their "natural state," are unable to practice self-control, and thus, free from accountability. She learns that women's character and worth derives from artificial factors like her clothing rather than her humanity. She understands that her body is shameful and needs to be both hidden and revealed for male pleasure. These expectations are absolutely ridiculous and dehumanizing for women everywhere. At the end of the day, some women feel confident in a crop top and others in a hijab, and it is not up to others to decide for them. Despite what an entitled few believe, a girl should and must have full control over her body and with whom she shares it.

In another scene from the same project, Grace, a white teenager peeling her flying, dark curls from her shiny lips on this windy day, stands on a red milk crate, in character practicing for her social justice project, speaks her truth to the neighborhood as if she were addressing a group of young men:

> If you only knew. If you only fucking knew the pain that we endure, you wouldn't allow it to continue. If you only saw us as human beings – not sluts or temptresses or bitches or hoes or any of the one-dimensional tropes women are seen as so our pain can continue to be dismissed and unheard. Can you see us? The girls who were coerced into doing things we didn't want that leave us feeling empty and violated. Can you hear us? The

women whose trust was violated by people we love. Do you even want to know about the harassment and groping and stalking and physical, financial and emotional abuse? No? You don't? Well, too fucking bad. Because I want to show you. I want to tell you all of our stories. I want you to see our pain and hear the tears and the shame that choke our voices, but we will keep talking because you need to see that we are people, living breathing people that deserve safety and bodily autonomy and respect. We will keep talking for our sisters that can't speak their truths. I want to document our voices and our tears and our stories so you can know and people across the world can know and the next generation can know. Because if everyone knew the pain that rape culture causes, it would end.

Following her passionate speech, Grace opens a carton of sidewalk chalk and passes it around to the gathering crowd of observers and audience members. She draws a line in purple chalk and instructs them to write, on one side, statements of what they wished they could say to survivors of sexual assault and, on the other, to write messages to young boys, potential perpetrators before they commit acts of violence and to think about how to prevent sexual assault.

As this street theater shows, girls can infiltrate and interrupt public space with their performances. The audience follows them, never more than a few feet away and without the structure of being stuck in theater seats with the actors on a stage; they can directly interact at various points throughout the performance. As Laila described,

> In order to keep the audience actively processing and voicing their thoughts during our production, we addressed them directly whilst in character (personal communication).

These public space performances are for girls interested in communicating their message to people who do not (or cannot) buy a ticket to the theater. Performing in outdoor public spaces has multiple advantages. The leading strength of this method is that girls can literally take up space in visible, positive, crafty, and impactful ways and can reach people they might not otherwise have access to. By performing empowering, self-written texts, they can reverse assumptions about what young people are capable of. As crowds gather to hear their words and voices, the girls are in control of the stories they wish to communicate.

A challenge though of public performance is that the audience is more unpredictable, potentially belligerent, and possibly uninterested or angry that their public space has been repurposed for the duration of the performance. Holding people's attention outdoors on a busy street corner is challenging for the best performers and girls can quickly get frustrated or discouraged if they feel they are not being listened to. For directors collaborating with them on outdoor public performances, it is crucial to anticipate and prepare for every potential response. Almost every rehearsal for *This Is Not a Safe Space* was held outside in the spaces where we would eventually perform. This allowed the girls to be totally comfortable and adaptable to whatever the environment might bring. We got used to our hair blowing across our faces on windy days, parked buses blocking audience sightlines, and annoyed business owners glaring at us as we took up space on the sidewalk. We learned to keep things moving so that we never allowed audiences to linger too long in one space and potentially block customers from going into stores and hurting the local businesses. We wanted our show to celebrate the neighborhood and encourage people to shop locally and to that end, we made efforts to buy slices at the local pizza spot for lunch, snacks at the bodega, notebooks at the independent bookstore and to introduce ourselves and our project to as many folks with whom we interacted. This allowed residents and workers from the neighborhood to get familiar with us, engage with us throughout the process, understand our goals for the project and then feel some local connection with us during the performances. At one point, our portable generator stopped working and a man who had been watching us rehearse on his block for weeks and gotten to know us was quick to jump in and help us restart it. Public outdoor performances can build community within a neighborhood, which can lead to future collaborations and local support.

TikTok as a public commons

For a generation of young people, the very concept of "public space" might look less like Main Street and more like the Discovery tab on their TikTok phone app, a public space where they can post, view, share, and engage with recorded performances. Not live theater, but an interactive, sometimes politically charged space where millions of teenage girls and nonbinary young people are using performance tactics to draw attention to issues they care about. As girls studies scholar Gayle Kimball (2019) writes, by using social media and technology:

> In the safe space of their bedrooms, the Internet and the cell phone enable young women to express their voices, perhaps using a pseudonym, even to organize uprisings. They can get around family restrictions and desires to protect them by speaking publicly from a private space.
>
> (p. 41)

My favorite TikTok is an amazing thread of teenage girls lip-synching along to US Congressional Representative Alexandria Ocasio-Cortez's bold, accusatory speech to Representative Ted Yoho on the floor of the House of Representatives, in response to his non-apology for publicly accosting her on the steps of the Capital in July 2020. Remixed with Kendrick Lamar's song, "Humble," the screen fills with a girl putting on make-up, often dressed as the Congressperson, imitating her exact facial expressions and gestures as she lip syncs:

RepresentativeYoho put his finger in my face. He called me disgusting. He called me crazy, he called me out of my mind. He called me dangerous. RepresentativeYoho called me, and I quote, "A fucking bitch."

These videos often include hashtags encouraging viewers to vote for Democrat Joe Biden in the upcoming presidential election, and often include scrolling text highlighting Ocasio-Cortez's accomplishments and pleading that she run for president in 2024. Along with the closing audio, many of the girls apply Ocasio-Cortez's signature blood-red lipstick along with the grand finale:

I am here because I have to show my parents that I am their daughter and that they did not raise me to accept abuse from men.

Hearted by millions of viewers this "AOC Challenge" blazed through the app and inspired thousands of girls to learn her speech and create these inspiring videos. By literally tasting the words of a powerful woman in their mouths and taking time to practice embodying her, girls might gain a more intimate understanding of what it might feel like to stand up to a powerful man and the system he represents, all while remaining safely in their homes. For teenagers and kids scrolling through the addictive app, they can stumble upon and learn about how this powerful young Puerto Rican woman took a common yet unacceptable experience of an older white man condescendingly insulting her based on her gender, and pushed back. And as they listen to AOC's voice coming out of the lips of teenagers, they might also imagine themselves and their peers speaking out against misogyny.

TikTok as a vehicle for activism has been well-documented. Taylor Lorenz, a *New York Times* technology reporter told "Nightline" (Singh et al., 2020). "TikTok is a place where teenagers go to post information about how to protest, where protests are happening, what's happening on the ground." Because of its video format, creators need to make engaging and entertaining pieces to ensure their messages will be heard among the millions posted every day. As an app with a primarily teenage demographic (nearly 50 percent of teenage internet users in the US have downloaded TikTok, compared to just 9 percent of overall US internet users) (TikTok Revenue and Usage Statistics, 2020), it has become more and more popular during the Covid-19 pandemic when young people are physically distancing, quarantining, and unable to congregate as before.

Another significantly impactful performative TikTok action/prank brilliantly devised and executed by teenagers came to sweet fruition at President Trump's June re-election campaign rally in Tulsa, Oklahoma. Hoping to fill a nearly 20,000-seat arena despite the Covid-19 pandemic, Trump aggressively boasted about his expected crowds and claimed over a million people had tried to reserve tickets. Well, he wasn't wrong. Thanks to several hundred teenagers, it did appear that the event was "sold out," because as part of their grand strategy to humiliate Trump, bruise his fragile ego and show that he might not have the full support he needed to win the election, they used TikTok to create hundreds of videos that were shared and liked millions of times encouraging their peers to reserve free tickets to the rally, and then (cough, cough) get sick and not show up. They were successful and of the anticipated "million," only 6,000 people actually showed up, leaving two thirds of the stadium empty and the "overflow" arenas dismantled hours before to avoid further embarrassment (Lorenz et al., 2020).

Significantly, TikTok is not primarily a space for progressive-minded young people, as it attracts both liberal and conservative teenagers, including millions of young Trump supporters who wear Make America Great Again hats and lip-sync along to the president's speeches. What it offers to young people is a space to connect globally through quick performed texts, performances, or dances. Especially as most of the young people in the world are experiencing social and physical isolation as a result of coronavirus lockdown policies, their phones are their lifelines. Without other means to perform in public spaces, they can record themselves spewing their opinions, ranting, dancing, or speaking their truth, expecting that somewhere, somehow, someone might be listening.

Public space as a site for performance goes back so many thousands of years that it is more significant to consider that *private* space is actually the anomaly. When the cost of theater for audiences, particularly young people who have limited dispensable income is too often prohibitively unaffordable, it is no wonder that so many of them grow up without considering it as an option for their creative expression or as a form for their protest. If there were more examples of live, free, performances in outdoor or other public venues, more teenagers might have stumbled upon it often enough to pique their creative energies. The limited examples in this chapter don't include other possible sites for public performance and I encourage readers to research local spaces in your own communities, and encourage the young people you work with to share with you the public spaces where they and their friends hang out. Maybe your next performance will be at the mall, on the boardwalk, in the library or on the public bus. When more young people see their peers using performance to speak their truths and advocate for what they need, maybe they will be inspired the next time they're ranting about injustice, to gather friends, make a performance and reach new listeners.

Note

1 See "26 Ways to be in the Struggle Beyond the Streets," compiled by Piper Anderson, Kay Ulanday Barrett, Ejeris Dixon, Ro Garrido, Emi Kane, Bhavana Nancherla, Deesha Narichania, Sabelo Narasimhan, Amir Rabiyah, and Meejin Richart. https://issuu.com/nlc.sf.2014/docs/beyondthestreets_final

6 "Finally someone hears us"
Considering our audiences

"Who needs to hear this?" I would argue is the most important question to ask young people at the beginning of the theater devising process, as they start to share the personal and fictional stories that will be the heart of their productions. Our job then is to strategize how to make sure that person or people are part of the audience.

When I asked viBe Theater Experience's Executive Director Toya Lillard in an interview who she wanted in her audiences, who needed to hear the words, voices, and performances created by Black girls, and who most needed to change in order for the lives of Black girls to begin to improve, she did not pause before launching into her response:

> The people who are responsible for the care of children, who are charged with protecting, caring for, educating children, should hear their stories. We did a performance and talk back at the [American Alliance for Theatre Education] conference and it was a room full of teachers. And these teachers were really searching for different ways of engaging them and they needed – they *wanted* the truth. And so, we got to remove these barriers that we create between children and adults and invite children to tell the damn truth because they're going to tell you, and we need to hear it. *We* are the ones that need to change, not them and don't be so arrogant as to think that you have so much to offer a child when you have a lot of internal work to do yourself and I'll end with this old adage, it's not an adage, I just read it in a meme (laughs). But it said, "If you are over the age of 40 and you do not have several mentors who are under 30, you are missing out on major cultural shifts." Yes, so I have many mentors that are under the age of 30 because of this work, because of viBe. Which inform me of the cultural shifts that I need to be aware of so that I can continue to do the internal work. And show up in a way that's helpful.

I love Toya's insights about where change needs to happen and her shifting of the power back into the hands of the young people as the experts of their experiences, and the holders of knowledge that adults need for all of our survival. I was in the room during the girls' presentation at that AATE conference and I remember the dynamics at play. The teachers were leaning in, scribbling in their notebooks, and listening deeply to the wisdom of the girls, asking them questions about what they could do to better support their own students. Sometimes those specific audience members make it through the doors or into the park for that original production, but once a show has been created, you might also find that the answer to, "Who needs to hear this?" has shifted.

The ensemble of Black girls from viBe Theater had spent the summer working on a theater production that I co-directed and was to be performed for their own friends, family, and community. When we had the opportunity to share excerpts of the show-in-progress in the middle of the summer, the girls were excited to be in this space where the traditional power structure flip-flopped and the panel of experts was a table of Black girls speaking out to a sea of older, whiter faces. When deciding on the "where" of their performance, some ensembles choose public spaces like a Chicago park or a Brooklyn street corner, and other groups think differently about who they want to cast as their audience. Whether it is the expansive potential of performing in the street or the limitation of performing for an invited group, the specific identities of the audience members matter.

"Real men show their emotions": an audience of boys

Stained by the lingering stench of sweat and the bleach to cover it up, inside a community center auditorium/gym/cafeteria, one of my favorite theater moments ever came to fruition. Rewind a couple of months as the group of girls I had been collaborating with had written a haunting play about a dystopian world where young people are gender-segregated into "Finishing Schools" for boys and girls where they are forced into traditional gender roles and punished for any attempt to resist oppressive stereotypes. After a discussion during our process about the root causes of the violence too many men enact upon women and girls, the young theatermakers decided they wanted to write a scene from the point of view of boys. They talked about how boys are conditioned to be aggressive and dominant and how they have witnessed the ways that the boys in their lives suffer from the pressure to conform to dangerous norms and tropes of masculinity (Way, 2011). I reached out to a friend and colleague who worked as the Executive Director of the Boys Club of New York, told him about this production and that the girls really wanted to perform it for an audience of teenage boys. Within weeks, we made it happen and the group of girls was speaking out on the wooden stage as 100 teenage boys slouched in rickety folding chairs, riveted.

This space mattered. The girls walked in to perform at the Boys Club of New York, a huge and historic structure committed to serving our city's boys. It was founded in the late nineteenth century as a space for boys whose fathers had been killed in the Civil War to participate in recreation activities, receive education support and foster a brotherhood among other boys. In the past 144 years, they have served more than one million boys. Though many of their staff members are women, it was rare for girls to enter the space and I remember getting lots of doubletake looks as we walked in and set up for our performance. Inside such an explicitly boy-centered space, the girls' performance felt braver, riskier, and more impactful than when they performed the same play a few weeks prior, in a theater space for an intergenerational and mixed-gender audience.

As the performance started, the boys seemed to be scrolling through their phones, tucking their heads into their hoodies or snickering across at each other, but slowly as the words and messages of the performance filled the space, I noticed the energy shifting in the audience. The boys' bodies went from leaning back to leaning in as they lowered their phones and actively listened to the girls' voices. When we got to the scene where the girls put on their basketball jerseys, baseball caps, and hooded sweatshirts and transformed into the boy characters, the audience was rapt. The text of the scene follows:

ALL: Don't be such a girl!

[Music blasts: "Turn Down For What?" by DJ Snake and Lil Jon]

SASHA/BOY 1:   Men don't cook, they say! Put down that pan and pick up a basketball. What's wrong with me wantin' to stay home and bake? I love baking cookies and brownies and cakes and pies. Chocolate chips, frosting all that! Everybody laughs when they see me in the kitchen but as soon as I come out with a batch of fried Oreos, everybody wants some. I'm tired of being harassed 'cause I bake instead of ball. I don't see how it makes me any different.

ALL: Don't be such a girl!

PENNY/BOY 2:   "Real men never feel scared." Ever since I owned up to being afraid of the dark, all the guys have teased me, picked on me, pushed me around, calling me a fraidy-cat. They always say, "Your wife is going to be braver than you, you pansy." And what if she is? What if she kills all the spiders in the bathroom instead of me? I don't see the big deal. All guys are different, man. If there's one thing this school taught me, it's that everybody's got their own problems. And if I have the balls to tell mine, I'm not really afraid.

ALL: Don't be such a girl!

KELLY/BOY 3:   Because beauty isn't women deep. Because yeah, I thread my eyebrows too. People always assume men should be rugged, un-moisturized, hairy creatures. Fact: I shave three times a week because I hate being hairy, doesn't make me feel manly – it makes me feel … hairy. Because I know my products better than my mom – sugar, olive oil, and honey – great natural exfoliator by the way – They think they can laugh me into embarrassment. I say it's not a crime to be hygienic, and a man!

ALL: Don't be such a girl!

BRANDY/BOY 4:   'Why do you listen to Mariah Carey all the time? Her music is so girly!' Does it matter? All guys try to be tough and not show their emotional side, but that's all fake. Real men show their emotions and stop hiding behind Drake. Like have you ever listened to Mariah Carey

Christmas album? It is the best! Whenever I listen to the album I always have to put All I Want for Christmas on repeat! If more men will embrace their emotions, most relationships would be saved.

ALL: Don't be such as girl!

KELLY/BOY 3:   Yo, you have any of the umm cake left over?

SASHA/BOY 1:   Yeah man, check the fridge. Fourth shelf and to your left.

KELLY/BOY 3:   Thanks, D. Your future wife is never gonna leave the kitchen.

CLARA/BOY 4:   Lol no, I actually wish they would teach us how to cook here and maybe even paint.

KELLY/BOY 3:   Ain't that right, D?

SASHA/BOY 1:   Yeah.

KELLY/BOY 3:   All they have us doing … is lifting weights and suppressing emotions.

BRANDY/BOY 4:   We the men, the future husbands

ALL: On my honor, I will succeed in upholding the core values of the Men's Finishing Academy: strength, power, ambition and fortitude. I abandon all weakness and fear forever more. Boys of today, warriors of tomorrow, strapping and relentless, we stand ready to lead.

[Music repeats: "Turn Down For What?" by DJ Snake and Lil Jon]

During the post-show discussion, the first thing the boys in the audience wanted to talk about was this scene. "How did you write that?" one asked. "Did you show it to any [boys] while you were working on it?" The performers responded and described their process. Some mentioned that they lived with brothers and spent time with boyfriends who had expressed some of the feelings captured in the script. Brandy asked, "Did it feel real?" And the smiles and head-nodding from the audience was the response she wanted to see, and she grinned with pride and accomplishment. The girls shared that they worried about the ways that boys are pressured to conform to a dangerous masculinity as the boys nodded and sat a little taller in their seats. The dialogue was engaging and easy and went on for nearly an hour, longer than the actual performance and definitely more than most of our post-show conversations.

A few years later, I interviewed Sasha about what she remembered about that performance and the discussion that followed. She shared:

> They were like, amazed. They had so many comments and you know, they really received it well. And so, I was like, Oh wow! This is good, this is good. This is something that is like opening up you know. Opening up conversations with groups of people that I would have never like, I would have never sat down and had a conversation with a group of boys about these topics otherwise.

Though we did not collect any formal survey data or conduct individual interviews with the boys in the audience, this performance felt uniquely impactful. There was a palpable sense of giddiness from some of the boys who kept asking more questions about that scene. I imagined that so much of the pressure boys feel to conform to these codes of masculinity, seems (to the boys) to come from girls. They assume that the girls want them to be "extra" masculine, when actually the girls wished their boyfriends were more emotionally in tune with them. To listen to girls themselves speaking out about how they think this whole pressure for boys to not show emotion or express vulnerability is pretty dangerous, might help boys see through it as well.

It felt so useful for girls; a group often marginalized because of their gender, to be the ones calling out injustice against boys, the gender group often perceived as holding more power in society. The art form of theater as the space to showcase the ways boys often feel unable to express themselves was particularly jarring and potentially impactful. One of the girls later said that she could not really imagine a group of teenage boys making a play about the toxicity of masculinity and the pressures they face to conform to it. I hope that there are groups out there making these plays, with boys and nonbinary young people as the writers and performers calling out the harm that is incurred from accommodating to these dangerous norms of masculinity.

A global audience: girls "take over" the United Nations

The lights dim to black in the packed 650-seat negotiation room at the United Nations headquarters in New York City. A girl's voice penetrates the silence:

> Hello. If you are hearing this secret international radio broadcast, you are a teenager. There is a certain frequency of sound waves only young people can hear. We are calling to you today to let you know of our secret mission to take over the United Nations. We are speaking specifically to girls. We ask you to gather on October 9th, to finally get your voice heard. We girls are tired of being abused, trafficked, raped, objectified, controlled, and married too soon. We want to be heard. Come and raise your voice with us. October 9th. The United Nations Trusteeship Council. Be there and help us make herstory.

The speech above was written and recorded by 17-year-old Clara, a white girl who lives in New Jersey, and performed as part of an official International Day of the Girl 2015 celebration at the United Nations. It was part of a performance collectively created by a racially diverse ensemble of nine teenage girls in and near New York City and included writings from dozens of other girls from more than 20 countries on six continents. From 2014 to 2016, I served as the co-chair of the Girls Participation Task Force of the Working Group on Girls (WGG), and from 2014 to 2018, I co-produced and co-directed four theater productions as part of the annual International Day of the Girl: Girls Speak Out, at the UN. Through WGG, a nongovernmental organization affiliated with the UN, we sent out a global call to agencies around the world inviting girls to send in poetry, monologues, speeches, and stories about the challenges they face in their communities and the strategies and dreams they have to improve their lives and the lives of their local peers and sisters. We would ask the writing prompt, "What's it like to be a girl where you live?" and each year would include various sub-questions related to the UN's annual themes in line with their millennial development goals. Strategically considering the space where the performance would happen and the audience that would be there, a cohort of teenage girls in New York collaborated with a team of adults from the WGG to create the script that would be performed. We knew the audience would be a combination of teenage girls invited to attend through their schools or community organizations, high-level UN officials, UN staff and delegates, and people who work directly with girls, along with scattered friends and families of the performers. In addition to the live audience, the event was live-streamed through UN Web Television, translated in real-time into five languages, and was viewed online by people in more than 80 countries. All of these audiences were taken into account to construct performances that would have the most potential impact.

Girls' voices and bodies are rarely present in political spaces like the United Nations for too many reasons to list (Bent, 2013). Because girls are (mostly) full-time secondary school students, they are prevented from attending events during school days. As young people, they are rarely taken seriously as having significant contributions to make to discussions about policy issues, and as girls, they are often dismissed as caring more about their appearance, the gossip at their school, and pop culture than about global issues. However, by giving girls access to spaces such as the United Nations, they get motivated and inspired to insert their voices and to ensure that their stories are heard. Since the event included UN officials who work on girls' issues and who write policy recommendations that directly affect girls' lives, the girls wanted to ensure that these power players heard – and would remember – details and narratives about real girls' lives.

The girls explicitly commented on the unfortunate lack of girls' voices in political spaces as they devised a performance titled *The Takeover*. The full International Day of the Girl event itself encompassed much more than just the performance piece. It wove together four distinct groups of contributors: 1) the performance itself performed by the teenage girls live in a 650-seat chamber at the UN; 2) speeches from five actual girl activists from around the world who were funded through the WGG to fly to New York City and share stories about their activism; 3) research conducted and presented live by Girl Advocates (high school students who spend the year working on girls' issues within the WGG); and 4) testimonies and interventions from high-level UN officials such as the ambassadors of Turkey, Canada, and Peru; the Director of UN Women; the Director of UNICEF and other officials from UN agencies working to improve the lives of girls globally.

Allow the girls' narrative from the 2015 performance, shared in the unique space of the United Nations, to unfold: Adults have been running the world for far too long and have seriously messed things up. They have created – and been unable to end – violence, war, poverty, disease, climate change, gender injustice, education inequality, and a host of other local and global issues. Instead of waiting for the grown-ups to fix these problems, the girls decide they should run the world. Girls have vivid imaginations, creative ideas, a desire to collaborate, and a deep wealth of experience that has been marginalized and suppressed. In their fictional play *The Takeover*, a group of girls take over the UN and test their theory that with girls in charge, people everywhere would be better off. They barge into the UN, armed with letters from girls around the world, lock the doors so no one can come in or out, write a resolution that girls should run the UN, vote on the resolution (using the actual UN voting machines at every seat in the negotiation room), win, and declare girls the new global leaders.

The letters that the girls open throughout the performance are the actual texts that girls from around the world sent to us. We selected approximately 30 of these pieces, ensuring regional, content, and style diversity and staged them as monologues or edited (with the permission of the original writers) them into collaborative pieces. The pieces addressed local issues such as child marriage, access to education, female genital mutilation, girls' self-esteem, domestic violence, street harassment, and migration. Some excerpts from these include this piece from Valentina in Colombia about domestic violence (reader, please be warned that the monologue below contains details about an abusive husband/ father), an issue that impacts women and children in every country in the world. Written by a teenage Colombian girl, it was performed by an Ecuadorean-American, Bronx-raised girl in our New York ensemble:

> Violence isn't just a statistic. My name is Valentina. I'm 15 years old and I'm from Colombia. "No te procupes no va a pasar otra vez." Words I heard my mother repeat to me multiple times as I grabbed ahold of them hoping they were true. Colombia, well known for its tropical landscapes and amazing coffee, which by the way isn't false. Mami's coffee was to die for, well that was when she used to make coffee. An aroma that used to fill our small home, an aroma so strong and comforting that felt like a safety blanket wrapped around my small fragile body. Well, what Colombia isn't known for is its ongoing violence against its women. Ever since I could speak I knew that what my father was doing was wrong, but like my mother I chose to believe it was the last time and that it wouldn't happen again …
> The last time I saw my parents was when one night my father came home, drunk as usual and mami had gotten home a little later than usual as she was working a night shift at the hospital. That day my mother picked me up and we rushed home so she can cook for my father because like she always said and like her mother always told her "You cannot be a respect-able Latina if you cannot cook a good meal for your husband." Well, that night as I hid behind the sofa I saw my father throw the pot with oil at my mother, I saw as he grabbed and hit and hit her over again, I saw as he dragged her and left her in the bathroom and then left. That night my mother packed my bags and sent me to my aunt's house, that night was the night I realized I would never see my mother again because that night was

the night that "no va a pasar otra vez" became "no puede parar que pase otra ves." And that's why I'm here today.

This following piece written by Fawzia in Indonesia (excerpts below) was performed by Akila, an Egyptian-American Muslim New Yorker teen wearing a headscarf who could personally identify with the religion, but not the race and nationality of the writer:

> Asalamualikum is a standard salutation in Arabic meaning "peace be upon you" so Assalamualikum, may peace be upon you all. As a young Muslim female, I have chosen the role of wearing the hijab at the age of five because I thought it was simply an aesthetic and it was not forced on me. Ever since Islam has been depicted as a violent religion by the media all around the world, my heart shattered because it was claiming that the religion of peace has been bombing and killing others in the name of religion. I just kept asking myself, "Do they not read the Quran? Do they not understand?" Ever since, I was not only emotionally bullied, but the hijab was pulled off my head several times ... No sir, I come from a religion of peace and acceptance. No sir, in Islam we have more rights than men because God chose us to lift the weight of a beautiful infant in our body and not men. No sir, it should not deprive me of my womanly rights and social status and yes sir, I am an extremist. I am extremely kind. We Muslim women wear the hijab and voluntarily wear the veil to show that we are in control of our own body. This hijab is allowing me to make sure you are dealing with my brain and I am now not allowing you to judge me on how curvy I am. Now I am asking you to carefully judge me on what I have to say and not what I have to offer to your eyes, but to your alluring mind. This is more than just a cloth that has been banned by governments around the world; this is the tapestry of my struggle and the stance of Muslim women practicing their independence.

Though powerful for audiences to hear the stories performed live, casting across culture, race, ethnicity, religion, nationality, and socioeconomic class had its challenges and pushed us to the edge of what I felt was ethically responsible in terms of representation. We were always weighing the power of these girls' stories to be performed at the UN with the potentially awkward at best or offensive at worst disconnect between performer and writer. Our New York ensembles were diverse in terms of race, ethnicity, nationality, and religion, but we could never match every identity marker of the writer with that of the performer. We weighed options of inviting the original writers to record themselves performing their pieces, or possibly even Skyping into the event and performing "live," but these ideas brought up a host of other issues including access to technology for high-quality video or strong internet, time zone incompatibility, language (all pieces were translated into English for the performance as the live audience was primarily English speakers) and the aesthetic concept that a live performer in the room with the audience was preferable to a recorded video. We also recognized the power of each girl in the ensemble performing several different stories, showing the audience the ways in which different topics and themes overlapped and held a fleeting universal power as we watched one girl's voice and body transform into several other "characters" throughout the performance.

The following poem about female genital mutilation was one submission created collaboratively by seven girls in Kenya. The New York ensemble delicately broke the poem into different pieces and performed it collectively as an ensemble of American girls who descended from Europe, Central America, and India. None could relate to this specific experience, though they connected with the root issues of violence against girls:

CLARA: EDUCATE ME, DON'T CUT ME
NEHA: Birth of a baby must be a blessed event
  But hers was short of a curse
CAMILLA: Daddy's face didn't shine, drums didn't make noise
  No shots were fired, no ceremony was held.
MAYA: The newborn was me,
  I am a girl
  In my culture, gender counts most
CLARA: A girl is not welcomed,
  A boy jubilation
NEHA: Raising cattle in the rangeland, family's highest priority
  They believe a girl has no hands for that.
MAYA: At five, I had to face the worst, it is always a dark age
  A woman had to cut across my genitals
  A midwife circumcised me, stitched me, infibulated me
  Where I used to have a clit, I have a black scar now
  Why inflict me with this pain, this real pain of primitive culture?
  The pain is so vivid to this day, two decades after it was done
CLARA: Through education I saw light
  And my granddaughters, daughters won't go through the cut
NEHA: Mum and dad, am I not a daughter?
CAMILLA: Dear brother, am I not a sister?
CLARA: Dear mankind, am I not a human being?
MAYA: EDUCATE ME, DON'T CUT ME.

As I consider the implications of American girls performing stories of violence and oppression specific to countries or cultures far away from their own, I analyze through the lens of the United Nations. The space matters. The UN is a global partnership institution created by 50 countries in a 1945 postWorldWar II charter and is "committed to maintaining international peace and security, developing friendly relations among nations and promoting social progress, better living standards and human rights."[1] I am deeply invested in the professional theater movement toward color-conscious casting where race is always a determining factor in casting, with an acknowledgment of the historical harm caused by white actors playing characters of color. I would feel differently about these performances we produced if they had been performed in spaces other than the UN. What felt most important and significant about the project was the goal that girls' stories from around the world would be performed live on the floor of the UN and become part of their historical archive. In our dream world, we would have the resources and capacity to bring the 30+ girls to New York for a couple of weeks to rehearse and then perform their own stories live. Though the limitations we faced and the choices we made for the New York girls to perform the stories added a layer of universality and a depth of cross-cultural empathy and understanding that was possible only through the Americans' sensitive portrayals. As directors, we committed considerable time in our process to honor and connect with the girls whose stories we were sharing and to never let the performers forget that they were speaking the stories of real people and that they had a heavy responsibility to do them justice.

Viv, whose family is from the Dominican Republic but was born and raised in Brooklyn, told me in an interview about her experience of performing the stories from girls from other countries:

> When I got to hear their stories, I felt my compassion grow, because I was like, now we're really zooming out into the world. I'm hearing other girls' stories, just as people in our audience hear our stories, we got to hear theirs. And I just felt like I was really open to everything that they were going through and a lot more of the struggles that are faced even past my own community. And it was really inspiring.

In turn, the girls who sent their stories had the experience of watching the Livestream of the performance from their schools or homes or community centers and see their words and stories brought to life by enthusiastic and passionate performers on the floor of the UN. Regrettably, we did not have much direct contact with most of the girls from outside the US or Canada who had submitted pieces for the performance. Because of their limited access to computers and the internet, much of the writing was sent to us through a staff member at the non-governmental organization in their country, and we communicated mostly with the girls by emailing back and forth with the adults who worked with them. This prevented any meaningful creative exchange beyond getting their approval for edits and making sure they knew about the Livestream of the performance.

As with most solid community partnerships, over the four years that I was part of the producing team of this unique event, we built a strong layer of trust with the technical staff at the UN as well as the workers at the missions that co-sponsored the event. With time, I felt more comfortable advocating on behalf of the girls and the project and seeing more clearly the levels of power and possibility at play. During the first year, we had staged the performance with the girls walking through the room, up and down the aisles, and interacting with the people in the audience. Little did we know that people don't really walk around much during events at the UN. We had a technical crisis! Since the event was to be Livestreamed to 80+ countries and the video cameraperson was set up to only record the front dias and projection screen, we feared that much of the action and performance would not be captured on the video. Plus, they only had three or four handheld wireless microphones and we had eight performers. Another technical crisis! Ok, these were not exactly crises to any seasoned theater director, but were a definite affirmation for me of how rare it was for the UN to produce live theater. Because our primary goal was making sure the girls' voices were heard and stories were released to the world, we had to weigh what – if anything – to let go of in terms of the creative vision for the event. It was equally important to model for the girls that we would not compromise our artistic integrity (without a fight) and that we would nego-tiate with the technical team and co-producers to ensure that the girls' work was seen and heard to the best of everyone's ability and resources. It would have been easier for the staff and team to cut all the inter-audience staging, let go of all the choreography and have the girls stand at shared microphone stands to recite the pieces. But we did not let that happen. Through discussions with the tech staff about what we needed, advocacy for financial resources to hire an additional video cameraperson to shoot the scenes in the audience and some inspired hustle from the awesome technical director there to find additional microphones in the vast building that could be made available for our perform-ance, we did it.

As a story of production management, this one is not particularly interesting. But as a cautionary tale for recognizing that the teenagers we work with might always be watching, paying attention, and making sense of the world, and their place in it, through how they witness power structures and who has the resources, relationships or privilege to challenge them in order to advocate for what they need, it is useful and educational. And the next year, Mike, the same technical director showed up at our production meeting with a smile and a confirmation that he had already secured additional mics.

I share these backstage stories as examples of the inherent and constant power structures within all spaces and the ways that we are always making choices about whether to accept or challenge the amount of power we have and are able to exert at any given time. I also name my own race, class, edu-cation, and age privilege that allow me to operate with comfort and agility in spaces such as the United Nations, and to engage with ease across the teams there to ask for what we need.

Although this performance obviously did not lead to girls making global policy decisions, high-level UN officials spent nearly three hours in a room dominated by the voices and stories of girls. The experience provided these leaders with context and detailed examples of the actual struggles girls face in their local communities and around the world. They had to publicly bear witness to these testimonies and could potentially be held accountable for hearing these stories, and then choosing not to act on finding solutions to the struggles the girls expressed. I am under no illusion that a three-hour performance at the UN-led to policies that would end female genital mutilation or child marriage or would ensure girls have access to free education globally.

There is a definite level of absurdity in the text that the girls from *The Takeover* created that exposes the power dynamics of age and to a certain degree of gender as well. There was always a sense from the adults that working on this project every year was a "feel good" effort and that the girls were there as tokens and accessories to show how much the grown-ups cared about girls' issues. There was clearly never a threat that the girls actually had power, or could take power away from the adults in the room, but for three hours, once a year, the digital names on the podiums and diases were changed from the country names of the ambassadors who usually sat in those seats to girls' names and there was something humorous and satisfying to see the words "GERMANY" or "NIGERIA" be replaced with "KAYLA" and "AASHA," as teenage girls stepped up and took their seats at the front of the room.

The impact of this event, in this very specific space, is more likely to splash ripples in the lives of the girls in the audience that day, the girls watching from computer screens or cellphones around the world and the girls performing and speaking out at UN podiums with their names sparkling on the digital dias. The hundreds of girls in the audience sat in the same negotiation chairs that some of the most powerful global leaders occupy. By being welcomed into this politically charged space, girls can begin to imagine themselves as future leaders and policymakers.

Performing for the media: theater as a campaign tactic

In 2012, the intergenerational organizers at SPARK Movement launched a multi-pronged campaign to demand teen magazines end their practice of digitally altering the faces, skin colors, and bodies of their models and commit to body size, racial and ethnic diversity in their pages and websites. As one part of our campaign, an idea hatched by Shelby Knox, the brilliant and seasoned Women's Rights Director at change.org and a member of our advisory board, we staged mini-performance events in very public spaces. One included a "mock catwalk," a long Maraschino cherry red carpet laid out on the sidewalk in front of the Conde Nast office building in midtown Manhattan to draw attention to Teen Vogue's refusal to meet our demands. A group of five, smiling teenage girls with different skin colors and body sizes wearing brightly colored SPARK tank tops, strutted up and down the "runway" with handmade signs proclaiming, "Let's get REAL: All girls are BEAUTIFUL!" and "Teen Vogue #KeepItReal!" Did we promote this sidewalk spectacle for weeks to make sure tons of people came? Did we find the most trafficked corner in Times Square for maximum visibility? Were we hoping to gather a crowd of thousands? No. Nope. Not really. The performance was created and staged entirely to attract local and national media in order to put global public pressure on *Teen Vogue* to meet with us and make a public statement promising to end their racist and body-shaming tactics. And the crowd of reporters from most mainstream media sources affirmed that we were in the right place at the right time as they swarmed around the girls, barraging them with questions and thrusting cameras and microphones into their faces.

A few weeks earlier, we had staged a mock photoshoot isn front of the offices of *Seventeen Magazine* for the same purpose and we were wildly successful. As cameras rolled and flashed from CNN, MSNBC, Fox, and ABC we knew that our message and campaign goals would be amplified. At that point, we had about 25,000 signatures on our petition, written by SPARK activist 14-year-old Julia Bluhm calling for *Seventeen Magazine* to include a photo spread without digital alterations (Bluhm, 2012), and we had already attracted an impressive buzz of press, but the coverage was slowing down and we needed more to push the campaign over the finish line and get a meeting with *Seventeen*'s Editor-In-Chief. We needed live performance. By staging these simple theatrical sketches, we were giving the photographers a dynamic photo or short video to include as strong and engaging visual content in their piece, beyond the usual talking heads. We were providing more sparkling substance to encourage them to write another article or shoot another news segment. We knew that the only way we could win this campaign was to get enough visibility from the mainstream media that *Seventeen* could not ignore our demands, or they would look like they were ignoring teenage girls, their only significant consumers. As ABC News reported:

> Julia Bluhm, an 8th grader from Waterville, Maine, has recently become a crusader against airbrushed ads. The 14-year-old traveled to New York City Wednesday to lead a protest, which was set up like a mock photo shoot, on the doorstep of the offices of the Hearst Corporation.
>
> (Davis & Millman, 2012)

And it worked. We were eventually invited in to the *Seventeen* offices and Julia and I sat down with their head, Ann Shocket, for a meeting. Everything was meticulously staged for the cameras from the platter of pink cupcakes we were served to the selfie Ann took with Julia and promptly posted to social media. This performance of intergenerational solidarity, of a powerful adult listening to an earnest and passionate teenager was precisely the image *Seventeen* – and SPARK – needed. Within weeks *Seventeen Magazine* published a "Body Peace Treaty," vowing to, among other things, "never change girls' body or face shapes; celebrate *every kind of beauty* in our pages. Without a range of body types, skin tones, heights, and hair textures, the magazine – and the world – would be boring!" (*Seventeen Magazine*, 2012).

Was it the performance that won the campaign? Yes and no. Without question, we would never have secured a meeting with the editor of *Seventeen* without the global media attention to the campaign. The 80,000 people who eventually signed the petition would never have known about it if it had just been, as the media always wanted to pretend, one lone eighth-grade girl who wrote a petition and posted it on change.org. It was various performance-based tactics that led to the impact. First, "casting" Julia in the role of petition writer, though unintentional at the time, was significant and proved to likely be key to the success of the campaign. The real story, also extensively documented elsewhere (Brown, 2016; Edell, Brown, & Tolman, 2013), though never through a performance studies lens, is that among the SPARK team of girl activists, we were discussing ideas for our next campaign and on one of our group chats with around 15 girls and three adults, we started brainstorming about the issue of Photoshopping in teen magazines and its potential impact on girls through a lens of body image and racism. After discussing who wanted to work on writing a petition as one part of the campaign, Julia volunteered. She shared a story about her experience as a ballet dancer and noticing all the ways her friends complained about their bodies and made the connection between the unrealistic portraits of girls in magazines such as *Seventeen*.

It was somewhat random that Julia happened to be the girl who wrote the petition, but in hindsight, she could not have been better suited to "fit" that role. She is white, thin, blonde, soft-spoken, a little shy and from small-town Waterville, Maine. She is likely the least possible threat to the institutions of power such as the corporate media conglomerations that publish magazines. As a "sweet" white girl, she seemed like she could be a younger version of the anchorwoman or the granddaughter of the CEOs. We tested this theory a bit through the casting of the follow-up campaign, to encourage *Teen Vogue* to make the same promise as *Seventeen*.

This time, the strategy devised by the adults, was to foreground more diversity from the lead activists, knowing that they would be performing in the media spotlight as Julia had. We asked Emma and Carina to co-lead the next phase, also ensuring (or so we thought) a message that leadership is collaborative and not the efforts of one, lone hero. Carina, a Puerto Rican 16-year-old, had thick curly hair and a fuller figure. Emma was 17, tall, white, and lean with a unique style and was often mistaken for a professional fashion model. Both girls went to high school in New York City and were smart, bold, outgoing, articulate, confident, and easily willing to challenge adults when they disagreed with them. Their performances in this role of activist leaders could not have been more different than Julia's. And the impact on their audience was different as well. We noticed several instances of blatant racism when Emma and Carina would do a joint interview and later the journalist would describe Emma as "the leader," as if Carina were her sidekick. Our meeting with the editor of *Teen Vogue* was more contentious and heated than the princess treatment Julia received at *Seventeen* headquarters. And the results? Their campaign was successful in engaging audiences and gaining global media attention, but never "won" the official ask of a promise to end digital enhancements and a commitment to diversity. *Teen Vogue* editor Amy Astley's response was defensive, aggressive, and belligerent with denial. Though there were also powerful moments when Carina shared her experiences of racism and sizism and the impact of never seeing girls who look like her in the pages of magazines. The fact that Carina herself was expressing her feelings and story on mainstream television was also considered a campaign win, and could have likely had the exact impact on teenage girls watching as the rest of our campaign's goals.

What was the specific role of the performances? As an activist organization, we knew that in order to be successful, the best campaigns also include the best tactics of performance. We need to be specific about our casting, specific about our audience and find fresh ways to tell personal stories in order for audiences to empathize and connect with the people demanding change. We also need enough "spectacle" to attract the attention necessary to pique people's interest in the content of the action. Over the years, our various campaigns would either achieve our articulated goal or not, but I always knew that the real "win" was in these performances: placing girls in the spotlight to share their stories in mainstream media and begin to change the face (and body) of what leadership and activism looks like.

Putting the audience in a box: performances on Zoom

I remember pushing my three-year-old son on a swing at our neighborhood playground, after school on a Friday in mid-March 2020 as I laughed with my mom-friends and we made plans to all go to the zoo that Sunday so our kids could run around and imitate the baboons. I didn't realize that it would be seven months until I would be with any of them again, and that we would be outside, wearing masks and standing six feet apart from each other. On March 12, life as we knew it in Brooklyn, in New York, in the US, in most of the world, pretty much shut down. Boxes of mac and cheese were delivered from the grocery store and immediately wiped down with bleach, lipsticks grew dusty on my countertop as I didn't want to stain my newly Etsy-purchased homemade cloth facemasks. Theater rehearsals screeched to a halt, shows were postponed two weeks, then a month, then quietly announced they would perform via Zoom. Audiences went from sitting in a dark theater breathing the same air as the performers to sitting at their kitchen tables while their cats climbed onto their keyboards and tried to nuzzle the camera. Though internally the collective feeling was rage, frustration, and despair, the actual sounds of 2020 were more like silence as we all retreated into our homes to protect ourselves, our loved ones, and our neighbors from Covid-19. And inevitably, virus-enhanced injustices in the world related to massive job losses, inadequate health care, lack of childcare, a toxic presidential election campaign, unbearable stress, anxiety, and systemic racism bubbled over the boiling point and we witnessed a massive increase in the visibility of a continuing racial justice revolution.

The urgency of the multiple crises, paired with the inability and/or danger of live gatherings, especially as the weather grew colder meant that most activist performances shifted online. Though initially frustrating and disappointing for theater artists, this new digital space also revealed many opportunities. Suddenly, the entire assumption of who your audience could be explodes. People from around the world can log in to your live performance or if they are not available, performances can be recorded and watched anytime and anywhere. In the weeks before the US election, I collaborated with Dahlia, a 17-year-old girl in Omaha, Nebraska who wrote a personal performance monologue that she performed on election night 2020, at an interactive, online event with Jewish clergy. A few benefits of live theater on Zoom are that the audience can respond; from anywhere in the world with an internet connection, in real time through the text chat box. What we miss in audible laughter, snaps and applause, we can gain in specific and thoughtful written feedback and live dialogue. On the evening of November 3, in the hour after the polls closed, as Americans collectively held their breath as voting machines chugged along in their tallying and news anchors pretended that the massive maps with the constantly changing blue and red states were accurately predicting a winner, Dahlia sat at her desk, face framed by spirals of brown curls, looked into the green light of the camera at the top of her computer screen and shared her story:

> Hi everyone, my name is Dahlia, and I am so grateful to be speaking with you this evening. When I took Rabbi Tamara up on the opportunity to come here tonight, she asked me, "Great, what can you do?" and I sat there, staring at my phone because that was the question I have been asking myself for the past eight months. "What can I do?" Right now, I am sitting in a place of particular vulnerability. I'm a 17-year-old woman in Omaha, Nebraska staring at my future dead in the face, unable to conceivably predict what's to happen next, and I'm in control of none of it.
>
> I am no stranger, however, to vulnerability. I'm a triple organ transplant recipient who was raised on a steady diet of hand sanitizer and self-isolation. Throughout my atypical childhood, I fantasized about what being a normal teenager was going to look like: School dances, musical opening nights, sleepovers with friends. And while I got some brief tastes of those things here and there, now I'm back to where I was six years ago, fantasizing yet again about what's to come, but this time I am consciously afraid.
>
> I am going to use this time to be vulnerable with you all and put a human story to the statistics. If the Affordable Care Act gets repealed, I will lose the insurance for my anti-organ rejection medication. If abortion becomes criminalized, I would be in serious danger if I ever had an unplanned pregnancy, and if I get Covid, I could get very sick. These are all truths I am conscious of at 17 years old, and I have no voice in any of them. I can feel the normalcy of my life ending before it even had the chance to begin.
>
> Now, this isn't a speech about why you should vote for Biden. If it were, I know I'd be preaching to the choir. And if you haven't voted by now, it may be a little late. This speech is about recognizing that you are not alone in your struggle and your fear today, over the past eight months, and even during these last four years. I want us all to think back to where we were on this night four years ago and how we knew everything was going to

change. This is the moment before our whole life will change once again. That's pretty magical.

I'd like everyone to now pull out a notebook or a Word document because we're all going to be a little vulnerable this evening. I want everyone to think about: Where your sense of hope is this evening? Where is your sense of joy? What can we remind ourselves of humanity to get through that period? I'm going to give you about five minutes to write, and then we'll share out.

She later told me in an interview how inspiring the event was and how powerful it was to connect with so many people from all over the country at such a prescient and super charged time as election night. Before the pandemic and the ubiquity of Zoom, we likely would have never engaged so frequently and so often with people from such different regions and across age, race, and power lines. She told me:

And especially living in Nebraska. I definitely kind of felt like – oh my gosh I have all these aspirations in terms of theater and in terms of activism and like, I felt very alone in that because people aren't very social activist minded or creatively minded here.

Because of Zoom's technology, she was able to reach an audience she never would have connected with in a live performance in Omaha.

The Zooming of performance has provided a uniquely new mode of engaging audiences and we are truly witnessing the birth of a new art form – a hybrid live performance/video/interactive space that both utilizes the spontaneity and real-time connectedness of live theater with the creative potential of pre-recorded video or digital storytelling. Zoom also allows a remarkable accessibility. Your audience can be anywhere in the world, yet safely inside their homes. For audience members with disabilities, they can sit, watch and engage with all the necessary accommodations they might need from closed captions to a comfortable and safe place to sit or stand or physically connect in any way that feels good for them.

The strongest example I experienced of activist performance on Zoom was educational theater doctoral student, artist, and organizer Quenna Lené Barrett's *Rewriting the Declaration*. "Catalyzed by the Movement for Black Lives, *Re-Writing the Declaration* is a devised, participatory play inviting audiences to center Black women, and femmes, nonbinary, and trans folx of color, in order to free us all" (Barrett, 2020). On her website, describing the history of the project, Quenna wrote:

As I read the Declaration of Independence, I realized that the United States of America's founding documents were never intended to include many of the people who call this country home. The justice system doesn't protect black and brown people for many reasons, in large part because it wasn't designed to. Because of these and other shortfalls, I wondered what would happen if I were to rewrite the Declaration as an artistic, performative, and participatory rendering of a new and more inclusive document, utilizing participatory performance, photography, and theatre-based workshops.

Though she was working with young adults playing teenagers, not with actual teens, I still found much of her approach and final production useful for those of us attempting to create meaningful, interactive and dynamic live performance on Zoom. What she and her ensemble built was an educational, funny, whimsical, passionate, and haunting exploration of the founding document from the United States with an intentional focus on the people excluded from it. The performance told the nonlinear story of a classroom of Black and Latinx high school students of multiple gender identities as they seek to unpack the overt and buried meanings of the document. The Zoom format allowed the audience to engage as "students" in the class and respond to questions, offer personal experiences or new content for the collective rewriting of the declaration. The show was a dizzying and satisfying adventure through the history of racism and white supremacy in the US and the current racial justice crisis while offering hope and tools for audience members to engage with and apply the content to their own lives. Zoom allowed me to engage in a "live" performance in the midst of a lockdown, as a single mother with limited childcare, while helping my four-year-old son do a puzzle on our living room floor.

The creative team engaged the audience in playful, thoughtful activities that kept us connected to the storytelling and active participants in the performance. For example, in one scene they asked us, "When you hear the phrase 'a seat at the table,' what does that mean for you?" Then they showed a video montage of a people of various gender and racial identities responding, and asked the audience to add our responses in the chat. They made ample use of the "Poll" function in Zoom by asking us to vote on different directions the performance could go or on creative responses to questions posed. After asking us to vote on how we would build our "table" that everyone would have a seat at, we could choose between, "glitter colored, heart-shaped, made of justice, finished with reparations" and other witty, but provocative options. They continued throughout the production to offer opportunities for audience members to volunteer on-screen or through commenting and voting; the result was one of the most engaged, interactive theater experiences I've had as an audience member – live or virtual.

Quenna described her thoughts about the ideal audience and how that related to her goals for the show and the unique value of producing it on Zoom:

> Yeah, that was a huge question for us, who do we want to come see this? …We absolutely wanted it to center joy and pleasure. Celebrate these identities and so it felt important to have these folks who were somewhat on our side already. And so, I think that's who showed up, like a lot of family members came for the cast, my own family. And like folks from across the

globe, really, they were from the UK and India, and you know [one of the performers]'s from Trinidad and so her family from there showed up. I think it made it accessible in a way that like typically we wouldn't be able to support folks and go see their plays.

Another value to the Zoom performance is that it can be easily recorded and still maintain much of the experience for the audience, unlike watching a recording of a play meant to be staged in a theater. And in terms of the larger activist mission, the recording allows for an evolution of promotion and engagement that could give the project wings so it can stay in the air for much longer than a typical theatrical run. Quenna is a true visionary, and she is also thinking strategically about how to use the recording to advance her goals for the project:

> Does it get released with a more blown out version of the website? And something that I've always thought about is how can people continue to interact with it? It happens through the [rewriting of the Declaration of Independence as a document]. And this is where the policy conversation continues, and how it can lead to further activism and engagement.

Through a longer-term engagement with an ever-expanding audience, artists like Quenna can create this hybrid theater/video/Zoom work with young people and continue to add to it as it grows and expands for the greatest possible impact.

Another incredible organizing opportunity that Zoom has enabled is the widespread accessibility of interactive social and racial justice trainings. In the summer and fall of 2020, not a week goes by when I am not invited to attend or register for another Zoom webinar to discuss structural racism,[2] white people working to end racism,[3] phone banking for the 2020 presidential election,[4] antiracist parenting,[5] standing up and standing by to end street harassment,[6] and countless others. Through the Zoom interface, workshop, and training participants can control how engaged they feel comfortable getting by turning their video on or off, commenting in the chat or sitting back and watching and listening. Through breakout rooms, folks can have more intimate guided conversations about the issues raised during the seminar. Also, the often sliding scale costs of many of these trainings make them affordable for the folks who need them most and obviously excludes the additional expenses related to transportation and accommodations needed to attend such trainings in the past. Though tangential to my focus on girls, performance and activism, I would be remiss to not acknowledge the usefulness of these trainings for my work and growth as an antiracist and youth-centered gender justice organizer.

Performing truth to power

When considering the audience, as I have repeatedly advocated for through these pages, we ask the girls before and after they write or create, "Who needs to hear this?" as the first step in power mapping[7] how change might occur. There is one audience that young people who participate in theater programs within community-based organizations, are often called upon to perform for: the donors and funders. I write this section with all the guilt and shame of a director who has done much of what I am about to critique. I hold myself accountable for the potential harm these performances might have incurred and hope to offer different frameworks for understanding how we can and must do better. Allow me to set the scene:

We are in the private event room upstairs at an exclusive wine bar with exposed brick and naked light bulbs dangling from the ceiling. We are in an expansive, expensive shiny white living room with leather sofas and glass tables. We are in a decadent ballroom with the remains of the dinner's beef medallions with wild mushroom sauce and the wheat berry pomegranate arugula salad. A white lady clangs and dings her fork on her wine glass until the room hushes. The mostly white crowd of adults in sparkling jewel-colored cocktail dresses, in jackets and ties, in heels, and with goatees gather around a cleared away area. The white lady welcomes everyone. She probably holds her hand over her heart as she shares a story about a "troubled" teenager who came to her organization, quiet, lonely, and shattered by trauma and then within weeks or months was performing on a stage. She might shed some tears. So might a few people in the crowd. She will thank everyone for coming. She will thank some big banks. She will thank some family foundations who made their money by exploiting their workers who look like the images of the smiling Black and Brown children and teenagers on the screen slideshow rotating behind her. She will thank another foundation who changed their name so people would not recognize that they made their money by marketing cigarettes to children. Then she will say that the *real* reason everyone is there is because of the amazing and inspiring and awesome and amazing and inspiring and awesome young people and don't we really just want to hear *their* voices? And everyone will put their drinks down so they can clap. And as Black and Brown servers weave through the room offering avocado lamb kabobs and kale empanadas, a group of Black and Brown teenagers will appear and will dutifully perform pieces from the show they had written months before to be performed on a stage with lighting and the audience a safe distance away. In golden light from the chandeliers or the flickering candles, they will sing and dance stories of overcoming trauma. When they take their bow, the audience will put their glasses down again and erupt in applause. The teenagers will leave, the adults will lift their glasses again as they wander the room and bid on auction items, hoping that this year they will get the weekend house rental in the Berkshires or the tickets to Hamilton.

These transactional "show pony" performances can feel necessary for so many youth arts/education/activist organizations sweating on the hamster wheel of nonprofit fundraising where they rely on the unrestricted funds that individual donors can provide.[8] On the one hand, there is absolute validity to the idea that if we accept that a tax-exempt organization needs to raise money in order to operate and serve the community, then during the fundraising events, it can be vital that the current and potential donors see what they are supporting. If the young people are *not* present at all, the event feels disconnected from the mission of the organization and relies entirely on the organization's staff to talk *about* the young people it "serves" and often inadvertently exploits or objectifies them by sharing stories of their personal struggles and how the organization's work has "saved" them. This process can wreak of the "white savior complex" whereby white people with power feel good about engaging in activities and endeavors that seem to improve portions of the lives of "disadvantaged" people of color, though avoiding any real systemic change or personal sacrifice. Teju Cole, the Nigerian-American writer, and cultural critic, describes the phenomenon as "not about justice. It's about having a big emotional experience that validates privilege" (Cole, 2012).

On the other hand, often, young people performing at fundraisers and galas tell me afterwards how much fun they had and how memorable the experience was for them. They talk about the decadent food, the chance to get dressed up and that they loved the opportunity to perform and be the center of attention. So many adults want to talk to them after the performance, ask about their experiences within the project and tell them how amazing their performance was. What's not to like?

In terms of an actual assessment of its impact, these sites of performance for donors, board members and other VIPs in attendance, such as elected officials or community leaders, can literally ignite significant change, if change is quantified through attainment of resources and the potential of a shifting of the perspectives of people with power. Oftentimes, local elected officials are invited to these events and they attend for the opportunity to get their photograph taken surrounded by smiling girls of color. They can use this image to signify to their constituents and voters that they care about girls, about young people, about Black people, about the arts, about social justice. They can use the site as a chance to publicly state their support for policies or funding that can actually improve the lives of the young people. Though their celebration of this complex narrative attempts to validate a misleading assumption that one theater experience can be enough to change the lives of marginalized young people (Balfour, 2009). And the girls are useful props and backdrops that provide evidence of the local leader's investment in the cause. Is the discomfort I often feel and the exploitation of the girls' (often unpaid) creative labor a fair trade for the resources we receive as part of the bargain?

If we did not have to imagine that the hands clapping in our audiences are also the hands that feed us, we would have more liberty to create work that names and implicates those with the power to make changes that directly improve the lives of vulnerable people. I have had just one truly terrible experience in my work where a brilliant Muslim Arab girl created a piece of writing that named many of the violent truths about Israel's occupation of Palestine and a pattern of sexual assaults of Palestinian women and girls by Israeli soldiers. The piece offended one of our board members who did not want to be perceived to be in solidarity with the views of this girl. She also felt that publishing the writing could impact our potential future funding from Jewish women's funding networks, and other issues related to her own work and the current and potential future work of her husband as her family gave money to our organization. It was a complicated situation and nearly all my attempts to stand up to the board member and support and stand by the girl, fell short. I deeply regret that it led to this amazing girl stepping away from the project entirely. I see stories similar to this repeated across youth-based organizations all the time, where the adult leadership, out of concern for funding, makes choices that prevent the young people from fully expressing themselves, or worse, do more harm.

I spoke recently with the former artistic director of a girls' theater company who revealed stories to me about how the white executive director would ask her to direct more "stories of trauma" from the girls of color, because those were the stories funders wanted to see. She told me, "But that's where the money was, so that's where the direction of the organization wanted to go – like, oh it's mental health."

viBe Theater executive director Toya Lillard spoke in a podcast interview with the Arts Management in Technology Lab aptly titled "Using an Abolitionist Framework in the Arts" (Johnson, 2020):

> We're comfortable with white people at the helm, speaking on behalf of communities of color, because we assume that those communities don't have the resources or capacity to speak up for themselves. We know that's not true. We know that that thinking only supports capitalist hierarchies. We understand that it only fuels this nonprofit industrial complex that causes harm and under-resources the organizations that are really doing impact.

In order to dutifully critique the nonprofit industrial complex and its ruptured and rotten core is to understand the way capitalism functions (and dysfunctions) in the US. As Ibram X. Kendi writes in *How to Be an AntiRacist*, "To love capitalism is to end up loving racism. To love racism is to end up loving capitalism. The conjoined twins are two sides of the same destructive body" (2019, p. 163). Dana Kawaoka-Chen, executive director for Justice Funders, spoke on a panel convened by Grantmakers in the Arts (2020) and offered an astute analysis of how we must reimagine the funding structures for community-based organizations. She said:

> It begins with transforming our underlying approach to capital, away from an approach where individuals and institutions have the right to endlessly accumulate capital and make decisions on how it should be allocated for the public good and towards an approach where the collective capacity of communities most impacted by extraction and exploitation are able to produce them themselves, give to and invest directly in what their communities need and retain the returns generated from these investments.

We are still a long way from finding sustainable methods for doing creative activist work with young people outside of the traditional nonprofit organizational structure, but I am inspired by the work of activists and organizers of color who have, by the necessity of struggling to survive within a racist world, found new ways to reimagine allocation of resources.

Author and social justice activist Sonya Renee Taylor launched *The Body is Not An Apology* (2018), a powerful initiative that includes workshops, trainings, presentations, books, and consulting work. When asked why she incorporated as a for-profit benefit corporation and not a tax-exempt nonprofit organization, she brilliantly preached:

1) I believe social change needs to be at the center of our economic systems, not the margins.
2) Those doing the most impacting work should not have to scramble in competition for small pots of foundation funding.
3) As long as equity and justice work is considered "charity" it will always be what we fund last and cut first.
4) I know that if we leverage our resources we have the collective economic and social power to ensure that everybody with a body has what they need to thrive.

Though it is beyond the scope of this book to imagine healthy and sustainable alternatives to the nonprofit industrial complex, I am inspired by those radical thinkers and artists such as Sonya Renee Taylor and Toya Lillard who are manifesting new ways of engaging in reciprocal, community-building, creative practices that nurture both the artists and the audiences and are supported by the communities who have the most at stake in their success.

When I consider all the different ways that audiences appear, support, interact, and engage with the theater created by teenagers, I offer an alternative way of answering the question, "Who needs to hear this?" that we ask so often. The assumption sometimes is that the person who needs to hear is the person who needs to change, but maybe the person who needs to hear these words is also the person who needs to heal, and listening to stories that they relate to and connect with allows them to feel less alone.

Notes

1 un.org
2 raceforward.org
3 trainingforchange.org
4 peoplesaction.org
5 embracerace.org
6 ihollaback.org
7 "Power mapping" is an often-used and highly effective campaign tool for identifying who has the power to make the change you want to see, and then literally

mapping the other people closest to that person and developing targeted strategies for fostering relationships and connecting with each person along the map. "A power map reveals avenues of influence available to an organization. The method allows a group to see how a particular target is influenced and to see connections between these influences" (Democracy for America Training Academy, pp. 150–152). Often for marginalized folks, the people who most need to hear their stories are the ones with the power to actually do something to shift their circumstances and end the systemic oppressions they struggle with. The power map helps us see the layers of relationships and connections we already have in order to get closer and closer to the person with the power to make the change.

8 Receiving grant money from foundations often requires extensive labor in the writing of the grant proposals, managing site visits, assessing the project to the guidelines of the foundation and submitting a final grant report. Additionally, many foundation grants are restricted to "program expenses" and often cannot be used for core and essential expenses such as rent, salaries, insurance, or fundraising expenses. In contrast, money that individual donors give can be spent on anything and rarely if ever demands follow up beyond an official thank you letter that the donor can use for a tax write-off.

Conclusion

Ripples of change

Theater and change: impacting the audience

> Every year after every program, the girls have to perform the play [that they've written] in front of their school staff – the principal and the teachers and the students. At [Oladele's charter school] they had a rule that stated that you couldn't wear head wraps, that head wraps were unprofessional, and they weren't allowed on school grounds. And Oladele, as a Nigerian-born girl, was just like, "This doesn't make any sense. Like what's going on?" And I was like, "Yea, I feel you. So, what do you want to do about it? You want to write something about it?" She was like, "Yeah. I'm gonna write something about it." And so, she wrote something and the week before we had to perform, she came to me with like, "I don't know if I can do this." … But she did it. She did it very beautifully and the principal saw the poem. She saw the performance and within the next week, the ban was lifted. Yeah. You can wear head wraps every day. And Oladele, the best part about that story is that Oladele was a freshman when it happened. So, she got to enjoy the four years of her high school career being able to be in her head wrap because of something that she did and the power that she took back. So, yeah.
>
> (interview)

With smiles and tears, I listen to this recording from my interview with viBe Theater Experience's artistic director Monique Letamendi. Girls are using theater to change the world, I now can write. And yes, there are other stories such as Oladele's where a girl sees injustice, has the support and the resources to use performance, shares her story, speaks her truth to power, and a policy is changed. Theater works. Case closed.

Yet this is one story of hundreds, maybe thousands. Yes, it happens. But what if Oladele had spent months creating her poem, then performed it, then … nothing happened. The headwrap ban persisted. Would it have been a "failure?" Check the "no change" box? How much control did Oladele really have over her principal? If the metric is about evaluating exactly how a specific process or production ignited a specific shift in policy or mass awareness–raising and activist cultivation, excluding Oladele's amazing accomplishment, the girls' performance projects in this book would seem an insignificant sweat drop in the ocean of social change. When I reflect on how I assess whether one of our shows had the intended impact, I try to imagine all the different possibilities for what might have been happening for audiences. For Oladele's poem, the intended audience member who had the power to make change was her principal, but her performance was likely just as impactful for students witnessing one of their peers bravely speaking out to critique something unfair. It is quite literally tossing change into a fountain. The first splash might be hitting your target, but the ripples continue to move the water.

I have lingered in the aisles, in the lobbies, in the restrooms, outside the subway entrances after productions and listened to countless audience members grab my hand, hug me or lean in close to tell me that the performance they just saw has changed the way they think about public schools, about racism, about gentrification, about girls. They have promised me that, after listening to the performance, they would now treat their daughter, their student, their sister, their neighbor differently. Did I call them six months later to check in about how they had changed their behavior? Did I track them through surveys or emails or requests for interviews? No. I have scant evidence that would hold up in a court of law or even on a grant report to document these ripples of social or personal change. And yet, the enthusiasm from girls and their audiences who keep returning, keeps me going. The trust I have in how change actually begins and functions in the world – the performance might not be the bonfire that burns down the systems of corruption and oppression, but it can be the crackle of the spark that strikes the first match.

I want the theater we make to offer clear paths for audiences to hear the narratives in our performances, learn strategies for how to make necessary changes in themselves and then understand how to apply those changes in their greater community to collectively build towards social justice. The stories are the beginning, but the collective performance and call to action are the wings to let the meaning soar. Not every show has such a specific demand as Oladele's, but every story likely offers the possibility of change. Theater can be a funhouse of stories, filled with different sized mirrors that expand and contract and swirl around, so each viewer sees themself reflected or distorted or represented through a cacophony of tones and lenses. Yet even within theater's ability to hold multiple truths and this dizzying array of stories, there is never a magical guarantee that by hearing any one story, audience members will spontaneously change their mind about an issue and jump up to take action.

Applied theatre scholar Dani Snyder-Young replaces the sugary coated "theater-can-change-the-world" mantra with a healthy spoonful of wasabi. It burns at first, makes my eyes water, but then after an initial jolt, everything goes back to the way it was. As one example of asking a play to carry the weight of social change, Snyder-Young writes about a Chicago production that addressed the dangers of gentrification in a rapidly changing urban neighborhood, and its potential to change the hearts and/or minds of middle-class, white, likely gentrifying audience members. She analyzed the experience of a talk-back following the production that revealed that the white, privileged audience members seemed to be wearing "blinders that prevented [them] from really hearing what the play was trying to say." She continues:

> When change would potentially cause an audience member stress and anx-
> iety, they actively avoid it. As a result, privileged audience members interpret
> theatrical performances in ways supporting their existing worldviews, even
> if it requires ignoring substantial elements of the world they have seen … If
> spectators put their own view of the world on the theatre they watch, the
> power of hegemonic discourse and structural oppression undermines the
> political efficacy of artistic projects with goals of making progressive social
> change … Theatre is not enough; change has to happen in the real world.
>
> (2018, p. 300)

Theater is one byway among many on the path of life's journey. It is not meant to be the final destination, but as part of life's adventure, it might be a useful rest stop, recharging station, or detour that sets us on a different path. Engagement in the theater, whether as an audience member, writer or performer is unlikely to be the solitary experience that ignites personal or political revolution, but the process itself of either witnessing or creating stories that resonate, can connect us to ourselves and to others and reveal our shared humanity with an audi-ence. This change is not instant, will not happen overnight, or possibly even over years, but through the performance process, new stories about how we survive, co-exist, and thrive become part of us all as we move forward through the world and make choices that impact ourselves and others. Theater director Anne Bogart writes:

> Artists and scientists are activists. They look at the world as changeable and
> they look upon themselves as instruments for change. They understand that
> the slice of world they occupy is only a fragment but that the fragment is
> intrinsically connected to the whole. They know that action matters.
>
> (2014, p. 12)

It is my belief that the experiences at the intersection of performance and activism, plant "story seeds" in both the artists and audiences. These seedlings might grow up and sprout into new understandings about race, class, capitalism, and gentrification that could ignite certain audience members to engage in anti-gentrification protest or in drafting and passing legislation to protect local businesses and families. Or they might stay as small seeds, buried for months or years until a day when one of those audience members makes the choice to buy her coffee at the local café instead of the new Starbucks. And for others, as Snyder-Young's example implies, the seed might just settle there and never take root. But assuming the messages of the production failed because the audi-ence could not articulate how they were changed in the minutes following the production, misunderstands how people can evolve over time. You can't turn from red to blue without spending quite some time, splashing around in shades of purple. Just because change is not visible immediately, does not mean it has not already been seeded.

Theater and change: impacting the girls

When I look at my own practice, my own political awakening, and my perceived impact on my community, I see the slow and gentle progression of my values and beliefs crystallizing over decades while I was taking risks, making mistakes, reading books, seeing theater, making theater, finding support, talking with people, making more theater, watching films and discovering my own voice and personal mission. Can I pinpoint any specific moments or conversations or pieces of art I consumed where I can say with confidence, "This! This is what *changed* me from an entitled, privileged, sheltered, white girl to a confident, theater-producing activist who (tries to) stand up to injustice in the world!" Sigh. No. Life is not a math equation where $x + y = z$. Sometimes we get to z without y at all. Or we never get to z, because we realize x was actually ok. For me, actually, when I'm really thinking about what *impacted* me or when I might ever authentically use the phrase "... and that totally changed my life," I remember and reflect most upon the mistakes I made and then the new, wobbly, fawn steps I took toward rediscovering how to move forward after.

As a kid, I was given space to use art and theater as tools to help me make sense of the world. There were two experiences that, in 20+ years of hindsight, did reroute me onto my current path, the first very immediately and the second, much, much more sloth-like, taking-a-week-to-crawl-down-a-tree slowly. As a 17-year-old high school senior, feeling somewhat dismissed and overlooked, I directed a production of Peter Schaffer's *Equus*, a play that I used as my mouthpiece to critique what I felt were people with power not recognizing and respecting the energy and passion of me and my friends. I cast a girl in the role of a man and felt that I was pushing against gendered assumptions about women and power, though I can now recognize I was also trying to make sense of my own insecurities about what I felt girls could achieve. That experience was "transformative" for me in that it literally transformed my life goals and my confidence in my abilities as a creative leader.

Before the *Equus* project, I saw myself as a passionate but mediocre actor and decent designer who loved theater, but did not really see it as a viable future life or career. I was frustrated by the lack of agency I felt in my collaborations with well-intentioned adult directors and took it upon myself to do something differently. By deciding I was going to produce and direct a full show, something no one my age that I knew personally had ever done, I had my first real experience as a leader. It was scary, I was intimidated. I remember being up all night before the first rehearsal, overpreparing and trying to stage the whole show in my notebook and terrified that one of the actors (aka: my closest friends) would ask me a question I couldn't answer and reveal me to be a fraud and a kid in over my head. But as the rehearsal weeks went by, I trusted my instincts more and more, and also started to see through example and experience that my not having the answer all the time was not a sign I was a "bad director," but that inviting the ensemble and design team into the process and co-answering the questions demanded by the script, we were actually collaborating and finding creative solutions together, better than any of us could have done on our own. I walked away from the process with a new framework for what the role of the director is in a production, and then significantly over time, I can also see how this experience as a novice director started to shape choices and behaviors I was making in my life outside the theater. I was discovering new tools for resolving conflicts among my friends. I was becoming a better listener. I was confidently taking on leadership roles at college and later, in my career.

So, it was theater, right?! Theater set me on this path. Well, yes. And, no. As an overachieving, ambitious, and self-motivated student, I was already primed to seek out new opportunities and to test my capacity in new situations. I was raised by loving and generous parents who always told me I could do anything I set my mind to and supported my dreams both emotionally and finan-cially. I had excellent teachers and role models along the way who guided me, supported me, validated me, looked like me, and provided both mirrors and windows into possible lives I could follow them into. I can say I was taking risks, but in reality, the stakes were low. If I failed as a theater director, I would likely have found another outlet and worked my way into a different passion, discip-line, or career. Certainly, theater helped, and gave me a viable container for my creativity, visions, and values.

Then, at 18, as I began to imagine ways theater could also be a vehicle for the social justice work I was equally passionate about, I took a directing Shakespeare class in college. There, I created a project that now fills me with fear and dread when I imagine the possibility of leaked photographs from the production and I exhale with relief that I could explore, be vulnerable, make painful mistakes, and learn from them decades before social media sites like Twitter, TikTok, or Instagram could document shame-filled images or texts that could later destroy me. As a white teenage girl, I was "discovering" racism and sexism and how understandings and misunderstandings of power corrupt, warp and poison our relationships and our actions. As a theater activist, I felt charged up and ready to make performances expressing my eager, uninformed musings about racism and patriarchy. For one of my class projects, I decided to focus on these issues.

Without much research or consultation with any Black people, I created a mash-up performance project where I took text from *Othello* and text from *Romeo and Juliet* and crafted a script where the characters Othello and Juliet meet and interact. That might have been fine, but I went further. Too far. I cast a white cisgender, straight man as Juliet and a white woman as Othello and began with the actors putting on their make-up, which consisted of "Othello" rubbing dark brown foundation over her pale white skin until she was entirely in Blackface and "Juliet" smearing excessive purple eye shadow, pink blush and red lipstick over his features in a mockery of a hyper-femme aesthetic. The performance spiraled gulpingly downward from there. There were nods to minstrelsy and bows to appropriated gay male, effeminate posing. I remember feeling like I was doing something daring and being excited to share it. At the time, I was proud of the performance and it was praised by my professor and fellow students. I got an A in the class. I don't remember when, over time, I began to remember it with a suckerpunch of nausea in my stomach. I was wrong. Dangerously wrong, and I made an inexcusable and unjustifiable mistake with this project. I cannot defend it through the lens of my youth or that "it was a different time." I am sorry I made that piece. I take full responsibility and I wish I could apologize to all of the Black people and queer people whom I likely offended through my racist and homophobic choices, ignoring centuries of violent oppression and assuming race, gender and sexuality were performances that could be applied (and removed) like liquid foundation. In very different ways, this project changed me, too. Not the kind of change I would write about in a grant report, but the kind of deep soul excavating change that contributed to my shift from talking about how racism is bad to actually taking actions in my life to work toward dismantling it. The crawling self-awareness that I had unintentionally created something racist, pushed me to see how white people like myself do harm all the time and that we need to make greater efforts to interrupt and repair that harm.

I share these stories to show how challenging it is for individuals to recognize moments that led to change, and yet we ask this of theater projects all the same. What did it actually change? Where is your evidence? The principal changed the unjust policy? Great, change accomplished! She didn't? Sorry, no change. When considering this question of impact, I refer readers to the *Research In Drama Education*'s special 2007 issue, and Michael Etherton and Tim Prentki's editorial introduction with the provocative title, "Drama for Change? Prove It! Impact Assessment in Applied Theatre." They write:

> Where there is no message or issue at the heart of the process but rather the encouragement to the community to develop self-confidence and assume control over their own lives, to transform themselves, in other words, from the objects into the subjects of their development, it is much more difficult to assess whether such a personal transformation has led, in the long term, to the wider social impact envisaged. Some applied theatre activists maintain that personal transformation is all that they should properly aim for; and that social impact is for other kinds of agency.
>
> (Etherton & Prentki, 2006, p. 147)

I take Etherton and Prentki's words, as well as research focusing on individual young people's capacity to change through engagement in activist programs, to heart for the work that I do, and as I have written throughout this book, I will synthesize again here: I have found that collaboratively creating activist performances might not always change the world in specific and measurable ways, but it is likely to have an impact on the girls who create it, and the people in their immediate circles. And those girls might then take the skills, confidence, relationships, and experiences they had in their theater processes and use them for further social justice work. The creativity and agency they practiced through their activist theatermaking become prized tools in the toolbox they will use throughout their lives. And the world will change. We just need to let go of the pressure to name and document every rung on the ladder.

In another example, Marti, a recent college graduate who had participated in activist theater with The Arts Effect's All-Girl Theater Company while she was in high school, shared:

> I truly think that I wouldn't be where I am today without [co-directors] Katie and Meg, and without the Arts Effect. Growing up, I was always into dance. I was always into theater. But in middle school we were putting on shows like Grease, and [The Arts Effect], it really changed the way I interact with the people in my life as I grew into a kind of political theater activist. Theater that was talking very honestly and very vulnerably about things that we as young women were facing … So, I came into, I came into my time at [college] knowing that I wanted to study political science, I wanted to study women, gender and sexuality studies … I'm seeing a future in politics or a future in law as something that I'm really excited to do. And all of that is because of this foundation that Katie and Meg lay out for us.
>
> (interview)

Twenty years from now, Marti might be in a position of power in the world, in government or business or law and her future actions might have worldwide consequences. She might write legislation or sit on a bench as a judge and her experiences as a teenage theater activist might inform the decisions she makes that impact the lives of the most vulnerable people.

In the applied theatre field, focusing on changing the individuals who hold most of the power might sometimes feel upside down when engaging in process-based performance projects with marginalized folks. In "participant-centered" models of theater making, the burden of change often seems to lay in this vague, hard-to-quantify goal of "transformation" (Nicholson, 2005; Taylor, 2003) and we struggle to precisely articulate the ways that performance might have ripples of impact across different communities and classes of people.

Australian applied theatre practitioner and scholar Michael Balfour (2009) breaks down the implications of applied theatre projects where the actual theatermaking is tangential to individual transformation goals, often problematically mandated by the donors or funding agencies. He argues:

> in resisting the bait of social change, rehabilitation, behavioural objectives and outcomes, perhaps (and it is a small perhaps), applied practice might more readily encounter the accidental, and acknowledge that what applied

[theater] does is not always linear, rational and conclusive in its outcomes, but is more often messy, incomplete, complex and tentative.

(p. 357)

Absent any archive of data that promises to unquestionably prove that because of any one, single theater project, a particular young person or a specific piece of legislation was spun around in a 180 degree change of heart and doctrine (and as a passionately and unabashedly qualitative researcher), I lean on the stories. The arcs of complicated and sometimes fulfilling lives that stretch over time with occasional sprouts of radical joy and extreme productivity and dip down into depths of depression, apathy, and destructive behavior. The experience of being heard, of being taken seriously, validated in a public space and witnessing the potential of your story's impact, matters.

Where is the evidence?

In my original imagining of this book, I envisioned an epilogue chapter that would answer the question, "Where are they now?" with delightful vignettes about how the girls I wrote about in earlier pages have grown up into accomplished, agentic, fulfilled superstars who speak their mind, confidently pursue their dreams and engage in practices to improve their communities. I started reaching out to adult women with whom I had collaborated as teenagers to try to learn if and how they made sense of their past theater experiences and how these experiences might have impacted any part of their lives today. As I saw their faces on Zoom, I noticed how much and how little they seemed to have changed in the past five, ten, or 15 years since I'd last seen them. We laughed and cried together as we remembered all the special moments we had shared and how much we had grown. You have a daughter now?! You're a teacher in the school you graduated from?! You're still best friends with Toni?! You married Cedric, that boyfriend you were dating in high school?! Oh my God, YES, I saw Kristy in the Fame movie, wasn't she amazing! I was flooded with so many feelings and a face aching from my stretched smiles. I knew I could never attempt or want to fit these stories into boxes that quantitative, longitudinal studies would want me to check. How many former girls graduated from college? How many were never incarcerated? How many work in social justice fields? How many have leadership jobs? How many completed graduate school? How many voted in the last election? How many volunteer at least once a month? How many own a blazer? Own a computer? Own a car? Own a home? How many? How many? How many? How many?

I burn with frustration at the assumptions so many of these studies make about what is important to count and to track, and how we can attempt to quantify personal growth and transformation as if it happens on a bar graph with an encouraging line reaching from the lower left to the upper right corner. I remember the ways we had talked about change, power, and structural oppressions as we attempted to challenge injustice in the projects we made together and I see how so many of those systemic injustices we discussed when they were teenagers are as strong as ever, a decade later. I could share the stories about Raine. Raine, a radiant Black girl who never held back from speaking her mind, was deeply involved with viBe and had written and performed in productions every year of high school. She burned with confidence and rage and once wrote and recorded a song with us called, "I hate you," whose lyrics included:

> Wait, stop, let's think for a minute
> It's my world, bitch, I just let you live in it.
> I'm running the show, I'm the coach of the team
> I'm a motherfucking queen if you know what I mean
> I'm not 50 Cent, but I run New York now
> And you're just lucky I won't kick your ass out.

I remember one day I was surprised to see her arrive really early to rehearsal to work on our show. I asked if she didn't have school that day and she just simply stated, "Oh, I stopped going to school. It's boring." I paused and asked what she was doing all day if she wasn't in school and she told me, "I've been writing a novel." I asked if I could read it and within a week, she sent me an amazing manuscript, a 300-page novel about drama among teenagers in Brooklyn. It was brilliantly written and an extraordinary accomplishment. She wasn't failing school, school was failing her. Yet the theater was a space she could thrive. She eventually did graduate high school, is now completing her dissertation to earn her PhD in psychology, and she is a professor teaching college courses such as Psychology of Oppression. When I asked if she would meet with me for an interview for this book, she said she was interested, but the timing never worked out because she was on vacation in Tulum, Mexico, Facebook photos showing her radiating joy and calm on a beach at sunset. Was it the theater space that allowed her to explore her creativity or her own self-motivation that drove her to write a novel? Or was it her supportive parents who came to every show and stood by her? Our joys and successes don't come with a DNA strand claiming "33 percent parental support, 18 percent white privilege, 9 percent my kindergarten teacher, 22 percent nondisabled body, 6 percent talent, 12 percent that theater program I did when I was 14."

As important as it is to share stories of traditional "success" such as Raine's trajectory, I never want to imply that the only ways to quantify "success" are through higher education, middle-class jobs, and luxury vacations. The fact that Rosemary, as a 30-year-old Black woman is still living in the same public housing apartment she had grown up in and is struggling to piece together a livable income from one retail job to the next, does not mean our activist theater project "failed" or that Rosemary "failed." It means we still live in a world where race, class, gender, and immigration barriers are nearly impossible to surpass (Bronfrenbrenner, 1979).

For girls like Rosemary, the additional obstacles she faced throughout her life were likely beyond what a performance project could reverse. Yet before drawing a conclusion that if theater isn't going to "save" a girl, why bother, I still see traces of the pride and excitement Rosemary has maintained when she talks about music and singing. Rosemary's unique, gorgeous voice is a bellowing, ruby-toned, pitch-perfect one and to this day, I still listen to the songs she recorded with us and the powerful content of her lyrics and her singing lifts my spirits and makes me smile even in my dreariest moments. Her performance had changed *me*. I ran into her on a Brooklyn street corner a couple of years ago and she lit up when she saw me and my son. We laughed together and shared memories and I told her how her music still pierces my heart. She asked if I had any copies of the CD she recorded way back when and I promised to send her a few. She said she wanted to share it with her boyfriend and was thinking about starting to sing again. Maybe the performances she created as a teenager are offering her positive energy and motivation and strengthening her relationships. Maybe she'll record again and impact more listeners. Or maybe she'll sing to and with the people she loves and music will bring them joy.

I could write about Clara, one of our rare young white, middle-class women whose trajectory in the five years since we made shows together include graduating from an elite, private university and securing a competitive entry-level job at a progressive consulting agency. Was it her theater experiences that gave her the cultural capital, creative literacy skills, and belief in herself to soar through early adulthood? Possibly. Or as a white girl who attended well-funded schools with ample arts opportunities and parents with the resources to seek out and pay for extracurricular theater programs, summer camps, and girls' leadership opportunities, was she already primed to excel through school and beyond? She had a unique opportunity to participate in a theater program from the age of five through high school where she wrote plays with her peers, with the help of an inspiring and supportive teacher. She grew up with that theater program and articulated the role of theater in her development, reflecting,

> Having done theater for so long, I sort of had more of an ability to stand up for myself … I think theater is one of the worlds where if you demonstrate you're willing to work hard, it usually is rewarded.

For white, middle-class girls like Clara – and me, yes. When invited to reflect back on her interview, she later added:

> I don't necessarily believe that all hard work gets rewarded in the theater. I've seen plenty of hard-working kids get screwed over. The theater and its powerbrokers are certainly not immune to racism, sexism, classism, ableism, and so on. I do believe that the theater world is open enough that people who don't fit into societal standards and who deeply love the work are sometimes able to carve out space for self-expression and be rewarded in some capacity.

I also must chime in here and state that Clara, even with all her privileges, was also a girl who worked extremely hard. She was one of the smartest, most motivated, generous, passionate, and ambitious teenagers I have ever worked with. And it's not that her family never struggled – her grandmother was forced into a marriage at 14 and by the age of 28 had had ten pregnancies and seven children. Clara's mother was a strong and inspiring role model who had overcome significant obstacles in her life and gently encouraged her, but Clara also sought out opportunities for herself along the way. She was one of the girl advocates at the United Nations when I first met her and was writing her own speeches and presenting them in massive UN negotiation rooms, advocating in front of world leaders on behalf of girls' issues worldwide and holding adults accountable. Her experiences as a performer and playwright offered her additional tools for her to sharpen her public speaking skills and better articulate her thoughts and ideas. She has a deep awareness of her own racial privilege that she seemed to learn more about through her diverse theater and activist experiences as an adolescent along with her experience at a progressive women's college. She is interested in pursuing a career in politics and policy and I have little doubt that she will continue to be part of social and political justice movements that will lead to legislative and policy change that could impact the lives of people more marginalized than she. When I shared these past paragraphs with Clara, she responded in an email:

> The way you wove my story into this chapter is really interesting, particularly with the comparison to Rosemary. In this excerpt, you ask whether I was primed to succeed in school and in my career. I can say with all certainty that yes, I was not only primed for the life I am living, but expected to reach a certain level of success. It's very striking how much my background informed my present and the privilege that that carries. In my current self-work, I'm attempting to detach my achievements from my self-worth, and I am constantly confronted by the ways that capitalism shapes the way we interpret our value.

Clara's wise words remind me yet again of the ways certain privileges pave a well-worn path toward a capitalist definition of "success," and the buried costs to both achieving and not achieving these "rewards." For girls like Clara and others who spend lifetimes pushing themselves forward along competitive career tracks, there is the potential to ignite mental health ruptures related to binding one's identity with one's career. These repercussions might lead to stress, anxiety, and depression or a lifetime of feeling just never quite good enough. Girls leadership expert Rachel Simmons (2018) addresses many of these issues and offers strategies for guiding girls to healthily overcome them in her book, *Enough As She Is: How to Help Girls Move Beyond Impossible Standards of Success to Live Healthy, Happy, and Fulfilling Lives.*

From the King James Bible to Voltaire to the most common attribution of Peter Parker (aka: Spiderman)'s Uncle Ben, we recognize the significance of the teaching: "With great power, comes great responsibility." I have never forgotten an experience I had when I was an undergraduate student at Brown participating in a volunteer program called SPACE (Space in Prison for the Arts and Creative Expression) where, along with many other students, we would create and facilitate arts workshops with women incarcerated at the Rhode Island women's prison. Roberta Richmond, an artist, and leader committed to criminal justice reform, was the extraordinary warden at the time. During our orientation with her, she stood before us, a cluster of mostly white, very earnest 19, 20, and 21-year-olds, and told us how she really felt about our presence there. She said something like (it was 20+ years ago and I don't remember the exact words, but the message was crystal clear):

> Welcome. You all think you're coming here to change the world. You think your theater and poetry and dance workshops are going to change these women's lives. You think they're going to leave prison and never return because of what *you* taught them about art and creative expression. That they'll build confidence and trust themselves and each other. Maybe. But unlikely. I greenlight this program every year, not for what it will do for the women, but for what it will do for *you*. You all are going to graduate with your Ivy League degrees and you are going to be the ones who run the world. You will run companies. You will serve as judges. You will be in executive positions where you have the power to hire people. And because of your experience *here,* you will remember these women. You will never forget that they have dreams, families, intelligence, passion, generosity and humanity. And when you can, you will hire them. You will support them. You will advocate for them. *That* is why you are here doing your theater workshops.

And she was right. I have never forgotten them, and I think about some of my friends who I co-facilitated with who are now college professors, lawyers, journalists, and health care professionals and I have seen the threads of our experiences at the Adult Correctional Institution weave through their lives. I remembered Warden Richmond's words recently when one of the women from that cohort posted on Facebook that she was organizing volunteer book drives for people incarcerated in prisons, and another was recently telling me about the compassionate and healing work she does as a psychiatric nurse at a public hospital.

I hope it goes without saying at this point that the point of engaging in performance work with marginalized people is absolutely not solely for the benefit of the privileged facilitators. Yet, I offer these stories as contributions to the ecosystem of change and name the usefulness of recognizing the potential impact creating theater has on different players within the project. It is not the job of the marginalized to convince people with power that they are human and deserve the same levels of support and care as everyone else in our communities. And yet, we unfortunately live in a world where the systemic dehumanization of Black and Brown people is too rampant.

As I am writing these final pages of this book, a Facebook message pops up on my screen from a former girl (now woman) who had been in many viBe shows in the early 2000s. A few days after the murder of yet another Black teenager by a police officer's gun, she writes:

> So I've been thinking about this for a while now but tonight I feel like it's time to really take action on it. I'm considering starting a program in Columbus, Ohio similar to viBe. The program was therapeutic for myself and others and I feel now more than ever girls where I am can benefit from that form of expression. I was wondering if you would have time at some point to set up a call with me and let me pick your brain a bit about the steps you and chandra took to get the ball rolling and allow me to bounce some ideas that I have off of you.

With tears in my eyes, I replied an exuberant YES, and we connected and started a conversation about how she might create spaces for girls in her community to share their stories, to be heard.

Where do we go from here?

Girls dip their quills in the bloody pools of heart juice to write their lives
Ink on paper
Pencil scratch in diaries
Thumb clicks of a text message
Girls have been telling stories
To any and every one who is ready to listen
Listening to girls requires ears that tilt downward
Lean in close for a whisper or back up for a snort
Listening to girls requires volume that matches their laughter
Lips that can smirk curls around the corners
Eyebrows that know the route north
At high speed when called for
I've been listening to girls
Since I was a girl
My white, wrinkled skin is at first a gatekeeper challenging me and her
To defy expectations of what I can hear
And what she can say

As I search for a container for my final thoughts, I follow my own directives to the girls I make theater with. What do I need to say? Who needs to hear it? How do I want to say it? I think about *you*, my audience who has traveled

with me along this journey as I make sense of how girls are using performance, demanding to be heard. I consider what it takes to listen to them, to be in
relationship with them, to support them to find the most creative vehicles for
their urgent voices. And I consider, deeply, all the ways that I have shown up in
this work. My whiteness, my age, my education, my access. As a white woman
who has been creating theater with Black and Brown girls for so long, I am
recognizing my responsibility to step back from leadership roles in this field, to
support and offer guidance (when invited) to the Black women who are long
overdue to get the resources they need to step fully into their power. As we have
witnessed a racial justice revolution rise up around many parts of the world
this year, conversations about whiteness, white privilege, and white supremacy
are rampant in my communities. As I ask myself how I can best be a true ally,
accomplice, and co-conspirator in this movement, the girl I am listening to
most is my 14-year-old self. I am pulled and drawn and called to her voice and
the voices of her white friends trying to make sense of the segregation, racism,
and inequality around them, the shame, vulnerability, and self-silencing about
what their own roles have been in upholding this world that was benefiting
them and hindering their neighbors.

I am ready to pivot again, to choose-my-own-adventure to the page I've yet
to turn to. I can smell the seeds of my next project, a devised theater performance with white, middle-class, teenage girls where we will start the unpacking
and necessary process of acknowledging the harm we have done and using performance to imagine and manifest our way through to a new world. I believe
in our theatermaking and trust this is the process I know and love best to use
our stories to transform ourselves and our communities.

Works cited

A Long Walk Home. (2020). www.alongwalkhome.org

Aapola, S., Gonick, M., & Harris, A. (2005). *Young Femininity: Girlhood, Power and Social Change*. New York, NY: Palgrave Macmillan.

Action Play. (2019, January 15). https://actionplay.org/about-us/

Allardice, L. (2018, May 12). Jesmyn Ward: "Black Girls Are Silenced, Misunderstood and Underestimated." *The Guardian*. www.theguardian.com/books/2018/may/11/jesmyn-ward-home-mississippi-living-with-addiction-poverty-racism

Alrutz, M. & Hoare, L. (2020). *Devising Critically Engaged Theatre with Youth*. New York, NY & Abingdon: Routledge.

American Association of University Women. (1992). *How Schools Shortchange Girls*. Washington, DC: AAUW Educational Foundation.

American Psychological Association. (2007). *Report of the Task Force On The Sexualization of Girls*. Washington, DC: APA.

Bagcal, J. (2018, December 20). Student from York College in Jamaica named NYC's 2019 Youth Poet Laureate. QNS.com. https://qns.com/2018/12/student-york-college-jamaica-named-nycs-2019-youth-poet-laureate/

Balfour, M. (2004). *Theatre in Prison: Theory and Practice*. Portland, OR: Intellect Books.

Balfour, M. (2009). The Politics of Intention: Looking for a Theatre of Little Changes. *RIDE: The Journal of Applied Theatre and Performance*. 14(3), 347–359.

Bandura, A. (1997). *Self-Efficacy: The Exercise of Control* (1st edn). New York, NY: Worth Publishers.

Banham, M. (2004). *A History of Theatre in Africa*. Cambridge: Cambridge University Press.

Barrett, Q. L. (2020). Re-Writing the Declaration. Quennalene.com. www.quennalene.com/re-writing-the-declaration

Beare, D. & Belliveau, G. (2007). Theatre for Positive Youth Development: A Development Model for Collaborative Play-creating. *Applied Theatre Researcher/ IDEA Journal*. 8, 1–16.

Beauboeuf-Lafontant, T. (2009). *Behind the Mask of the Strong Black Woman: Voice and the Embodiment of a Costly Performance*. Philadelphia, PA: Temple University Press.

Behar, R. (1996). *The Vulnerable Observer: Anthropology that Breaks Your Heart*. Boston, MA: Beacon Press.

Bent, E. (2013). A Different Girl Effect: Producing Political Girlhoods in the "Invest in Girls" Climate. *Studies of Children and Youth*. 16, 3–20.

Bent, E. (2019). Unfiltered and Unapologetic: March for Our Lives and the Political Boundaries of Age. *Jeunesse: Young People, Texts, Cultures*. 11(2), 55–73.

Bickerstaff, S., Barragan, M., & Rucks-Ahidiana, Z. (2012). "I Came in Unsure of Everything": Community College Students' Shifts in Confidence. CCRC Working Paper No. 48. Community College Research Center, Columbia University.

Black Women's Blueprint. (2011). An Open Letter from Black Women to the SlutWalk. www.huffpost.com/entry/slutwalk-black-women_b_980215.

Blanchet-Cohen, N. & Rainbow, B. (2006). Partnership between Children and Adults? The Experience of the International Children's Conference on the Environment. *Childhood. 13*(1), 113–126.

Bluhm, J. (2012). Seventeen Magazine: Give Girls Images of Real Girls. change.org

Blumenkrantz, D. (2016). *Coming of Age the RITE Way: Youth and Community Development Through Rites of Passage.* Oxford: Oxford University Press.

Boal, A. (1979). *Theatre of the Oppressed* (C. A. & M. L. McBride, Trans.). New York, NY: Theatre Communications Group.

Bogart, A. (2001). *A Director Prepares: Seven Essays on Art and Theatre.* New York, NY: Routledge.

Bogart, A. (2014). *What's the Story? Essays About Art, Theater and Storytelling.* Abingdon & New York, NY: Routledge.

Bogart, A. & Landau, T. (2005). *The Viewpoints: A Practical Guide to Viewpoints and Composition.* New York, NY: Theatre Communications Group.

Brenner, L., Ceraso, C., & Cruz, E. D. (2021). *Applied Theatre with Youth: Education, Engagement, Activism.* New York, NY & Abingdon: Routledge.

Brice, P. (2017, January 25). TED Talk: Using play for everyday activism. www.mattiebrice.com/ted-talk-using-play-for-everyday-activism/

Brodkin, K. (1998). *How Jews Became White Folks and What that Says about Race in America.* New Brunswick, NJ: Rutgers University Press.

Bronfrenbrenner, U. (1979). *The Ecology of Human Development: Experiments by Nature and Design.* Cambridge, MA: Harvard University Press.

brown, a. m. (2019). *Pleasure Activism: The Politics of Feeling Good.* Chico, CA & Edinburgh: AK Press.

Brown, L. M. (1998). *Raising their Voices: The Politics of Girls' Anger.* Cambridge, MA: Harvard University Press.

Brown, L. M. (2003). *Girlfighting: Betrayal and Rejection Among Girls.* New York, NY: New York University Press.

Brown, L. M. (2016). *Powered by Girl: A Field Guide for Supporting Youth Activists.* Boston, MA: Beacon Press.

Brown, L. M., Edell, D., Jones, M., Luckhurst, G., & Percentile, J. (2016). "'I Love Beyoncé, But I Struggle With Beyoncé': Girl Activists Talk Music and Feminism." In Warwick, J. & Adrian, A. (Eds), *Voicing Girlhood in Popular Music and Culture* (pp. 56–76). New York, NY & Abingdon: Routledge.

Brown, L. M. & Gilligan, C. (1992). *Meeting at the Crossroads: Women's Psychology and Girls' Development.* New York, NY: Ballantine Books.

Brown, R. N. (2009). *Black Girlhood Celebration: Toward a Hip-Hop Feminist Pedagogy.* New York, NY: Peter Lang.

Brown, R. N. (2013). *Hear Our Truths: The Creative Potential of Black Girlhood.* Urbana, Chicago, & Springfield, IL: University of Illinois Press.

Brown, R. N. & Kwakye, C. J. (2012). *Wish to Live: The Hip-Hop Feminism Pedagogy Reader.* New York, NY: Peter Lang.

Brown, R. N. & Lomax, T. (2020). Collectively Building Anew: The Department of African American and African Studies. https://cal.msu.edu/news/collectively-building-anew-the-department-of-african-american-and-african-studies

Brumberg, J. J. (1997). *The Body Project: An Intimate History of American Girls.* New York, NY: Random House.

Bryer, J. R. & Hartig, M. C. (2006). *Conversations with August Wilson (Literary Conversations)* (1st US-1st printing edn). Jackson, MS: University Press of Mississippi.

Business of Apps. (2020, October 30). TikTok Revenue and Usage Statistics. www.businessofapps.com/data/tik-tok-statistics/

Cahill, H. (2008). "Resisting Risk and Rescue as the Raison d'Etre for Arts Interventions." In O'Brien, Angela and Kate Donelan (Eds), *Arts and Youth At Risk: Global and Local Challenges* (pp. 13–31). Newcastle upon Tyne: Cambridge Scholars Publishing.

Cardi B. (2018). "I Do" [song]. On *Invasion of Privacy*. Atlantic Records.

Cargle, R. (2020, September 28). [Photo of quote by Rachel Cargle]. www.instagram.com/p/CFsPUOhnab7/?utm_source=ig_web_copy_link

Charlton, J. I. (2000). *Nothing About Us Without Us: Disability Oppression and Empowerment.* Berkeley, CA: University of California Press.

Chenowith, E. & Pressman, J. (2020, October 16). This Summer's Black Lives Matter Protesters Were Overwhelmingly Peaceful, Our Research Finds. *The Washington Post.*

Christensen, M. (2019). "Baby Suffragettes": Girls in the Women's Suffrage Movement across the Atlantic. *The Thetean: A Student Journal for Scholarly Historical Writing. 48*(1), 7.

Cohen-Cruz, J. (2005). *Local Acts: Community-Based Performance in the United States.* New Brunswick, NJ: Rutgers University Press.

Cohen-Cruz, J. (2006). "Storytelling: Redefining the Private: From Personal Storytelling to Political Act." In Cohen-Cruz, J. & Schutzman, M. (Eds), *A Boal Companion: Dialogues on Theatre and Cultural Politics* (pp. 103–113). New York, NY & Abingdon: Routledge.

Cole, T. (2012, March 8). Teju Cole [Tweet]. Twitter. https://twitter.com/tejucole/status/177810262223626241?lang=en

Coles, N. A., Larsen, J. T., & Lench, H. C. (2019). A Meta-Analysis of the Facial Feedback Literature: Effects of Facial Feedback on Emotional Experience are Small and Variable. *Psychological Bulletin. 145* (6), 610–651.

Collins, P. H. (2000). *Black Feminist Thought: Knowledge, Consciousness and the Politics of Empowerment.* London & New York, NY: Routledge.

Conner, T. S., DeYoung, C. G., & Silvia, P. J. (2016). Everyday Creative Activity as a Path to Flourishing. *The Journal of Positive Psychology. 13*(2), 181–189.

Conroy, C. (2009). *Theatre & The Body.* London: Red Globe Press.

Cox, A. M. (2015). *Shapeshifters: Black Girls and the Choreography of Citizenship.* Durham, NC: Duke University Press.

Cox, A. M. (2018). *Gender: Space.* New York, NY: Macmillan Interdisciplinary Handbooks.

Crenshaw, K. W. (1991). Mapping the Margins: Intersectionality, Identity Politics, and Violence Against Women of Color. *Stanford Law Review. 43*(6), 1241–1299.

Crenshaw, K. W., Ocen, P., & Nanda, J. (2015). *Black Girls Matter: Pushed Out, Overpoliced, and Underprotected.* New York, NY: Center for Intersectionality and Social Policy Studies, Columbia University.

Crenshaw, K. W. & Ritchie, A. J. (2015). "Say Her Name: Resisting Police Brutality Against Black Women." New York, NY: African American Policy Forum.

Davis, E. C. (2017). Making Movement Sounds: The Cultural Organizing Behind the Freedom Songs of the Civil Rights Movement (doctoral dissertation) https://dash.harvard.edu/handle/1/39987965

Davis, L. & Millman, J. (2012, May 12). 8th Grader Petitions Seventeen Magazine to Feature Un-Airbrushed Photos. ABC News. https://abcnews.go.com/Entertainment/8th-grader-petitions-seventeen-magazine-feature-airbrushed-photos/story?id=16266445

Democracy for America Training Academy. (2008). DFA Training Manual. http://uploads.democracyforamerica.com/0005/4009/DFA_Training_Manual_2008_-_Chapter_14_Power_Mapping.pdf

DiAngelo, R. (2018). *White Fragility: Why It's So Hard for White People to Talk About Racism.* Boston, MA: Beacon Press.

The DisAbility Project. (2020). That Uppity Theatre Company. www.uppityco.com/about-1

Durham, A. (2011, Spring/Summer). Hip Hop Feminist Media Studies. *International Journal of Africana Studies. 16*(1), 117–140.

Edell, D. (2010). "Say It How It Is": Urban Teenage Girls Challenge and Perpetuate Cultural Narratives by Writing and Performing Theater. (unpublished doctoral dissertation). New York University. New York, NY.

Edell, D. (2013). "Say It How It Is": Urban Teenage Girls Challenge and Perpetuate Stereotypes by Writing and Performing Theater. *Youth Theatre Journal. 27*(1), 51–62.

Edell, D. (2015). "Girl Uninterrupted: Using Interactive Voice Diaries as a New Girls' Studies Research Method." In Johnson, D. & Ginsberg, A. (Eds), *Difficult Dialogues About 21st Century Girls* (pp. 55–76). Albany, NY: SUNY Albany Press.

Edell, D. (2018). "Theatre and Girls' Resistance." In Cox, A. M. (Ed.), *Gender: Space* (211–224). New York, NY: Macmillan Interdisciplinary Handbooks.

Edell, D., Allicock, K., & Duran, L. (2021). "Listen to Us! Teenage Girls Creating Theatre for Social Change." In Brenner, L. S., Ceraso, C., & Cruz, E. D. (Eds), *Applied Theatre with Youth: Education, Engagement, Activism.* New York, NY & Abingdon: Routledge.

Edell, D., Brown, L. M., & Montano, C. (2016). Bridges, Ladders, Sparks, and Glue: Celebrating and Problematizing "Girl-driven" Intergenerational Feminist Activism. *Feminist Media Studies. 16*(4), 693–709.

Edell, D., Brown, L. M., & Tolman, D. L. (2013). Embodying Sexualisation: When Theory meets Practice in Intergenerational Feminist Activism. *Feminist Theory. 14*(3), 275–284.

Edell, D., Christophe, N., & Shawlin, T. (2018). "'This is Not A Safe Space': Sparking Change Through Activist Theater." In Talburt, S. (Ed.), *Youth Sexualities: Public Feelings and Contemporary Cultural Politics* (pp. 23–35). Santa Barbara, CA & Denver, CO: Praeger.

Einwohner, R. L., Hollander, J. A., & Olson, T. (2000). Engendering Social Movements: Cultural Images and Movement Dynamics. *Gender and Society. 14*(5), 679–699.

Ellis, C. & Bochner, A. P. (2017). "Foreword." In Pensoneau-Conway, S. L., Adams, T.E., & Bolen, D. M. (Eds), *Doing Autoethnography* (pp. vii–ix). Rotterdam, Boston, MA, & Taipei: SENSE Publishers.

Emdin, C. (2016). *For White Folks Who Teach in the Hood... And the Rest of Y'All Too.* Boston, MA: Beacon Press.

Erikson, E. H. (1968). *Identity: Youth and Crisis.* New York, NY: WW Norton & Co., Inc.

Erlick, E. (2018). Trans Youth Activism on the Internet. *Frontiers: A Journal of Women Studies. 39*(1), 73–92.

Etherton, M. & Prentki, T. (2006). Drama for Change? Prove it! Impact Assessment in Applied Theatre. *Research in Drama Education: The Journal of Applied Theatre and Performance. 11*(2), 139–155.

Fordham, S. (1993). "Those Loud Black Girls": (Black) Women, Silence, and Gender "Passing" in the Academy. *Anthropology & Education Quarterly. 24*(1), 3–32.

Fraden, R. (2001). *Imagining Medea: Rhodessa Jones and Theater for Incarcerated Women.* Chapel Hill, NC: University of North Carolina Press.

Freire, P. (1970). *Pedagogy of the Oppressed.* (M. B. Ramos, Trans.). New York, NY: Continuum.

Friedman, J. (2011). "You Can Call Us that Name But We Will Not Shut Up." www.youtube.com/watch?v=LMicqYFVL5A&feature=emb_logo

Gallagher, K. (2000). *Drama Education in the Lives of Girls: Imagining Possibilities.* Toronto: University of Toronto Press.

Gallagher, K. (2007). *The Theatre of Urban: Youth and Schooling in Dangerous Times.* Toronto: University of Toronto Press.

Gallagher, K. (2014). *Why Theatre Matters: Urban Youth, Engagement, and a Pedagogy of the Real.* Toronto: University of Toronto Press.

Garrison, E. K. (2000). U.S. Feminism-Grrrl Style! Youth (Sub)cultures and the Technologies of the Third Wave. *Feminist Studies. 26*(1), 141–170.

Garza, A. (2020). *The Purpose of Power: How We Come Together When We Fall Apart.* New York, NY: One World.

Gaunt, K. D. (2006). *The Games Black Girls Play: Learning the Ropes from Double-Dutch to Hip-Hop.* New York, NY: New York University Press.

Gill, R. (2007). "Critical Respect: The Difficulties and Dilemmas of Agency and 'Choice' for Feminism." *European Journal of Women's Studies. 14*(1), 69–80.

Gill, R. (2008). Empowerment/Sexism: Figuring Female Sexual Agency in Contemporary Advertising. *Feminism & Psychology. 18*(1), 35–60.

Gilligan, C. (2004). "Recovering the Psyche: Reflections On Life-History and History." In Winer, J. A., Anderson, J. W., & Kieffer, C. C. (Eds), *The Annual of Psychoanalysis, Volume 32: Psychoanalysis and Women* (pp. 131–147). Hillsdale, NJ: The Analytic Press.

Ginsberg, A. & Johnson, D. (2016). *Difficult Dialogues About 21st Century Girls.* Albany, NY: State University of New York Press.

Girl Scouts of the USA. (2017, October 6). *The G.I.R.L. Agenda Powered by Girl Scouts Launches.* www.girlscouts.org/en/press-room/press-room/news-releases/2017/g-i-r-l-agenda-powered-by-girl-scouts-launches-promote-civic-action1.html

Gonick, M. (2003). *Between Femininities: Ambivalence, Identity and the Education of Girls.* Albany, NY: SUNY Press.

Gordon, H. (2007). Allies Within and Without: How Adolescent Activists Conceptualize Ageism and Navigate Adult Power in Youth Social Movements. *Journal of Contemporary Ethnography. 36*(6): 631–668.

Gordon, H. (2010). *We Fight to Win: Inequality and the Politics of Youth Activism.* New Brunswick, NJ: Rutgers University Press.

Graber, R., Turner, R., & Madill, A. (2016). Best Friends and Better Coping: Facilitating Psychological Resilience through Boys' and Girls' Closest Friendships. *British Journal of Psychology. 107*(2), 338–358.

Gray, A. (2019, June 4). The Bias of "Professionalism" Standards. *Stanford Social Innovation Review.* https://ssir.org/articles/entry/the_bias_of_professionalism_standards#

Gray, E. (2018). *A Girl's Guide to Joining the Resistance: A Feminist Handbook for Fighting for Good*. New York, NY: HarperCollins.

Greene, M. (1988). *The Dialectic of Freedom*. New York, NY: Teachers College Press.

Hanna, K. (undated). "What Is Riot Grrrl?" *The Riot Grrrl Collection* (compiled by Lisa Darms). New York, NY: The Feminist Press CUNY.

Harris, A. (2004). *All About the Girl: Culture, Power, and Identity*. Abingdon & New York, NY: Routledge.

Harris-Britt, A., Valrie, C. R., Kurtz-Costes, B., & Rowley, S. J. (2007). Perceived Racial Discrimination and Self-Esteem in African American Youth: Racial Socialization as a Protective Factor. *Journal of Research on Adolescence*. 17(4), 669–682.

Hatton, C. (2003). Backyards and Borderlands: Some Reflections on Researching the Travels of Adolescent Girls Doing Drama. *Research in Drama Education*. 8(2), 139–156.

Hernandez, J. (2020). *Aesthetics of Excess: The Art and Politics of Black and Latina Embodiment*. Durham, NC & London: Duke University Press.

Higginbotham, E. B. (1993). *Righteous Discontent: The Women's Movement in the Black Baptist Church, 1880–1920*. Cambridge, MA: Harvard University Press.

hooks, b. (1984). *Feminist Theory: From Margin to Center*. New York, NY & London: Routledge.

hooks, b. (1999). *Ain't I A Woman: Black Women and Feminism*. Boston, MA: South End Press.

hooks, b. (2000). *Feminism is for Everybody: Passionate Politics*. London: Pluto Press.

hooks, b. (2003). *Rock My Soul: Black People and Self-Esteem*. New York, NY: Washington Square Press.

Hughes, J. & Wilson, K. (2004). Playing a Part: The Impact of Youth Theatre on Young People's Personal and Social Development. *Research in Drama Education*. 9(1), 57–72.

Jacobs, C. (2020). *Ready to Lead: Leadership Supports and Barriers for Black and Latinx Girls*. Girls Leadership. https://cdn.girlsleadership.org/app/uploads/2020/07/GirlsLeadership_ReadytoLeadReport.pdf

Johnson, A. (2020, December 10). Toya Lillard: Using an Abolitionist Framework in the Arts. *Arts Management and Technology Lab*. Podcast. https://amt-lab.org/podcasts-interviews/2020/12/toya-lillard-using-an-abolitionist-framework-in-the-arts

Johnson, M. (2018). *How I Resist: Activism and Hope for a New Generation*. New York, NY: St. Martin's Press.

Jones, P. (1996). *Drama as Therapy: Theatre as Living*. New York, NY: Routledge.

Juhl, K. & Smith, L. (2013). Adapt the Space! Working with People of Diverse Abilities. In Bowles, N. & Nadon, D. R. (Eds), *Staging Social Justice: Collaborating to Create Activist Theatre (Theater in the Americas)* (pp. 186–193). Carbondale, IL: Southern Illinois University Press.

Kaufman, M. & The Tectonic Theater Project. (2001). *The Laramie Project*. New York, NY: Vintage Books.

Kawaoka-Chen, D. (2020, June 16). Coronavirus Response: Building a Future That Reimagines Systems for Justice [video]. Grantmakers in the Arts. https://howlround.com/happenings/coronavirus-response-building-future-reimagines-systems-justice

Kay, K. & Shipman, C. (2018). *The Confidence Code for Girls: Taking Risks, Messing Up, and Becoming Your Amazingly Imperfect, Totally Powerful Self*. New York, NY: HarperCollins Publishers.

Kearney, M. C. (2006). *Girls Make Media*. Abingdon & New York, NY: Routledge.

Kendi, I. X. (2019). *How to Be an Antiracist*. New York, NY: Oneworld.

Khan-Cullors, P. & Bandele, A. (2020). *When They Call You a Terrorist: A Black Lives Matter Memoir*. New York, NY: St. Martin's Griffin.

Kim, S. (2019, September 28). Across From UN General Assembly, A Day Full of Youth Activism and Disability Inclusion. *Forbes*. www.forbes.com/sites/sarahkim/2019/09/27/we_day_un_disability_inclusion/

Kimball, G. (2019). Media Empowers Brave Girls to be Global Activists. *Journal of International Women's Studies*. *20*(7), 35–56.

Kirschner, M. (2011, October 4). A 17-Year-Old Does SlutWalk. *Ms. Magazine*. https://msmagazine.com/2011/10/04/a-17-year-old-does-slutwalk/

Koonce, J. B. (2012). "Oh Those Loud Black Girls!": A Phenomenological Study of Black Girls Talking with an Attitude. *Journal of Language and Literacy Education*. *8*(2), 26–46.

Kosciw, J. G., Greytak, E. A., Bartkiewicz, M. J., Boesen, M. J., & Palmer, N. A. (2012). *The 2011 National School Climate Survey: The Experiences of Lesbian, Gay, Bisexual and Transgender Youth in Our Nation's Schools*. New York, NY: GLSEN.

Kramer, L. (1985). *The Normal Heart*. New York, NY: Samuel French, Inc.

Kuppers, P. (2013). *Disability and Contemporary Performance: Bodies on the Edge*. Abingdon & New York, NY: Routledge.

Kushner, T. (1992). *Angels in America: A Gay Fantasia on National Themes*. New York, NY: Theatre Communications Group, Inc.

LaBennett, O. (2011). *She's Mad Real: Popular Culture and West Indian Girls in Brooklyn*. New York, NY: New York University Press.

Lamb, S. & Brown, L. M. (2006). *Packaging Girlhood: Rescuing Our Daughters From Marketers' Schemes*. New York, NY: St. Martin's Press.

Lampert, N. (2013). *A People's Art History of the United States: 250 Years of Activist Art and Artists Working in Social Justice Movements*. New York: The New Press.

Leadbeater, B. J. & Way, N. (Eds) (1996). *Urban Girls: Resisting Stereotypes, Creating Identities*. New York, NY: New York University Press.

Leadbeater, B. J. & Way, N. (Eds) (2007). *Urban Girls Revisited: Building Strengths*. New York, NY: New York University Press.

Lipkin, E. (2009). *Girls' Studies*. Berkeley, CA: Seal Press.

Lloyd, C. & Levitan, S. [Producers]. (2009–2020). *Modern Family*. Los Angeles, CA: Lloyd-Levitan Productions.

Lorde, A. (1984). *Sister Outsider: Essays and Speeches*. Berkeley, CA: Crossing Press.

Lorenz, T., Browning, K., & Frenkel, S. (2020, November 6). TikTok Teens Tank Trump Rally in Tulsa, They Say. *The New York Times*. www.nytimes.com/2020/06/21/style/tiktok-trump-rally-tulsa.html

Maddow-Zimet, I., Kost, K., & Finn, S. (2020, October 6). *Pregnancies, Births and Abortions in the United States, 1973–2016: National and State Trends by Age*. Guttmacher Institute. www.guttmacher.org/report/pregnancies-births-abortions-in-united-states-1973-2016#fn0a

Masters, B. M. (2020, April 15). We Are Not Afraid: The Montgomery Gospel Trio and Protest Songs for Freedom. www.williamsonhomepage.com/spring_hill/community/we-are-not-afraid-the-montgomery-gospel-trio-and-protest-songs-for-freedom/article)

McAuley, G. (2000, June). Theatre, Film, Performance: The Role of the Spectator. In *Sydney Society of Literature and Aesthetics Conference*, Sydney University.

McRobbie, A. (2008). Young Women and Consumer Culture. *Cultural Studies*. *22*(5), 531–550.

Menakem, R. (2017). *My Grandmother's Hands: Racialized Trauma and the Pathway to Mending Our Hearts and Bodies*. Las Vegas, NV: Central Recovery Press.

Minaj, N. (2014). "Feeling Myself" [song]. On *The Pinkprint*. WB Music Corp.

The Miracle Project. (2019). https://themiracleproject.org

Mitchell C., Reid-Walsh, J., & Kirk, J. (2008, Summer). Welcome to This Inaugural Issue of Girlhood Studies. *Girlhood Studies: An Interdisciplinary Journal*. 1(1), v– viii.

Moraga, C. & Anzaldúa, G. (1981). *This Bridge Called My Back: Writings by Radical Women of Color*. Watertown, MA: Persephone Press.

Morgan, J. (1999). *When Chickenheads Come Home to Roost: A Hip-Hop Feminist Breaks it Down*. New York, NY: Simon & Schuster.

Morris, E. W. (2007). "Ladies" or "Loudies"? Perceptions and Experiences of Black Girls in Classrooms. *Youth & Society*. 38(4), 490–515.

Morris, M. W. (2016). *Pushout: The Criminalization of Black Girls in Schools*. New York, NY: The New Press.

Morris, M. W. (2019). *Sing a Rhythm, Dance a Blues: Education for the Liberation of Black and Brown Girls*. New York, NY: The New Press.

Mutchnick, M. & Kohan, D. [Producers] (1998–2006). *Will and Grace*. Los Angeles, CA: KoMut Entertainment.

Myers, S. (2009). (Re)Embodying Girlhood: Collective Autobiography and Identity Performance in Rude Mechanicals' Grrl Action (unpublished doctoral dissertation). University of Texas, Austin, TX.

The National Coalition for the Homeless. (n.d.). www.nationalhomeless.org/

National Research Council & Institute of Medicine. (2002). Community Programs to Promote Youth Development. Washington, DC: National Academy Press. www.nap.edu/openbook/0309072751/html/index.html

Nelson, B. (2011) "I Made Myself": Playmaking as a Pedagogy of Change with Urban Youth. *Research in Drama Education: The Journal of Applied Theatre and Performance*. 16(2), 157–172.

The New York Tribune. (1912). Girl Speaks Sans Riot. www.newspapers.com/image/467712339/?terms=%22dorothy%20frooks%22&match=1

Nicholson, H. (2005). *Applied Drama: The Gift of Theatre*. New York, NY: Palgrave Macmillan.

Nuamah, S. A. (2019). *How Girls Achieve*. Cambridge, MA: Harvard University Press.

O'Brien, A. & Donelan, K. (Eds) (2008). *Arts and Youth At Risk: Global and Local Challenges*. Newcastle upon Tyne: Cambridge Scholars Publishing.

Ogle, S., Glasier, A., & Riley, S. C. (2008). Communication Between Parents and their Children about Sexual Health. *Contraception*. 77(4), 283–288.

Orenstein, N. (2020, January 22). "Our Monologues" Show Replaces "Outdated" "Vagina" Tradition at Berkeley High. *Berkeleyside Nonprofit News*.

Orenstein, P. (1995). *Schoolgirls: Young Women, Self-Esteem and the Confidence Gap*. New York, NY: Anchor Books.

Paley, A. (2019). *National Survey on LGBTQ Youth Mental Health*. The Trevor Project. www.thetrevorproject.org.

Partners for Youth with Disabilities. (2018). *Partners for Youth with Disabilities*. https://pyd.org

Paul, C. & Tamaki, L. (2018). *You Are Mighty: A Guide to Changing the World*. New York, NY: Bloomsbury Children's Books.

Pendzik, S., Emunah, R., & Read Johnson, D. (2017). *The Self in Performance: Autobiographical, Self-Revelatory, and Autoethnographic Forms of Therapeutic Theatre.* New York, NY: Palgrave Macmillan.

Phipps, A. (2014). *The Politics of the Body: Gender in a Neoliberal and Neoconservative Age.* Weinheim: Wiley.

Pride Youth Theater Alliance. (2020). Pyta-Online. www.prideyouththeateralliance.org

Raymond, D. (1994). "Homophobia, Identity, and the Meanings of Desire: Reflections on the Cultural Construction of Gay and Lesbian Adolescent Sexuality." In Irvine, J. M. (Ed), *Sexual Cultures and the Construction of Adolescent Identities* (pp. 115–150). Philadelphia, PA: Temple University Press.

Renold, E. (2018). "Feel What I Feel": Making Da(r)ta with Teen Girls for Creative Activisms on how Sexual Violence Matters. *Journal of Gender Studies.* 27(1), 37–55.

Rich, K. & Sagramola G. (2018). *Girls Resist! A Guide to Activism, Leadership, and Starting a Revolution.* Philadelphia, PA: Quirk Books.

Robinson, T. & Ward, J. (1991). A Belief in Self Far Greater than Anyone's Disbelief: Cultivating Resistance among African American Female Adolescents. *Women and Therapy.* 11(3/4), 87–103.

Rogers, L. O., Rosario, R. J., Padilla, D., & Foo, C. (2021). "[I]t's Hard because it's the Cops that are Killing Us for Stupid Stuff": Racial Identity in the Sociopolitical Context of Black Lives Matter. *Developmental Psychology.* 57(1), 87–101.

Rosin, H. (2012). *The End of Men: And the Rise of Women.* New York, NY: Riverhead Books.

Rush, C. (2011, February 18). Cop Apologizes for "Sluts" Remark at Law School. *TheStar.com.* www.thestar.com/news/gta/2011/02/18/cop_apologizes_for_sluts_remark_at_law_school.html

Salami, B., Hirani, S., Meherali, S., Amodu, O., & Chambers, T. (2017). Parenting Practices of African Immigrants in Destination Countries: A Qualitative Research Synthesis. *Journal of Pediatric Nursing.* 36, 20–30.

Sandahl, C. & Auslander, P. (2005). *Bodies in Commotion: Disability and Performance.* Ann Arbor, MI: University of Michigan Press.

Schechner, R. (2013). *Performance Studies: An Introduction* (3rd edn). New York, NY & Abingdon: Routledge.

Schroeder, N. (2020, June 20). Young, Black Activists Lead Charge at Protest-Themed Juneteenth Celebration in Portland. *Bangor Daily News.* https://bangordailynews.com/2020/06/19/politics/young-black-activists-lead-charge-at-protest-themed-juneteenth-celebration-in-portland/

The Sentencing Project. (2018, May 1). *Report to the United Nations on Racial Disparities in the U.S. Criminal Justice System.* www.sentencingproject.org/publications/un-report-on-racial-disparities/

Shepard, B. (2005). Play, Creativity, and the New Community Organizing. *Journal of Progressive Human Services.* 16(2), 47–69.

Simmons, R. (2018). *Enough As She Is: How to Help Girls Move Beyond Impossible Standards of Success to Live Healthy, Happy, and Fulfilling Lives.* New York, NY & London: Harper.

Singh, A., Kim, D., & Yang, A. (2020, July 24). How Young TikTok Users Are Making their Activism Go Viral. *ABC News.* https://abcnews.go.com/US/young-tiktok-users-making-activism-viral/story?id=71950082

Slater, J. (2012). Self-advocacy and Socially Just Pedagogy. *Disability Studies Quarterly.* 32(1), http://dsq-sds.org/article/view/3033

Snyder-Young, D. (2018). "Despite Artists' Intentions, Emancipated Spectatorship Reinforces Audience Members' Existing Attitudes and Beliefs." In Woodson, S. E. & Underiner, T. (Eds), *Theatre, Performance and Change* (pp. 295–302). Cham: Palgrave Macmillan.

Solar Bear Deaf Youth Theatre. (2020). https://solarbear.org.uk/deaf-youth-theatre/

Spathis, J. & Kennedy, K. (2017). *Wake, Rise, Resist! The Progressive Teen's Guide to Fighting Tyrants and A*sholes.* New York, NY: So's Your Face Press.

Streeter, J. R. & Olusanya, N. (2021). "From Vision to Implementation: Re-examining Essential Practices for Applied Theatre with Youth." In Brenner, L. S., Ceraso, C., & Cruz, E. D. (Eds), *Applied Theatre: Working with Youth.* New York, NY & Abingdon: Routledge.

Stop Street Harrassment. (2014). *Unsafe and Harassed in Public Spaces: A National Street Harassment Report.* www.stopstreetharassment.org/wp-content/uploads/2012/08/National-Street-Harassment-Report-November-29-20151.pdf

Taft, J. K. (2004). "Girl Power Politics: Pop-culture Barriers and Organizational Resistance." In Harris, A. (Ed.), *All About the Girl: Culture, Power, and Identity* (pp. 69–78). New York, NY & London: Routledge.

Taft, J. K. (2011). *Rebel Girls: Youth Activism and Social Change Across the Americas.* New York, NY: New York University Press.

Taft, J. K. (2015). "Adults Talk Too Much": Intergenerational Dialogue and Power in the Peruvian Movement of Working Children. *Childhood. 22*(4), 460–473.

Taylor, D. (2003). *The Archive and the Repertoire: Performing Cultural Memory in the Americas.* Durham, NC: Duke University Press.

Taylor, P. (2003). *Applied Theatre: Creating Transformative Encounters in the Community.* Portsmouth, NH: Heinemann.

Taylor, S. R. (2018). *The Body Is Not an Apology: The Power of Radical Self-Love.* San Francisco, CA: Berrett-Koehler Publishers.

Territory Acknowledgement. (2020). Native-Land.ca – Our Home on Native Land. https://native-land.ca/resources/territory-acknowledgement/

The Sentencing Project. (2018, May 1). *Report to the United Nations on Racial Disparities in the U.S. Criminal Justice System.* www.sentencingproject.org/ publications/un-report-on-racial-disparities/

Thompson, J. (1998). *Prison Theatre: Perspectives and Practices.* London: Jessica Kingsley Publishers, Ltd.

Thompson, J. (2003). *Applied Theatre: Bewilderment and Beyond.* New York, NY: Peter Lang.

Tolman, D. L. (2002). *Dilemmas of Desire: Teenage Girls Talk about Sexuality.* Cambridge, MA: Harvard University Press.

Tolman, D. L. (2018). "Slut Shaming as a Crisis of Connection: Fostering Connections to Fuel Resistance." In Way, N., Ali, A., Gilligan, C., & Noguera, P. (Eds), *The Crisis of Connection: Roots, Consequences, and Solutions* (pp. 188–210). New York, NY: New York University Press.

Townsend, T. G., Neilands, T. B., Thomas, A. J., & Jackson, T. R. (2010). I'm No Jezebel; I Am Young, Gifted, and Black: Identity, Sexuality, and Black Girls. *Psychology of Women Quarterly. 34*(3), 273–285.

Turner, V. (1967). *The Forest of Symbols.* Ithaca, NY: Cornell University Press.

Van Gennep, A. (1960). *The Rites of Passage.* (M.B Vizedom & G. L. Caffee, Trans.) Chicago, IL: The University of Chicago Press.

viBe Theater Experience. (2020). *Why Us?* https://vibetheater.org/impact

Wang, L. (2018). This Woman Had the Best-Ever Response to Slut-Shaming. Bust.com. https://bust.com/feminism/194866-samirah-raheem-slutwalk.html

Washington Post. (2016, October 7). Watch: Donald Trump Recorded Having Extremely Lewd Conversation about Women in 2005 [video]. https://tinyurl.com/54h8wbjz

Way, N. (2011). *Deep Secrets: Boys' Friendships and the Crisis of Connection.* Cambridge, MA: Harvard University Press.

Wernick, L. J., Dessel, A. B., Kulick, A., & Graham, L. F. (2013). LGBTQQ Youth Creating Change: Developing Allies against Bullying through Performance and Dialogue. *Children and Youth Services Review. 35*(9), 1576–1586.

Willett, J. (1977). *The Theatre of Bertolt Brecht (Plays and Playwrights)* (new edn). North Yorkshire: Bloomsbury Methuen Drama.

Wilson, J. & Pippins, A. (2019). *Step Into Your Power: 23 Lessons on How to Live Your Best Life.* Minneapolis, MN: Wide-Eyed Editions.

Winn, M. (2011). *Girl Time: Literacy, Justice and the School-To-Prison Pipeline.* New York, NY: Teachers College Press.

Wolf, S. (2005). "Disability's Invisibility in Joan Schenkar's *Signs of Life* and Heather McDonald's *An Almost Holy Picture.*" In Sandahl, C. & Auslander, P. (Eds), *Bodies in Commotion: Disability and Performance* (pp. 302–318). Ann Arbor, MI: University of Michigan Press.

Woodson, S. E. (2015). *Theatre for Youth Third Space: Performance, Democracy, and Community Cultural Development.* Chicago, IL: Intellect Books.

Woodson, S. E. & Underiner, T. (2018). *Theatre, Performance and Change.* New York, NY: Palgrave Macmillan.

Young, I. (2004). "Five Faces of Oppression." In Heldke, L. & O'Conner, P. (Eds), *Oppression, Privilege, & Resistance* (pp. 37–63). New York, NY: McGraw Hill.

Zabot-Hall, M. (2020, June 4). Where Was the Peace 400 Years Ago? JGirls. https://jgirlsmagazine.org/2020/06/where-was-the-peace-400-years-ago/

Zarrilli, P. B., Williams, G. J., & Sorgenfrei, C. F. (2006). *Theatre Histories: An Introduction.* New York, NY & Abingdon: Routledge.

Organizations, projects, and resources

The following (in no way complete!) alphabetical list represents a smattering of organizations, projects, and resources that address activism, performance, and girls though not always all three. Some are co-ed activist youth theater groups, others are girls' activist organizations. Most hug the coasts of the US as projects outside major cities can lack the resources for detailed websites and online information. All the words have been directly quoted from their organization's website. If you are or know a girl interested in making activist performances, I encourage you to connect with one of these organizations – go to a show, make a donation, volunteer, ask for a job or join their programs. If you don't see one in your hometown, consider launching or creating your own (perhaps the topic for my next book …).

Act Like a Grrrl

Nashville, Tennessee

ALAG is an autobiographical writing and performance program that inspires female-identifying teenagers (ages 12–18) to write about their lives and transform their thoughts into monologues, dances, and songs for public performance. As GRRRLS find their voice and speak their truths on stage, they develop the self-confidence, personal agency, and leadership skills to live more empowered lives. During the program, the GRRRLS explore their innermost selves and are introduced to strong adult women who model the power of living authentic lives and pursuing their chosen dreams.

https://actorsbridge.org/act-like-a-grrrl/

AGENDA: A Young People's Guide to Making Positive Relationships Matter

Wales

AGENDA is an online curriculum developed with young people for young people that supports your right to speak out about and change things that matter to you. AGENDA is an online guide with equality, diversity, children's rights, and social justice at its heart. It connects you to the creative ways young people in Wales and beyond are challenging gender-based and sexual violence.

https://agenda.wales/

The AMY Project

Toronto, Ontario, Canada

The AMY (Artists Mentoring Youth) Project offers free performing arts training programs serving young women and nonbinary youth. AMY breaks down barriers to participation by providing meals and transportation; accessible, queer and trans inclusive, and anti-racist environments; one-on-one mentorship; and more.

www.theamyproject.com

Carolinas Pride Theatre Ensemble

Charlotte, North Carolina

Teen and young adult artist-activists committed to using theater arts as a tool to impact social change. Young performing artists using theater arts as a tool for social change!

www.facebook.com/CarolinasPrideTheatreEnsemble/

CAT Youth Theatre

New York, New York

CAT Youth Theatre is a free, after school program that invests in young people and inspires them to thrive – on stage and in life – by creating socially relevant, artistically sophisticated original plays while learning vital life skills enabling them to become self-confident, compassionate and accountable; develop relationships across differences; build community; and be prepared to act as contributing citizens.

www.creativeartsteam.org/programs/cat-youth-theatre

Changing Lives Youth Theater Ensemble at Creative Action

Austin, Texas

Changing Lives is an ensemble of teen artist-activists that create and tour original, youth-led performances focused on violence prevention, healthy relationships, and social justice. Through the powerful medium of peer education and theater, Changing Lives gives young adults the knowledge, skills, and confidence to support healthy relationships and stand up against violence and bullying as courageous allies.

www.creativeaction.org/programs/teen-programs/changing-lives/

A Company of Girls

Portland, Maine

At A Company of Girls, girls come together after school and learn about theater, the arts, and social skills. It is a safe place where they can discuss issues that are important to them. It is also a fun place, just for them, where they can discuss "girl things."

www.acompanyofgirls.org/whowhatwhy

Dark Girls

Syracuse, New York

Dark Girls is a critical media literacy program for Black middle and high school girls, which uses writing, arts, performance, and dance.

https://mysouthsidestand.com/younguns/danforth-middle-school-launches-the-dark-girls-project/

Dramagirls

Chicago, Illinois

The Dramagirls program paired middle school girls in Chicago with female artist mentors in an artistic exploration of creativity and leadership. The program encouraged participants to draw from their personal experience and imagination to create annual performances featuring spectacle techniques. From 1996 to 2009, over a thousand youth and mentors participated in the program.

Girl Be Heard

New York, New York

Girl Be Heard is uniquely positioned to engage youth and open up dialogue about social justice issues affecting their communities – from gun violence to sex trafficking. We run afterschool and weekend education programs in underserved areas where all of our girls' theatrical work is generated. We build self-esteem, grow individual talents (step dancing, singing, rapping, and acting), and empower girls to become leaders in and advocates for their communities.

www.girlbeheard.org

The Girl Project

Lexington, Kentucky

The Girl Project is an arts meets activism program designed to inspire, educate, and empower girls of all ages to challenge the mis-representation of girls and women in American media culture through performing arts education. The Girl Project provides girls with the creative, cognitive, and emotional tools necessary to challenge this negative message and envision positive possibilities for themselves and their futures.

www.thegirlprojectky.org/

Girls Leadership

Philadelphia, Pennsylvania

We teach girls to exercise the power of their voice through programs grounded in social emotional learning and provide programs for girls, workshops for families, and professional development training for teachers, guidance counselors, and non-profit staff. Girls Leadership centers gender and racial equity in our work to address the internal and external barriers to leadership development.

www.girlsleadership.org

Girls Learn International

Chapters throughout the US

Girls Learn International (GLI) empowers and educates middle and high school students to advocate for human rights, equality, and universal education in the US and around the world. Student-to-student, and student-to-parent, GLI is building a movement of informed advocates for universal girls' education and a new generation of leaders and activists for social change.

www.girlslearn.org

Girls Rock Camp Alliance

Chapters throughout the North and Latin America, Europe, Africa, Asia, and Australia

The Girls Rock Camp Alliance is an international membership network of youth-centered arts and social justice organizations. We provide resources and space for community building to our membership in order to build a strong movement for collective liberation.

www.girlsrockcampalliance.org/

Girls Write Now

New York, New York

Girls Write Now mentors underserved young women to find their voices through the power of writing and community.

www.girlswritenow.org

Global Girls, Inc.

Chicago, Illinois

Our mission is to use the performing arts to equip African-American girls with skills that nurture their individual growth and inspire them to use their talents for positive change in their communities and throughout the world.

www.globalgirlsinc.org

Go Girls

Oakland, California

Go Girls!™ is a girl empowerment program – winter, spring, summer day camps and after-school clubs – just for elementary and middle school-aged girls and gender non-conforming kids. By making theater, art, music, and media, girls learn the skills to love themselves and each other, and make bold and brave choices in their lives and communities.

www.gogirlsoakland.com

Grrl Action

Austin, Texas

Grrl Action began in 1999 as a summer workshop in creative writing and perform-ance designed to empower girls to find their public voices and build confidence while collaborating with young women from diverse socio-economic and cultural backgrounds. In 2007, Grrl Action expanded and added a year-round performance-based artistic education program enabling young women from age 13 to 18 to plan and execute individual, long-term artistic projects, working across the disciplines, alongside professional female artists as their mentors. Participants can expand their practice beyond the theater space and into their everyday lives and communities, making them not only better writers and performers, but better citizens, activists, and role models.

https://twitter.com/grrlactionatx

A Long Walk Home

Chicago, Illinois

Founded in 2003, A Long Walk Home, Inc. (ALWH) is a Chicago-based national non-profit that uses art to educate, inspire, and mobilize young people to end violence against girls and women.

www.alongwalkhome.org

LOUD: New Orleans Queer Youth Theater

New Orleans, Louisiana

LOUD is a group of outspoken, unapologetic queer and trans★ youth and their allies coming together in solidarity to build community and tell their stories, a space where youth can explore varied and fluid performances of queerness, learn theater making techniques and hang out.

https://neworleansqyt.wixsite.com/loud

Muslim Girls Making Change

Burlington, Vermont

Muslim Girls Making Change (MGMC), a youth slam poetry group created Kiran Waqar, Hawa Adam, Lena Ginawi, and Balkisa Abdikadir, is dedicated to social justice through poetry. Tired of having their voices ignored by older generations, they turned to slam poetry to be heard and to make a change. Since forming, these girls have competed at international levels, won numerous awards, performed widely, and help lead several local and nation initiatives.

www.muslimgirlsmakingchange.weebly.com

Project Pride

Kansas City, Missouri

Project Pride is a group of LGBTQ and straight allied teens creating theater that gives voice to their experiences, culminating in a production that challenges the assumptions and celebrates the diversity of the participants and audience.

www.thecoterie.org/project-pride

Radical Monarchs

Oakland, California

The Radical Monarchs create opportunities for young girls of color to form fierce sisterhood, celebrate their identities and contribute radically to their communities. The Radical Monarchs empower young girls of color so that they stay rooted in their collective power, brilliance, and leadership in order to make the world a more radical place.

www.radicalmonarchs.org

Rock 'n' Roll Camp for Girls

Portland, Oregon

Our mission is to build confidence and self-esteem through music creation and performance, empowering women, girls, and gender expansive folk through collaborative music creation, peer to peer mentoring, and advocacy for an equitable and inclusive society.

www.girlsrockcamp.org

The Rose Theatre's Broken Mirror Project

Omaha, Nebraska

Broken Mirror is a leadership and theater experience for female-identified and gender expansive youth who wish to examine the role gender plays in our society. The troupe uses poetry, improvisation, comedy, music, and more to create dynamic theater reflecting the questions, concerns, and triumphs of being a teen in today's world.

www.rosetheater.org/education/teens/

Say Sí – ALAS (Activating Leadership, Art & Service) Youth Theatre Company

San Antonio, Texas

Say Sí ignites the creative power of young people as forces of positive change. Committed to the creation of new and original performance work by, for, and about San Antonio youth, ALAS challenges students to draw from their own experiences, observations, and insights to produce theater of relevance to their lives and their communities. Emphasizing leadership skills and civic engagement, ALAS creates work that addresses community needs and concerns, challenges prejudices and social injustice, and celebrates diversity and difference. www.saysi.org/programs/alas-theater-program/

SOLHOT

Champaign–Urbana, Illinois and East Lansing, Michigan

SOLHOT (Saving Our Lives Hear Our Truths) is a space to celebrate Black girlhood in all of its complexity with Black girls and those who love and support us. In SOLHOT we dance, sing, discuss important issues, create art, and organize together to improve the communities of which we are a part. We do what needs to be done. The process of doing SOLHOT involves being together and deciding what our work will be based on the gifts, talents, and ideas of those who show up. More than anything we value Black girls' lives and create spaces to affirm Black girl genius.

www.solhot.com

S.O.U.L. Sisters Leadership Collective

Miami, Florida and New York, New York

S.O.U.L Sisters supports new leaders that have "lived and breathed" the inequalities of our legal, educational, and economic systems. Our mission is to mobilize systems-involved girls, femmes, and TGNC youth of color – Black, Brown, and Indigenous – to interrupt cycles of state violence, poverty, and oppression. Our four pillars are leadership, healing, social justice, and the arts.

https://soulsistersleadership.org/

SPARK Movement

Global / Online

SPARK arms activists, educators, community leaders, and girls themselves with the training and resources to foster coalition and partnerships in order to ignite and support a global youth-driven antiracist feminist movement.

www.sparkmovement.org/

Southern Girls Rock Camp

Nashville, Tennessee

Southern Girls Rock Camp (SGRC) is a summer day camp for girls and gender non-conforming youth aged ten to 17. SGRC's mission is to support a culture of positive self-esteem and collaboration among girls while building community through music. SGRC recognizes the potential of every young woman to be a strong, talented, creative, and empowered individual while providing a safe space where all kids rock.

www.southerngirlsrockcamp.com/

Stand Up! Girls

New York, New York

Stand Up! Girls is a nonprofit organization whose core mission is to educate, inspire, and equip girls from underserved communities with the communication skills necessary to succeed in and lead male-dominated workplaces. Through developing and performing stand-up comedy, our girls learn to own the room – be it a courtroom, operating room, or boardroom.

www.standupgirlsnyc.org/

"Playmaking for Girls" at Synchronicity Theatre

Atlanta, Georgia

Playmaking for Girls (PFG) is an innovative theater outreach program that aims to empower "with-hope" teen girls in the Atlanta-area. Many participants have been touched by the Department of Juvenile Justice system, and are living in group homes as wards of the state. Others have recently come to the United States as refugees from all over the world, and are acclimating to a new country and language. These young ladies come together as playwrights and actors, and through theater, are empowered to "find their voices" and "speak their stories."

www.synchrotheatre.com/about

Proud Theater

Madison, Wisconsin

Proud Theater is an award-winning, exciting, and innovative youth theater program whose mission is "to change the world through the power of theater and the theater arts, and to make a positive difference in the lives of LGBTQ+ and allied youth through the tenets of art, heart, and activism."

www.proudtheater.org/

True Colors OUT Youth Theater (at The Theater Offensive)

Boston, Massachusetts

The True Colors Troupe is an after-school theater program for gay, lesbian, bisexual, transgender, queer, and questioning youth and their straight allies, ages 12–17. Youth work with artists to create an ensemble to develop skills in performance, social justice, and community activism. Performance Squad is an advanced performing ensemble of LGBTQ young artists ages 18-25 that produce theater for schools and communities around New England and beyond.

www.thetheateroffensive.org/true-colors-out-youth-theater

viBe Theater Experience

New York, New York

viBe Theater Experience (viBe) provides girls, young women, and nonbinary youth of color (aged 13–25) in New York City with free, high quality artistic, leadership, and academic opportunities. viBe works to empower its participants to write and perform original theater, video, and music about the real-life issues they face daily. viBe's performing arts and training programs provide the platform for participants to amplify their voices and "speak truth to power," by creating an artistic response to the world around them.

www.vibetheater.org

The Viola Project

Chicago, Illinois

The Viola Project celebrates play and performance in young people while creating a foundation for young women to stand up, advocate for themselves, and demand inclusion: inclusion in the classroom, in the workspace, in the world, and on the stage. Why Shakespeare? Shakespeare's characters are determined to get what they need, to be understood, to be listened to. There is no better teacher for how to use language to make your voice heard than William Shakespeare.

www.violaproject.org

Working Group on Girls at the UN New York, New York

The WGG is a non-governmental organization working for girls, with girls at the United Nations helping to elevate the voices and needs of girls globally. It supports girls' full and equitable participation in international meetings and events, and it allows girls to advocate on their own behalf in local and global arenas.

www.girlsrights.org

Youth Empowerment Performance Project

Chicago, Illinois

YEPP strives to create a brave environment for Lesbian, Gay, Bisexual, Transgender, Queer, and Intersex (LGBTQI+) youth experiencing homelessness to explore their history, investigate new ways to address their struggles and to celebrate their strengths through personal, leadership, and community development programming that incorporate different art-expression forms.

www.wesayyepp.com/

Youth Speaks

San Francisco Bay Area, California

Committed to a critical, youth-centered pedagogy, Youth Speaks places young people in control of their intellectual and artistic development. By making the connection between poetry, spoken word, youth development, and civic engagement, Youth Speaks aims to deconstruct dominant narratives in hopes of achieving a more inclusive, and active, culture.

www.youthspeaks.org

Index

CPSIA information can be obtained
at www.ICGtesting.com
Printed in the USA
LVHW082033020822
725003LV00004B/144

9 780367 427115